BRED OF HEAVEN

One man's quest
to reclaim his Welsh roots

Jasper Rees

PROFILE BOOKS

First published in Great Britain in 2011 by
PROFILE BOOKS LTD
3A Exmouth House
Pine Street
Exmouth Market
London EC1R 0JH
www.profilebooks.com

1 3 5 7 9 10 8 6 4 2

Typeset in Transitional 551 by MacGuru Ltd
info@macguru.org.uk

Printed and bound in Great Britain by
Clays, Bungay, Suffolk

A CIP catalogue record for this book is available from the British Library.

ISBN 978 1 84668 299 5
eISBN 978 1 84765 422 9

The paper this book is printed on is certified by the © 1996 Forest Stewardship
Council A.C. (FSC). It is ancient-forest friendly. The printer holds FSC chain
of custody SGS-COC-2061

FSC
Mixed Sources
Product group from well-managed
forests and other controlled sources
Cert no. SGS-COC-2061
www.fsc.org
© 1996 Forest Stewardship Council

To the memory of Bert and Dorothy

Contents

'O bydded i'r hen iaith barhau' = O let the old language endure

Evan James (1856)

Author's Note

The business of writing about Wales brings up an inevitable question. Place names: to anglicise or Welshify? There is no real method in the choices I've made other than pure instinct. It would be perverse to refer to Caerdydd, Abertawe and Casnewydd when almost all of Wales knows them as Cardiff, Swansea and Newport. For most towns I have kept to that rule of thumb. So it's Carmarthen not Caerfyrddin, Llandovery not Llanymddyfri. But where there is simply an English transliteration, I've reverted to Welsh spelling. Thus Caernarfon rather than (the abomination) Carnarvon. Hence also the Llŷn peninsula not Lleyn. As for rivers, the Severn and the Wye are overwhelmingly known by their English names so I've stuck with them but it seems preferable to refer to the Tywi, the Taf and the Dyfi rather than the Towey, the Taff and the Dovey. Finally, most Welsh mountains do not have English names. But two famous ones do. In the case of Snowdon (and Snowdonia) I've – mostly – used the English rather than wilfully obfuscate with Yr Wyddfa (and Eryri). However, where the Welsh say and write Pumlumon, I simply cannot bring myself to go with Plynlimon, which may be just as pervasive but is plainly the orthographical product of an Englishman's failure to listen.

(And it goes without saying that it's Owain Glyndŵr, not Owen Glendower.)

Cyflwyno = Introduce

'Wales, *see* England.'

Encyclopaedia Britannica, 9th edition (1875–89)

YOU HAVE TO PAY to get in. The current cost, if you're in a car, is £5.30, though it's less for motorcycles and more for heavy goods vehicles. Pressing a note and two coins into a fleshy female palm, I deploy the lone word of conversational Welsh in my locker: 'Diolch.' Thanks. Then push my right foot down and accelerate into the land of my fathers.

Initially there's not much topographical discrepancy from the foreign field back at the other end of the bridge. Arable land trimmed into rectangles. Grey cloud flattens the light, as it often seems to this side. And now the tidal waters in my passenger window recede from view. I'm not really sure where I'm going. 'Croeso i Gymru', says the sign. Am I really welcome to Wales? I've been coming here since before I can remember, the atavistic summons dutifully answered at Christmas and in summer. Twice a year we ploughed over the old bridge, into the west, along roads which down the years became broader and smoother and faster until eventually it was possible to drive the ninety miles from the toll gate to my grandparents in not much more than an hour; South Wales was reduced to a race against time, the chain of conurbations whipping by in a blur of turn-offs. Newport. Cardiff. Swansea. Quite early on in my childhood the road signs began speaking in two tongues: Casnewydd, Caerdydd, Abertawe. Services: *gwasana-ethau*. Parking: *parcio*. How we laughed at that one: the foreign language indebted to the master. The car – in the 1970s we had a succession of Range Rovers which glugged petrol at the dipsomaniac rate of thirteen miles to the gallon – munched on the long column of tarmac and spat it out behind us.

All I knew of Wales was the road, and a house on a hill above the market town of Carmarthen. Caerfyrddin.

'Haven't you grown?' my grandmother would exclaim in her warm Welsh soprano as we squirmed out of her embrace, scrummed through the mock-Gothic porch and past her down the long welcoming corridor. We stayed for a night, sometimes two. My grandmother would leak tears as we snuck over the cattle grid and began the return journey back east. And when ninety miles later we crossed the Severn and accelerated into England, my entirely Welsh father would urge us to cheer.

This is the closest my childhood came to indoctrination. I could never quite work out what we were celebrating. I'm still looking for the answer. It's what has been bringing me back to Wales time and again: a sort of cultural bafflement, an unfulfilled sense of ancestral belonging. And here I am again. I've got a spare week and I've answered the westerly summons.

Suddenly I veer left. I've always sailed past this little corner of Wales. I decide to follow my nose and attempt to drive south towards the water. Flat, even sunken, and riven with ditches, the countryside looks neither English nor Welsh but Dutch. I follow a track down towards a sea wall and, turning off the ignition, set foot on Welsh soil. I clamber up the steps and there, arrayed in front of me, is the Severn estuary, the Bristol Channel. England fans out along the horizon. I breathe in briny air. Overhead, gulls squawk territorially. Before the wall was raised, high tides would have scurried inland and drowned the fields in salt water.

I turn my back to the water and gaze across the protected plain. Down below, a forthright child pushes its own rickety pram on the rutted road, while a young mother and a spaniel amble patiently alongside. Two grey-haired men arrive stoop-shouldered on expensive bikes and, in neon Lycra which faithfully highlights every contour of slackening bodies, bounce up the steps and onto the sea wall. One day I too will no doubt lever myself onto a crotch-partingly narrow saddle, grasp a pair of drop handlebars and try to pedal away from the inevitable flood tide of old age. I too will look ridiculous. As things stand, there's no need of death-defiance. At forty-three, for another couple of years my twenty-fifth birthday is still nearer than my sixty-fifth.

It's hard to say from here where the river ends and the sea begins. Somewhere below the surface of the wide waters, epic undercurrents have been arguing that one since the last Ice Age. It's hard also, it occurs to me, to say where my Englishness ends and my Welshness begins. My father was born and brought up in Wales. Six decades later my two daughters pushed their own prams in England. I've wanted to know this for ever. Do you come from where your parents come from? Or do you, like it or lump it, just come from where *you* come from? Which I may as well admit is why I am here.

Am I Welsh? How Welsh, in the end, is half Welsh? My yearning, my claim, has always been for my Welsh half to swamp the rest. But it's hardly had a chance. I've never lived in Wales. In fact I scarcely know it outside the little corner I've always visited: I've never been to the top of Snowdon or along the Rhondda Valley, barely even stopped in Cardiff or ever set foot in the mountainous middle. But on some inchoate level I sense that I love Wales. It feels like having a crush on a long dead star whose face you know only in the black and white shimmer of the silver screen.

These feelings of belonging have had to sprout from barren anglicised soil. If scientists in a laboratory were creating an upbringing designed to inculcate Englishness in a boy, they couldn't find a much better template than mine. My birth in London took place at a Welsh-sounding address: Gower Street. But everything else about the street is English. The Pre-Raphaelite movement was also born here. Illustrious residents include Charles Darwin, Mr Pickwick and the Royal Academy of Dramatic Art. I then grew up in the smartest crescent in the heart of the royal borough. Every morning we ran to our bedroom window in the garret and watched the Household Cavalry clop and clink glamorously along the Old Brompton Road. On Friday afternoons we clambered into the car and drove down south to the South Downs to spend ineffably English weekends on ponies and Choppers. We were sent to a school called Sussex House, and when we moved permanently to Sussex itself I stopped my tears like many a good English boy, put a little English bung in my little English rear and boarded: the immemorial English expulsion from the English home to the English public school. Envelopes crested with the family's heraldic device would arrive at school franked with a Dyfed postmark, containing chatty news from Wales in my grandmother's spidery hand. They would have been more or less indistinguishable from letters mailed thirty-five years earlier to my father. He was of that generation who were sent away to school in England at the age of eight and never really came back. Wales had been educated out of him. He liked to tell a story of how, touring Herefordshire one summer with his medical-school cricket team, he snuck out of the hotel under cover of darkness to steal the 'Croeso i Gymru' sign guarding the Welsh border as a trophy for the pavilion back in London. Not long after, he was driving his Welsh mother into Wales. 'Some vandals have removed the sign,' she said. He kept quiet. Later, his emotional detachment from the scenes of his youth manifested itself in the ritual we performed every time we crossed into England. In that succession of Range Rovers thumping back across the bridge, we'd hurrah and huzzah like junior zealots.

How Welsh can all that grounding make you? How Welsh can you be on the back of two visits a year? Eventually there came a time when if I wanted to go to Wales I had to travel under my own steam. It didn't take long for the wool to be pulled from my eyes. By train, and then – when my grandmother gave me her old Simca saloon with its handy orange disabled sticker – by car, I would push along the old corridor to Carmarthenshire with a budding awareness that we had been hoodwinked. Wales, it turned out, was not somewhere you had to get out of as quickly as your four wheels would carry you. In subtle and creeping ways it grew on me. But hold on, I remember realising one evening as loafy hills burned in the slanting western sunlight, Carmarthenshire's gorgeous. I was much taken with the diesel trains chugging picturesquely to and fro along the shore of the Tywi estuary. I started to feel possessive about the lowing castle at Llansteffan, a broken-toothed ruin put out to grass centuries ago but still pluckily commanding the heights. This would have happened when I was about twenty, and getting past my teenage indifference to landscape. I stopped looking at Wales through paternal eyes.

Many years and many visits to Wales later, and for all my shouting at the telly on match days, I'm still pretty much English. I certainly sound English. I'm like everyone else. I have a deep hankering to come from somewhere. Maybe it's because I'm a Londoner, but I feel rootless. My kind of middle-class Englishness lacks meaning, at least to me. Which is why I've drifted over the Severn this overcast Friday morning. A magnet has drawn me. The Welsh call it *hiraeth*: longing. But I'm nowhere near Welsh enough to start giving my feelings Welsh names.

It's on the sea wall where Welsh land and Welsh water meet that it occurs to me: to take the scenic route round Wales, do the whole circumnavigation. It suddenly seems the thing to do: to put a girdle round the old country. I have seven spare days, and no real idea how to kill them. I bet it doesn't get done much, if at all – coming in on the new Severn Bridge and several hundred Welsh miles later leaving on the old one. I can practically feel obsession, that omnivore of the male brain, sinking its talons in. This is a man-made project that will need rules and order. It will impose discipline and purpose. It will make sense.

Before I skip down the steps and into the car, I invent some instant guidelines. No islands, of which there are several (so Anglesey is out). Always stick to the road nearest the sea, however tiddly. And when I get close to the northern border, cut inland and drive down along the Welsh side of Offa's Dyke, the man-made ridge which once upon a time advised interested parties where England begins and Wales ends.

I unlock my car, lower myself behind the steering wheel, open the map to the relevant corner of Wales, reconfigure my milometer back to zero and turn the key.

What follows is a slow and winding crash course in Welshness, although the Welsh have a more resonant word for it: *Cymreictod*. On the surface at least, the induction is topographical. Knobbly headlands and beetling cliffs make way for windy strands of white powdery beach. Chimneys belch and cough. There are Georgian jewels and kiss-me-quick resorts. Estuaries bite deep chunks out of the coast. Turrets of innumerable castles prop up the clouds. Mountains tumble into the sea. Along the edge of Offa's Dyke delineating the old border with England, empty moorlands sound like the winds which howl about them: Eglwyseg, Berwyn, Y Mynyddoedd Duon.

At strategic points I get out and walk. And walk – over heathered moors, up looping paths, along deserted beaches, past trilling woodland streams, onto tufty headlands and into secretive coves. I walk among the stony remains of past incursions: castles raised by kings and barons, abbeys planted by monks, now roofless and naked to the heavens. Welsh weather permitting, it's usually possible to see along the tumultuous coast towards the site of the next ramble. And the weather, contrary to expectation, does permit. Friendly breezes shoo away the cloud cover. The sun is free to pick out blues and greens, the seas and meadows partitioned by seams of sand and rock. Once or twice it rains old women and sticks, as they colourfully say in Welsh, and I can't see beyond the fence. Otherwise it wouldn't be Wales.

The more I stop to clamber up hummocks and take in the view, the more I am baffled by something. When you can see so much of it in one go, the country seems no larger than a postage stamp. One miraculous dusk I sit on a drystone wall, picking at an Indian takeaway, and with the naked eye take in the entire sixty-mile semi-circular sweep of Cardigan Bay while Snowdon and her siblings bustle and bristle beyond the shore. I've only ever gawped at that from a plane before. Another golden twilight I look down on the long arcadian corridor of Clwyd, beyond it the whole commotion of North Wales as far as the eye can see, and in the distance the magnificent lonely peak of Cadair Idris. Wales, in short, doesn't go far. On the other hand, criss-crossed by a labyrinth of ridges and ravines, it goes on for ever. Its distances are in its ups and downs, in the intestinal coils of roads pushed this way and that by Welsh geology.

The binary nature of the place is of course underlined, even
enforced, by the names of things. Such has been the success of the
Welsh Language Society's rearguard action that this is a country
where you can be driving to two places at once: one with a Welsh
name, another known by a later English alternative. With only
myself to entertain I try to exhume a grandson's sepia memories of
Welsh pronunciation. The signposts are never slow to tease the
tongue: I pass through Dinbych-y-Pysgod and Abereiddy, Mwnt
and Tywyn and Gŵyr, Llanystumdwy and Rhydycroesau, Dwygyfyl-
chi and Penbontrhydyfothau. The consonants I'm sort of on top of,
but the vowels can seem as alien as Greek. It's as if they're encrypted
to bamboozle some nameless enemy. Forebears of mine knew their
way round every nook of the language. For all my efforts, Welsh
keeps its back turned to me. I look at a sentence without the first
idea which word's the verb. And yet the Romans left their Latin
DNA in the names for things: *pont* and *porth* and *castell*. Wales is a
broth, I tell myself, thousands of years in the brewing.

And then there is the quilt of voices. As I make my clockwise
circuit, the accents of the place sing and dance, narrow and fatten.
The voice of the capital has a tight, parsimonious tang. The Dyfed
accent swoops and dips in a hilly lilt. In Gwynedd delicate wispy
vowels flutter as if wind-borne. Across the porous border of Clwyd
come abrupt stabs of nasal Scouse, while further south in Powys
and Gwent impenetrable inflections form a kind of natural barrier
against the enemy over the hill.

By the end the milometer, measuring serrations in the coastline
and the jagged eastern edge of the country, has ticked over towards
850 or so long and very winding miles. That tally incorporates
wrong turnings, backtrackings, map-reading indecision and
evening sorties from my bed and breakfast to the pub for stout and
chips. There are also a pair of disastrous mishaps in which I

accidentally drive a good hundred yards into England. Manfully I control an obsessive-compulsive urge to turn round and snake back along another route and maintain the Welshness of my footprint. There are only so many country lanes, lurching and burrowing along the fertile length of the border, stuck behind ancient hatchbacks and swaying tractors or even bobbing dinghies on their stately way to water, that even the keenest born-again Welshman can take.

So by the time I drive deliberately back into England with a sentimental lump bulging in my throat, I am confused. On the one hand, I am so bloody Welsh you wouldn't believe it. On the other, I don't believe it myself. The symbolism of my chosen route is irrefutable. I have gone around Wales. It's where a lot of Wales is. But I haven't strayed into the heart of Wales, or into my own Welshness. I wonder if despite this immersion I can make any claim to be Welsh at all. Maybe it's all been just a mirage. I try to banish the thought, but a week after my week in Wales I can only look on helplessly as imperious England replants its flag in my head. I am disappointed with myself. The inference is clear. I must be culturally fickle. I'm no more than a flirt. Or, worse, a tourist.

I don't want to be like one of those American Celts who stick out like sore thumbs in pubs. It seems clear that Wales is not going to claim me voluntarily as one of its own. If I want to turn myself into a Welshman, I'm going to have to force the issue. I'm going to have to look for Welsh experiences, try to get Welsh stuff done. Some are born Welsh. Some achieve Welshness. I am going to thrust myself upon Wales.

So I'm going back in.

1

Dechrau = Begin

'Tell me where Wales begins.'

H.V. Morton, *In Search of Wales* (1932)

ONCE UPON A TIME we all spoke Welsh. Before the Normans came, before the Vikings, before the Angles and the Saxons brought their amalgamated Johnny-come-lately language, before even the Romans rowed across the seas, the inhabitants of the place we call England were, in effect, Welsh. The various invaders, who referred to the natives as Britons, successfully shunted the indigenous language back into the mountain fastnesses in the west, where what was once known as Brythonic evolved into the great survivor that is Welsh.

Did they but know it, compelling evidence confronts anyone who crosses the so-called English Channel and sees rising white cliffs, a geographical feature tightly allied with English identity, gleam across the water. The ferry pulls in at the dock. Vehicles nudge from its innards onto English tarmac. Drivers trickle through customs and excise, brandishing passports, their badges of nationhood. They are greeted by a sign: 'Port of Dover Ferry Terminal'.

The name 'Dover' is a modern transliteration of *dwfr*. *Dwfr* is

Old Welsh for water. The most English of ports with its blue birds and its chalky ramparts, which could not be much further east of Wales, takes its name from the island's oldest living language.

Like it or not, in the beginning was Welshness.

'So tell me, Bryn, what is Welshness?' As I work on my plan of campaign for Project Wales, there's no harm in going to the very top. I look straight into the blue eyes of Bryn Terfel, the international face of Wales. 'How would you measure Welshness?' I add, for good measure.

The face seems fashioned from rock. The jaw has a kind of jutting mass, a hewn heft. I am reminded of one of those monstrous capstones on the burial chambers that dot the long coastline of Cardigan Bay.

We are in a hotel not far from Caernarfon. Outside the fields are lush from summer rains. Into the mouth from which the famous bass baritone sound has emerged these twenty years, the great man has been shovelling forkfuls of pasta quills with roasted vegetables. But now the loaded fork hangs suspended. There is a ruminant pause. The blue eyes betray cogitation. And then he speaks.

'For me personally,' he says, 'a Welshman that sings, who speaks the language, lives in Wales, brought up, everything Welsh, education, through the medium of Welsh, being taught geography in Welsh, biology in Welsh, maths in Welsh.' The oracle has delivered its verdict, without recourse to main verbs. But there is no mistaking his meaning. Welshness sprouts from the soil. To define yourself as truly Welsh, you need to have learned about the birds and the bees and the isosceles triangle in the native tongue.

I swallow. According to the international face of Wales, my quest is over before it has even begun. I will never turn myself into a Welshman. I can give up now. But hold on, here comes more.

'Sometimes people might laugh at the fact that you haven't read things like *Madame Bovary*. But you've read your Welsh poets and your Welsh writers. That's something that matters. I read *The Mabinogion* to my kids most nights. I love to think that my children are growing up exactly as I did, through the medium of Welsh in primary schools. It didn't harm me at all.'

So Welshness is also about handing a legacy on to your children. I decide not to mention my own Welsh inheritance, the celebratory whoops as we cleared the Severn Bridge and raced into England. Nor my failure to enthuse my daughters about their quarter Welshness. I try to suppress the despondency in my voice.

'You're setting the bar quite high there, Bryn.'

He looks at me.

'This is only from my perspective,' he says. 'I love to have my roots firmly planted in Wales.'

I look back at him.

'You could come and live in Wales now?' he offers.

The bar is coming down. Not by much, mind. My life is in London: children, work, responsibilities. There really is no hope.

'And if you showed any enthusiasm towards the language you would be welcome here with open arms. There are two shops in my vicinity that are run by people who have come over from Liverpool, and not one morning have they said "good morning" in Welsh to me. I just need one word. It doesn't take much, does it?'

There's a mixed message in the blue eyes lodged in the midst of that giant face. They defy and they beseech. It's a very Welsh look.

'It is two hundred miles long and about one hundred miles wide. It takes some eight days to travel the whole length.' Thus wrote Gerald of Wales, author of the first effort to encapsulate in literature the essence of Wales and Welshness.

It is a structural quirk of travel literature that visitor speaks unto visitor. Gerald de Barri was born in Manorbier on the south coast of Pembrokeshire, and may have called himself Welsh, but the family tree has him down as three-quarters Norman. His *Description of Wales* was composed in Latin in the 1190s. Much travelled – he had crossed the Alps to Rome – he was nonetheless impressed by the forbidding wall which Wales presented to those approaching from England. 'Because of its high mountains, deep valleys and extensive forests, not to mention its rivers and marshes, it is not easy of access.'

This would remain a stock reaction for several hundred years. The mountains which had thwarted invaders also kept out visitors. It was in the eighteenth century that the trickle began, when roads became more passable and the leisured classes developed a new taste for luxuriating in the sublimity of untamed landscape. Daniel Defoe was one of the first literary travellers to gasp in awe as he confronted Wales's natural fortifications. 'I am now at the utmost extent of England west,' he noted in his *Tour Through the Whole Island of Great Britain*, 'and here I must mount the Alps, traverse the mountains of Wales.' The comparison with the Alps was apt, he enthused, 'but with this exception, that in abundance of places you have the most pleasant and beautiful valleys imaginable, and some of them, of very great extent, far exceeding the valleys so famed among the mountains of Savoy, and Piedmont.'

Wales's peaks and hollows were no longer unassailable to thrill-seekers. Indeed the first approving impression of Dr Johnson, arriving in the Vale of Clwyd in 1774, was that the place had been tamed: 'Wales, so far as I have yet seen of it, is a very beautiful and rich country, all enclosed and planted.' Travellers flocked west, several sending back dispatches which they would publish. The first impression was not always auspicious. The Revd Richard Warner, setting off on a walk through Wales in August 1797, was fleeced by the ferryman taking him over the Severn but consoled himself with improving thoughts of the river's classical lineage, known to Tacitus as Sabrina, and hymned by Milton. On landing in Wales he and a companion set out keenly to inspect the nation's monuments and ruins, only to meet an instant anticlimax. 'The ruins of Caldecot castle disappointed us,' he reported. 'In its appearance there is nothing striking or picturesque.'

Wales was particularly appealing to young men of unplacid temperament. No sooner did he penetrate Wales in 1798 than the excited young Turner was splashing its castles and crags onto canvas in untidy swirls and whorls. Walking into the Elan Valley as a very young man, the proto-revolutionary Shelley reported that 'this country of Wales is exceedingly grand: rocks piled on each to tremendous heights, rivers formed into cataracts by their projections, and valleys clothed with woods present an appearance of enchantment.' The sheer jaggedness of the place exercised a form of convulsion on his febrile mind. A few months later he introduced his young first wife Harriet to Wales. They had a treacherous thirty-six-hour crossing from Dublin. 'We had been informed that at the most we should certainly be no more than 12 hours,' wrote Harriet. 'We did not arrive at Holyhead till near 2 o'clock on Monday morning. Then we had above a mile to walk over rock and stone in a pouring rain before we could get to the inn. The night was dark and stormy.' It was only when day broke and Anglesey revealed its splendours that her pen seized up: '... the beauty of this place is not to be described.'

In dowdy middle age on a warm summer's day in 1824, Wordsworth had a more pleasant introduction to the north coast on a steam-packet from Liverpool with his wife and daughter. They 'passed the mouth of the Dee, coasted the extremity of the Vale of Clwyd, sailed close under Great Orme's Head, had a noble prospect of Penmaenmawr, and having almost touched upon Puffin's Island, we reached Bangor Ferry a little after six in the afternoon. We admired the stupendous preparations for the bridge over the Menai.'

Even the prospect of Wales, its beckoning landscape an eruption of the unfamiliar, had the capacity to restore the spirits of its visitors. George Borrow, author of the classic Victorian portrait *Wild Wales* (1862), sped towards the country by train in, he reports, a melancholy frame of mind 'till looking from a window I caught sight of a long line of hills, which I guessed to be the Welsh hills, as indeed they proved, which sight causing me to remember that I was bound for Wales, the land of the bard, made me cast all gloomy thoughts aside and glow with all the Welsh enthusiasm with which I glowed when I first started in the direction of Wales.' Francis Kilvert, arriving in 1865 to take up a position as a young curate in Clyro on the river Wye, recalled striding for the first time over the moor to Builth Wells. 'Then every step was through an enchanted land,' he wrote a decade later. 'I was discovering a new country and all the world was before me.'

And then there was the visitor who didn't know where England ended and Wales began. H. V. Morton, a journalist who popularised travel writing at the dawn of the motor-car age, pulled up on the border near Chirk, where there are no mountains forming a natural frontier, and had to ask. 'Your front wheels are in Wales,' he was told by a road sweeper, 'and your back wheels in England.' This was between the wars, when Welsh identity was in the doldrums, the language in steep decline and the mining industry rapidly shrinking after the Great Depression. Morton stood and watched the road sweeper 'sweep the dust of Wales into England'. Looking about him, he wondered why there was no sign to mark the border.

'Wales should see to this,' he concluded. 'Two million people, many of whom speak their own language, and all of whom are proud of their country and its traditions, should tell the traveller where it begins.' And with that, he motored into Wales.

How do you learn Welsh?

We've all had a go at a language. The Teach Yourself learning kits make it sound like assembling a toy aeroplane. Try our unique language-learning tool. Fluency always guaranteed. The common experience teaches us otherwise. Especially when our mother tongue is English. Built into the English-speaker's psyche is a consensus that speaking in other tongues will not be necessary. English has long since usurped French as the international language of diplomacy; indeed it has deracinated itself and transmuted into something so universal as to be known as globish, an intercontinental mulch of patois and webspeak. If this is your birthright, why on earth speak anyone else's lesser language? Let the mountain come to Muhammad. In the Microsoft Age, English is the thug in the playground, its bovver boot planted on the windpipe of vulnerable dialects and local lingos, starving them of air.

But there's one language which, despite a jolly plucky effort, English hasn't quite managed to murder. As it was right next door, it should have been easy to rub out Welsh, just as it all but managed with Irish. Prevailing attitudes of the empire-bestriding Victorian towards 'an antiquated and semi-barbarous language' were enshrined in an infamous diktat penned in London. 'The Welsh language,' *The Times* thundered in 1866, 'is the curse of Wales. Its prevalence and the ignorance of English have excluded and even now exclude the Welsh people from the civilisation ... of their English neighbours ... The sooner all Welsh specialities disappear from the face of the earth the better.' And so it was that the 1870 Education Act gave with one hand – free schooling for all Welsh children – but took away with the other: the outlawing of Welsh in the classroom. Naturally the language pupils spoke at home and among themselves would trip inadvertently off many a junior tongue throughout the day. The first to do so would have a wooden tablet hung round their neck bearing the letters *WN* for 'Welsh Not'. It would be passed from one miscreant to another until, at the end of the school day, the child who had possession of this instrument of linguistic oppression would be thrashed.

'*Welsh?!*' says someone when I mention that I'm thinking of taking Bryn Terfel's advice. Her face screws up into a twisted moue of distaste. Some things never change. Her eyes scrunch. Her cheeks pucker. Her mouth gathers into a tight, uncharitable little anus. I swear it's involuntary. In that face is printed a millennium's worth of accumulated hauteur. A plume of fiery wrath whooshes up somewhere in the furnace of my guts. I really ought to give her a thorough dressing-down, but I find that I'm too polite – too *English* – to do it myself. She admits, on being pressed, that she has never been to Wales.

Yes, Welsh.

These feelings are good, it occurs to me. If my knee-jerk reaction is to hate those who hate the Welsh, I must therefore be a little bit Welsh already.

The old English joke about Welsh is the same as the one about Polish. It's a language which, for whole sections of randomly juggled letters, seems to get by entirely without vowels. If you haven't been walked through the rules and regs of the Welsh alphabet, it has the look of a sardine can of consonants. Vowels being the breath of a language, Welsh seems bafflingly to subsist without air.

Even if native English speakers are not linguists, some are more inclined that way than others. I couldn't do the sciences – yes, I hold my hands up: I flunked matrices and enzymes and all that quantum stuff and guff. But I could always find my way around the floor plan of a new language. It was the kind of learning I was good at: the shapes of words, their sinews and musculature, their etymological kinship with root languages, alliances with sister languages, their migrations and false friendships – this was the stuff that fired my curiosity.

But the learning was all literary. We didn't do much speaking in class, or not in the relevant language. We did reading instead. When I left school I could wade through Balzac and Molière in the original. But in France I could barely order myself a bowl of soup. Spanish and German I've basically forgotten. Then at eighteen I went away and for the first time tried learning a language by speaking it. To this day Italian is the comfiest fit. The experience taught me that the classroom is not the best place to pursue oral fluency. Or not the classrooms I was in.

But old habits die hard. Just for starters, I decide to swallow a chunk of Welsh vocab. So one day, when I'm in Wales, I make my way to the back of *The Rough Guide to Wales* and hoover up their short glossary of useful terms. Being a guidebook, it mostly comprises boilerplate words and phrases for 'good morning' and 'cheers', 'town hall' and 'bed and breakfast' and 'how much is that breathable windcheater in the window'? Many of them are familiar to all-comers from the bilingual signage you see everywhere in Wales. *Araf* for 'slow', *gorsaf* for 'station', in which *f*, it says here, is pronounced like a *v*. In *heddlu* (police) that double *d* is a hard *th* sound, as in 'this' or 'thus'. Oh, but here's the first curveball. That *u*, *The Rough Guide* advises, is actually pronounced *ee*. You basically have to treat it as an encryption. Like Cyrillic. Or music.

In the guidebook there is also a list of topographical nouns. In any other language, you probably wouldn't want to know how they say 'mountain pass', or not for the first couple of years. But more than other languages I've learned, Welsh geography is written in the names on the signposts. *Llan*, to take the most in-your-face example, literally means an enclosed piece of land, though it has long since been taken to refer to the church found within such an enclosure. There are more than 600 Llans in Wales, from the modestly named Llan all the way through to Llanfairpwllgwyngyllgogerychwyrndrobwllllantysiliogogogoch (which has two Llans in it). *Aber*, another prefix, means river mouth. *Pwll* means pool; *nant*, stream; *cwm*, valley; *melin*, mill, and *maes*, field. And so on. At Aberystwyth is found the mouth of the river Ystwyth. Porthmadog is Madog's gate. Cwm Rhondda is the famous Rhondda Valley. And so on and on. The *w* in *cwm*, it turns out, is actually a double *o*, so there's another vowel to add to the collection. Mountain pass, by the way, is *bwlch*.

That's fifty or so words in the bag without even breaking sweat. I buy a little red book, write them down and start to learn, like the good old days of O-level vocab. Welsh on the left, English on the right. That's the way to do it. I tell myself it all seems quite easy.

This facility didn't take a direct route down the family tree. My father grew up in a bilingual environment. Welsh was the first language of both his parents. A Welsh-speaking grandmother lived with the family. 'But English was the language of the house,' he tells me. 'I can remember driving round Carmarthenshire with my father visiting cousins on farms. My father spoke Welsh to them and I didn't understand a word.' How was it? 'Very dull.'

His older brother by contrast – my uncle – was linguistically attuned. Perhaps because he spoke only Welsh till he was three, he learned languages for fun, much as other boys play with train sets. It was a feature of our childhood, asking our uncle how many languages he spoke. The official tally settled on nine. We used to list them, starting with English as well as, obviously, French, Italian,

Spanish and German. One Boxing Day in Carmarthen, when I was about seven and everyone else was out on horseback killing foxes, he taught me to count to a million in German. He wrote a Latin primer at six. For him this was a living language rather than a remnant of the classroom. When resigning from the priesthood in Rome in the year of my birth, he had had to write to Pope John XXIII in the lingua franca of the Vatican. Modern Greek was another of his, also Russian. He once even had a stab at Turkish, though that wasn't on the list back then. And finally there was Welsh, which he relearned at the age of twelve.

'I'm thinking of learning Welsh,' I volunteer when I see him.

'Wonderful,' he says. 'It's a marvellous language. You'll love it.' My uncle is an enthusiast.

'I've already learned the words for black mountain and coastal marsh,' I add. 'Seems pretty easy so far. Any tips?'

'Well, there is one real snag with Welsh.'

'What?'

'The system of mutating. It's absolutely horrid. Really nasty.'

'Yes, but what is it?'

'You're used to changing the endings of words in French or Italian. In Welsh they change the fronts of words.' He pulls a face as if suffering a mildly unpleasant back spasm.

'That seems manageable,' I say.

'Ah, but there's a bit more to it than that.' He proceeds to explain that, depending on circumstances, a word like *tad* (father) may actually change to *dad*, *thad* or *nhad*. He pulls more of an anguished face this time, as if hearing of a relative's slightly early demise.

I've never heard of such a counter-intuitive linguistic model. Change the *front* of a word? You might as well stick it in a priest's hole. Still, that's only one word that changes, in only three ways. Presumably there'll be a few like that, a small bunch of wildly misbehaving individuals you have to keep your eye on, like incurable show-offs in class. I am undaunted.

'That's just one word. Are there other examples of these ... what are they called?'

'Mutations,' he says. It sounds like a botch-up in a laboratory. 'I'm afraid so. As a system, it's more or less ubiquitous. Mutations are absolutely integral to the Welsh language. You just have to learn them.' This time his voice and face impart outright shock and horror.

And if the mountains denied ease of access, so did the rivers. The Bristol Channel – the Severn estuary – presented the same obstacle to motorists in the mid 1960s as it did to the Romans. Before they built the bridge the journey was interminable. We had a Singer estate in racing green which my father wove along Welsh A roads with, I suspect, a mixture of impatience and dread. Impatience to escape a car with three small fighting boys. Dread at the imminence of home. Not that I knew any of that then. I just felt sick. Sometimes I actually was sick, usually by the side of the road, but once, spontaneously, down the front of my jumper (knitted by my grandmother), into my lap and thence onto the permeable weave of the Singer's back seat. After that I was allowed in the front. I took to this privilege like an insufferable princeling. Whenever a car journey beckoned, I would assert my rights over both brothers without conscience or let-up.

'Why does he always get to go in the front?'

'Because he gets car-sick, poppet.' My mother called her sons 'poppet' a lot. Mothers did back then.

'We're only going to Chichester.' This from my older brother.

'Yeah, but it's bendy.' This from me, with a hard, vituperative edge. That was the answer to everything. It's bendy. Nowhere was bendier than Wales. After they built the suspension bridge it became less so, but my primacy had been established by then. I spent my entire childhood in the front.

The bridge gave rise to a competition. Who would be the first to spot it? Children are not good with distances. We'd set out from West Sussex, usually quite early, and soon after we hit the M4 we'd start scouring the horizon for the telltale turrets. On and on the road mowed west, but our quarry resisted all efforts to will it into sight. I had the advantage of course, being in the front seat and therefore closer, with a full windscreen to see through. It must be round this hill. It must be over that brow. It must be. It never was, not for aeons. We'd start to lose interest, get bored, perhaps be distracted by the prospect of a squabble.

'You're a dimmy.'

'No, you are, so there.'

'Am not.'

'Boys, look!'

'Are so.'

'Not.'

'Can you see what I can see?'

You rounded a hill and there, surprisingly close, would be the Severn Bridge, suspended as if from the clouds. Strangely fore-shortened by a trick of perspective, visible long before the stretch of water it spanned, it was a thing of mystery and fascination.

We had a ritual of driving up for a closer look. There was a service station called Aust built on the banks above the Severn. I know now that Aust Services was the direst shitpit and the thought of it caused my parents to sink into morbid depression, but to us it was a wonderland. We'd eat eggs, beans and chips – chips were forbidden at home because my mother objected to the lingering pong – and look up at the bridge magnificently filling the window.

Below it the Severn swam muddily by. And on the other side of the
bridge you could see Wales. Or so we thought. Actually you
couldn't. It took me decades to work out that Wales begins beyond
the Wye, not the Severn, and that the opposite bank was
Gloucestershire.

'How many miles to go?' We knew exactly how far it was from
the bridge to our grandparents. Children with no concept of distance ask such things frequently.

'Eighty-four … seventy and a half …' My father would turn
arithmetical. 'Sixty-eight and three-quarters …' The revolving
milometer kept us from fighting. 'Fifty-nine point nine …' Progress
was slow. In those days, somewhere after Cardiff, the motorway
petered out into a single carriageway and the numbers would click
along with agonising reluctance. 'Forty-seven and a third.' Sometimes there was nothing else for it but to peer out at Wales crawling
by beside us.

It looked nothing like England. Children don't notice countryside. They aren't interested in the character conferred by the lumps
and bumps of landscape. But they know a plug-ugly bungalow
when they see one. They also regard deviations from their known
environment as somehow deficient, and that was certainly how I
saw the towns and villages the Singer hared through in the days
before speed cameras. It sure as heck didn't look like home. The
road was lined with squat, drab housing, low-slung shops and
hatchet-faced pubs. I remember wondering by what right petrol stations, planted in the middle of nowhere, were permitted to exist
with such unfamiliar names. And overhead it was forever grey. From
those journeys along that snaking, snailing road, whether I was four
or five or eight or nine, I have not kept a single memory of the sun.

'Twenty-seven miles to go.'

The colour, such as existed, was all in the names of places. And what colours they were. As we drove on we'd ask my father to read them out.

'How do you say that one?'

'Cwmrhydyceirw.' My father had a musician's ear for sound and a trace memory of correct pronunciation: the rising terminals, the firmly placed stresses that made Welsh sound like both a statement and a question.

'And that one?'

'Pontarddulais.' I might not have liked the look of the western end of Glamorgan as it began to shade into Carmarthenshire, but I liked the sound of it.

'Thirteen miles!' The countdown now began to take on a breathless urgency. We really wanted to get there. The hours in the car – five, six; once even epically close to *eight* – were gladly behind us, done and dusted, gone and forgotten. In front of us lay the golden prospect. Ten miles. The car swept along. Eight and a half. My father would be driving faster by now. Seven. We were in the west. Six and a quarter. No other cars on the road. Five. We swung off the main road and up a hill. Four. Is it just a fantasy or did the sun shoulder aside the clouds around now? Three. 'Bags I hug Granny first!' Two. '*I'm* going to!' One and a half. We thumped along the lane, hearts almost bouncing out of mouths. 'No, I am!' One. 'She's *my* granny, not *yours*.' I was convinced that our grandmother was exclusively my possession, that my brothers had some other grandmother, as yet unmet, for them to visit as and when they chose. 'She's everyone's granny,' my mother would say, her own mother dead before we were all born. 'Mine!' And there with half a mile to go, it would spontaneously erupt out of nowhere, a flash fight over grandmaternal ownership. 'No, mine!' I may have made my older brother cry with my ruthless power-grab. And thus as we bore down on our destination, the atmosphere turned fretful with junior fomentation and puerile wrath.

'Look, boys!' My father creating a diversion. Carmarthen beckoning. You could see it on the right-hand side, parked proudly in
the valley with hills lofting into the distance beyond. Caerfyrddin.
Merlin's Castle. No sooner there than it disappeared behind a
hedgerow, then a brow, then a village of tiny modern houses that
had recently sprouted on the hillside. The car rattled as it passed
over a cattle grid guarding the entrance to the house. And there it
was: low and wide, mock-Gothic windows, a porch painted a glossy
black, the door a beckoning white. We exploded out of the Singer
and thundered towards the door. I don't remember if there was a
bell or a knocker, but that's because my grandmother would have
heard the car clearing the grate and the voices filling the air and we
would barely even get to the porch before the door, heavy and thick,
would creak heart-stoppingly open to bid us welcome to the prom-
ised land.

I am going back to school. 'Welsh Level 1, Module 1,' it says in the
City Lit literature. I've never gone anywhere near adult education
before, and am amazed on flicking through the thick catalogue to
find that you can learn more or less anything. Yoga is an option, as
is opera. So are sewing and self-defence, Afro-Cuban drumming
and personal development. You can make jewellery, study anatomy,
learn to podcast. There are options for folklore, myth and spiritual
studies, for the philosophy of photography. They will even teach
you creative writing. Of course all the usual languages are queuing
up, but so too are the unusual ones. You name it, they teach it.
Including Welsh Level 1, Module 1.

'Learn to speak Welsh on this lively course for beginners, with
the emphasis on the practical use of Welsh and the development of
your listening and speaking skills.' I am two weeks late for some
reason. The course has already started, but I've been assured over

the phone that there is still one place. I fill out the form, write out the cheque and join the multicultural queue. City Lit is one of those buildings in the capital around which individuals randomly cluster from all generations, all corners of the globe, each brought here by the prospect of self-improvement. We are all trying to qualify for something or other. Me, I seek qualification as a Welshman. Following Bryn Terfel's recommendation, I am making my entry through the portal of language.

The room looks full. Of women mainly, mainly of a certain age. Standing at the front is a thin youngish man of medium height with fair red hair. 'Sh'mae,' he says in a Welsh accent as I push open the door. From my *Rough Guide* vocab list I know that is some sort of greeting.

'Er, hello.' Why on these occasions does one feel oneself flush? 'I ... I've come along for Welsh Module 1, er ...'

'Well, the class is full actually.' The voice sounds uncommiserating.

'Oh, I was told there was one place left.'

'Oh.'

'Oh.' This is a face-off. Having shelled out ninety quid, I shan't be backing down.

'What's your name?'

'Jasper Rees,' I say, laying heavy stress on the surname. I am clearly Welsh, with a name like that. The less said about the first name ...

'James dw i – croeso.' Thus the first sentence of Welsh ever uttered specifically to me: he is James and I am welcome. And so, after twenty-three years, I resume my education.

'Iawn,' says James, turning to the class. *Iawn* means OK, another word I already know. 'Last week your homework was learning the days of the week. So let's run through them again together. Dydd Llun ...' The class embarks on a slow recitation. 'Dydd Mawrth.' I have of course missed the first two lessons. 'Dydd Mercher.' A sudden memory taps me on the shoulder: this is what it was like arriving at boarding school, being behind in Latin and French. 'Dydd Iau.' I detest being behind. 'Dydd Gwener.' What else have they already conquered? They seem practically fluent. 'Dydd Sadwrn.' Hm, that sounds like Saturday. I glance across to my neighbour's textbook, open on the days of the week. 'Dydd Sul.' Some of these words are not so far from French or Italian. *Dydd Llun* must be Monday, *Dydd Mercher* Wednesday. It's all doable actually. Why was I worried?

'Da iawn.' *Da* must mean good – as in *bore da* (good morning), *iechyd da* (good health/bottoms up). It's like embarking on a crossword, filling in the clues.

'Now remember that in Welsh they also have words for the *nights* of the week. So let's go through those.' The class draws a collective breath and …

This time they seem more hesitant. 'Nos Lun.' Clearly they can't pronounce the tricky double L on *Llun*. 'Nos Fawrth.' Eh? What happened to *Mawrth*? The class leaves big gaps after each *Nos* as they read James's lips. 'Nos Fercher.' Why isn't it *Nos Mercher*? What's with the *F*s? 'Nos Wener.' And now Friday – *Gwener* – has gone and lost its *G*. It's completely missing its initial letter. The nights of the week are disintegrating before my very ears.

'Has anyone noticed something odd?' This from James. I'll say. A woman raises a cautious hand.

'The letters have changed?'

'Yes, good. And why is that?' With ill-suppressed cockiness, one of the class's few men pipes up.

'Mutation.'

'Oh, here we go.' A woman at the back wall is already fatalistic about mutations.

'Da iawn. Because "nos" is a feminine noun it triggers a soft
mutation.' James grimaces. 'Nothing I can do about it, I'm afraid.'
My uncle pulled the same face and said the same thing. He wasn't
lying. They really do alter the *fronts* of words. For anyone used to
forming an opinion of a word by its first syllable, this seems almost
wilfully obstructive. It's like encrypting your face with a false moustache, or collagen, or a burqa. These slippery mutations are shape-
shifters and not to be trusted.

I look around the class to see who's coping with the news. They
seem outwardly calm, apart from one woman with rodenty cheeks
and suffering eyes. Who are these people? Who in London learns
Welsh? One assumes it's Welsh expats who have lost the language.
Or descendants like me who never had it. Or people who have
married a Welsh speaker. Whose children are being educated
through the medium of Welsh. You hear that a lot in Wales: *the
medium of Welsh*, as if language lessons are a form of seance, a communication with one's forebears. We are exiles and émigrés all
drawn to the same redemptive well.

And so the lesson continues. It's ninety minutes of intense
Welsh. Basically, a double period. I'd forgotten how one yearns for
the bell, how the minute hand crawls and creeps and all but grinds
to a halt. But I am diligent in my note-taking. My vocabulary list
lengthens as James explains how to introduce yourself in Welsh.
'Pwy dych chi?' he writes on the board. Who are you? 'James dw i,'
he's saying. He is James.

'Right, so let's all do an exercise.' There is a clatter and flap of
swing-round desks as the class rises as one and shuffles into the
open space. People look for someone to introduce themselves to. I
gravitate towards a woman with big blue eyes.

'Pwy dych chi?' she says. Oh God, she's fluent. The accent is
perfect – the *ch* properly abrasive. *Pwy* is pronounced 'poy'.

'Jasper, er, dw i.' My Welsh accent is direct from Harrow-on-the-Hill. 'Pwy dych chi?' Poowy ducky. It wouldn't get you served in one of those legendary pubs where they all apparently start speaking Welsh the minute an Englishman walks in. I am nonetheless speaking Welsh.

'Julia dw i,' she volunteers. 'Sounds a bit rude, doesn't it, just saying "Who are you?"' Julia is very perky, even flirty. Someone barges in with a notebook. 'Pwy dych chi?' It's a man with an alpha-male aura about him. 'Pete dw i.' I try others in the room. Sian is rather serious. Mike wades through like a schoolmaster taking registration. Karen comes next, hesitant, eager. Thus we work the space, a circling clump of adult learners effecting introductions in Welsh. In due course it's my turn with Alpha Pete. His accent is pleasingly shiter than my cut-glass abomination. Eventually I come face to face with the terrified woman. Her hair's in a bit of a bun.

'Pwy dych chi?' I ask.

'Anne dw i,' she says, not lifting her nose from her notebook. 'Pwy dych chi?' The sound stutters out like an old-fashioned tickertape newsfeed, jerky, robotic. Her face is a complex mesh of hurt, fear and seething rage. Languages do that to some people. 'Jasper dw i,' I reply. She'll never last. Not a chance. Me, I'm in it for the duration.

My pursuit of Welshness has started to give off a vibe. I exude some sort of aura that encourages people to venture polite recommendations. 'You should meet so-and-so,' they'll volunteer. 'He/she can tell you all about Welsh politics/flora/universities/carpentry/fauna/surfing/tweed/gastropubs/scriptwriting/whisky/glaciology/grunge/cheese/nineteenth-century vernacular architecture. You really should. It would be good for your research.' They are always things that every culture has, but on this occasion given an apparently Welsh twist. Welshness seeps into all sorts of areas, into not all of which I feel the need to tread. Sometimes they just say, 'You should meet my dad. He can tell you lots of stuff about Wales.' And I'll think, I've got my own, if it's all the same. Thanks, but *dim diolch* (no thanks). 'You should go to Patagonia.' The process of fending off unwanted advice is helpful. It allows me to clarify in my mind what it is I'm looking for. I am looking for experiences that can be had only in Wales. I am chasing the quintessence of what it is to feel Welsh.

Hence, one beautiful sunny afternoon, I find I am going backwards. Despite my very best efforts. Steering on water has its own perverse logic, which, for the moment, is to me elusive. I was never much the oarsman. If you are going to learn to be Welsh, this is where to start. In the world's mind, Wales and Welshness may both subsequently have found themselves attached to other things. But before wool, slate and coal, before song and the oval ball, before leeks and daffodils and all the other better-known brand concepts, there was the coracle. The coracle goes back thousands of years. And like the Welsh language it's still going. Just.

'Hold the paddle like this!' From across a stretch of water Bernard Thomas is hollering instructions. His right hand grips the notched head, his left halfway down the shaft. I imitate the hold and brandish the paddle.

'Now, I want you to bring the coracle over here.' Bernard is perhaps twenty-five feet away across the limpid green-brown river. I flap my paddle and, ever so gently, the distance between us grows. Bernard recedes and then, when I make a more forceful effort to move forward, he spins entirely out of view. Now I am going backwards, in circles.

Bernard is as old as the hills that have sent this river and countless others broiling down through clefts and chasms until calm settles upon them as they meander across flat lovely plains towards the nearing sea. It's easy to confuse the various waterways, at least in this south-western quadrant of Wales where coracling lives on. Defoe noted the odd coincidence of South Wales's alliter- ating rivers: "Tis very remarkable, that most of the rivers in this county chime upon the letters T, and Y, as Taaf, Tawy, Tuy, Towy, Tyevy.' Or as they say in Welsh, the Taf and the Tawe, the Tywi and the Teifi. (I've no idea what or where the Tuy is.) In this case we're on the Teifi. It begins its journey many miles back in the desert uplands of Mid Wales, makes its way through Tregaron and Lland- dewi Brefi, past Lampeter and Newcastle Emlyn, then slips through a quartet of fishing villages known for their association with the coracle – Cenarth, Abercych, Llechryd, Cilgerran – before fetching up at Aberteifi, the mouth of the Teifi, better known as Cardigan.

I have come to the right place to begin Project Wales. Bernard Thomas is the oldest Welsh practitioner of the oldest Welsh tradi- tion. By the time I meet him, he has been retired from coracling for a fortnight. He is eighty-eight, and has spent eighty of those years on the river. As a boy he went on the Teifi with his father; as a young man he used to like taking girls out on the river with a fly- fishing rod. It was at the end of the war that Bernard chose to become a coracle man, like his father before him, whose licence he inherited. The first thing he needed was a boat, but the coracle- maker in Cenarth refused to teach him how to make one. He claims that he dreamt how to do it instead. Using willow, hazel and calico, over the years Bernard has made hundreds, taught many others and indeed given a lot of boats away.

Three of them are parked on a low wall in the sun outside his small house in Llechryd when I pull up. They resemble beetles hunkering in a row. He is standing beside them, a fluffy limping dog at his feet. His face has something of that concavity which visits the cheeks of the extremely old. The voice, which sounded withered and feeble on the phone, has a bit more heft in person. He's lived here since 1946.

During the season, from April to August, he'd go out coracling. It was a nine-to-five job: from nine at night to five in the morning. Then, after two hours' sleep, he'd be back at work wiring houses. Every day the fishmonger would drive along the Teifi Valley buying the night's catch from the coracle fishermen. 'My average was around eight to ten salmon a night. The largest I caught was thirty and a quarter pounds. That was a *big* fish.'

Coracling being done in pairs, and the net held between two craft as they drift downriver, he's fished 'with many a chap' over the decades, including his son and latterly his grandson. But Bernard has often been out on his own too. On Saturdays in winter he would paddle out with his twelve-bore to shoot a duck for Sunday lunch. He'd also rescue sheep caught in the water, cows, and humans who had fallen in when drunk, or jumped in when depressed. Bernard even coracled across the Channel in the 1970s. It took him twelve hours.

Now that Bernard is no longer fishing, a tradition that stretches back 3,500 years is one step closer to extinction. No new licence has been granted since the 1930s. There's the inevitable Coracle Museum in Cilgerran. But the drift from living tradition towards the artificial respirator of heritage seems irreversible. Ten years earlier the fishmonger's van stopped coming. 'Everything's diminished,' he says. 'There's hardly any trout now, there's no eels coming up the river. *Siwin* [Welsh for sea trout] that have been introduced to the river is all that's there.' He blames the pesticides. If a deloused sheep takes a bath in the river it kills the fish for a mile downstream. 'They've turned the river Teifi into a gutter.' His grandson has already given up.

One more tourist with a paddle can hardly staunch the tide. But I want to be Welsh, and Bernard is willing.

To pick up a coracle you grab the little loops at either side of the boat, hoist it onto your back, then loop the longer cross-handle over your neck so that it sits on your shoulders. It takes me three goes. As I totter, Bernard slots the paddle over my left shoulder, the end rammed under one of the hazel slats to take much of the burden. I feel like Dick Whittington with a very big knapsack.

Once Bernard gets his coracle up, we'll be good to go. He leans down slowly, grips the handles and pulls. The coracle rises a few inches off the ground before he lets it drop again. He's like a weight-lifter sizing up a load. A second go. This time he puts more into it and does slightly better. But he can't manage to heave it up and swing it round on his back. Bernard lets the coracle drop and looks up at me.

'The sooner I'm fucking dead the better!' he wails. It's heart-rending: an old man suddenly bereft of powers that have sustained and defined him through all his long life. His voice filled with anger and disgust. This is the real reason Bernard has given up coracling.

'Here, let me carry it, Bernard.'

He looks at me in scorn. 'You can't carry two, boy!' The prospect of help horrifies him. 'Just give me a hand lifting it.' So I deposit my coracle and lift his on his back while Bernard mutters about being good for nothing but the knacker's yard. To think coracle men used to walk miles under one of these, down to the river at dusk, then back up at dawn, while also lugging a heavy catch. We set off along the road. It's a slow trudge down to the nearby river. Salmon fishers on the Tywi, noted the Edwardian angler and author

A. G. Bradley, look 'uncommonly like some prehistoric monsters waddling down to drink'. Gingerly, he struggles down a deep cut in the bank.

'Now,' says Bernard, 'put the coracle down and put it in the water.' Years of instructing have made him terse and peremptory. 'Stick your paddle in the ground like this and then put one foot in the coracle and then the other.' He demonstrates, the blade in the earth, the other end in his armpit. Three-legged, he nimbly transfers his weight into the craft. When I try my body tenses. I don't trust the coracle not to float off while I've only one foot in it. Won't the calico crumple under the pressure of twelve or so stone pushing through one leg? I'm not sure I believe the evidence of its 3,500-year history. But carefully I transfer my weight from land to water and somehow it works.

'Put a foot in each corner, please.' The lesson begins. My spread feet impart balance and steady the vessel. Bernard pushes off into mid-river, swishing the blade of his paddle like a tentacular extension of his anatomy. Me, I swirl about like a cork in a whirlpool. 'Use the paddle like this!' he calls, holding it in front of the boat, stroking across from starboard to port. He twirls the vertical blade through ninety degrees so that it cuts thinly across the water, then repeats the stroke. My effort is less efficient. I copy the motion. Though the Teifi runs gently westwards, my coracle jerks and bobs as if caught in a foaming torrent. Bernard continues his patient coaching. I grow fretful at the boat's obedience to my flailing instructions. One false swish and I'm spinning to port. Then back again.

'Like this!' I keep at it and lo, the coracle nudges forwards. I have inadvertently done something right. I try to do it again but the paddle is clumsy in my hands. More rotation. 'Not like that!' Bernard's thin voice carries across the water. I try to repeat the motion without error and, yes, now the coracle responds to the correct coaxing.

'Come to me,' flutes Bernard, like a wizened siren, and I do. The river between us disappears. He proposes that we paddle downstream with the current. And so I scoop and slice the waters, scoop and slice, scoop and slice. Bernard is to my right.

'Now I want you to row with one arm.' He shoves the handle end into his right armpit, then grips the shaft with his right hand and coaxes the blade through the water at the side of the boat. This is harder, and I lose direction. With each spin I overcompensate, with the result that the bow is like a spectator at tennis, head switching left and right. I am lured towards a thicket of branches overhanging the river. 'You don't want to bloody go in there!' I resume the two-handed technique and escape. 'Try again.' Oddly, if only for a few strokes, the boat succumbs. Suddenly I see it. We are several yards apart, Bernard on the north side of the river, me on the south. We are each paddling with one arm, leaving the other free to hold the net between the two coracles.

'You've got it, boy!' Bernard calls, his voice reedy and infirm. 'You've got it!' The river drifts underneath us. Further down I can see a stately bridge, the end of Bernard's half-mile of river. Beyond it Bernard would never dream of going. The sun blesses the green banks of the Teifi. Our paddles caress the ancient waters. I am doing the oldest Welsh thing of all, reaching back to the very beginning of Welshness. 'You've got it, boy!' I am afloat.

2

Credu = Believe

'A Welshman is abandoned on a desert island and builds a church.
It takes five years. Then he spends another five building another
church. Five years after that he's rescued, and someone says,
"What's that?" "It's a church." "And what's that over there?" "It's a
church." "So why have you got two?" He says, "I don't go to that
one."'

A Welsh joke, *Guardian* (2010)

'BEFORE THE DAYLIGHT shines abroad, come, people …'

It is half past three. In the morning.

'… let us praise the Lord …'

We are not far beyond midsummer, but in this corner of Wales
the dawn is not even a twinkle in the eye of the Almighty.

'… whose grace and mercy thus have kept the nightly watch
while we have slept.'

Not that I got much kip. Through the thick monastery wall
came the bone-shaking rumbles of a snoring priest. I was granted
probably two hours. Now here I am at vigils, singing along with ten
monks robed neck to ankle in flowing white. It is, I repeat, half past
three *in the morning*. No one, surely, loves God this much.

It's less singing than chanting, featuring those small but

surprising musical intervals that occur only in plainsong. There are
no crashing major chords in the Cistercian songbook. Or indeed
chords at all. It sounds like the harmonic line to a missing melody:
up a tone here, down a minor third there – you never quite know
where the next note is heading. It is calming, though. Verily, it
could smooth the corrugated brow of a furious insomniac.

'O give thanks to the Lord, for he is good': Psalm 105. We are
operating a call and response system. The monks in the right-hand
stall sing one verse, then the monks on the left sing the other. I am
directly behind the abbot, bald and bespectacled, who has his back
to me. There are two others with me in the pews: priests. One of
them, I'm not sure which, is the snorer. They are here for a week's
worth of retreat. Which, in pursuance of Welshness, is sort of why
I am here too. Only not for a week. One day in the life of a Cistercian will do for me.

We reach the end of Psalm 106. 'Glory be to the Father,' they
chant, and as they do so they solemnly bow their heads. 'And to the
Son.' It really is abominably early. 'And to the Holy Spirit.' I only
ever get up at this hour to catch dirt-cheap flights from Stansted.
'As it was in the beginning …' They raise their heads. '… is now
and ever shall be …' The brothers are here every day of the year. '…
world without end …' Every day of their lives. 'Amen.'

One of those brothers is my uncle. His name nowadays is Teilo,
after the Welsh saint. Upon entering the monastery, and in order
to avoid having the same name as another monk, he changed it
from the one my grandparents gave him. Brother Teilo has been
on Caldey for a decade, initially as a novice. Having resigned from
the priesthood as a young man, he made his solemn profession at
the age of seventy-three. Others joined somewhat earlier: one
monk has been in the abbey since 1948. The Cistercians themselves have occupied it since 1929. It was the first monastery of

the order to reopen in Wales since Henry VIII dissolved the lot of them in the 1530s.

Gerald of Wales, writing in the twelfth century when the Cistercians were still quietly spreading their benign influence through Wales, approved of the order:

> Give the Cluniacs a tract of land covered with marvellous buildings, endow them with ample revenues and enrich the place with vast possessions; before you can turn round it will be ruined and reduced to poverty. On the other hand, settle the Cistercians in some barren retreat which is hidden away in an overgrown forest: a year or two later you will find splendid churches there and find monastic buildings, with a great amount of property and all the wealth you can imagine.

From the eleventh century until the Reformation, the Cistercians were everywhere in Wales. The tourist board is eternally grateful for the abbeys all over the country, which people still flock to see – Tintern, Strata Florida, Cymer, Valle Crucis, Neath and Margam and so on. There are thirteen of them in all. None now have so much as a roof between them, or indeed many walls. But here in these remote fastnesses is where the Cistercians left their footprint. They were the Welshest order, supporters of Welsh poets and kings. The grave of the greatest Welsh bard, Dafydd ap Gwilym, is at Strata Florida. In the early 1400s they put their weight behind Owain Glyndŵr in Wales's last glorious battle for independence. Give or take a 400-year moratorium in their activities, they are still here, praying and working and keeping themselves to themselves. And Brother Teilo is one of them.

'O Lord, open our lips,' chants a monk, also classically bald, to the right of the abbot. While you're at it, O Lord, perhaps you might open mine eyes. In every sense. I am Godless, not to mention sleepless.

I arrived on the last boat the previous afternoon. Fishing vessels act as ferries for tourists from the docks at Tenby. The last one chugs out of port at three in the afternoon. It's always empty and if you're staying at the abbey there's no charge. The crossing can be the purest bliss. Gulls squawk, the engine chugs, the wind caresses your cheek, and as the sun beats on Caldey Sound you can look along the soft slopes of Pembrokeshire towards the Gower off in the east. The beckoning island fills the horizon, beside it to the west the lumpy crag of St Margaret's Island. The abbey from afar is white-walled and red-roofed. Above and behind is a lighthouse which at night-time winks its warning to boats in the Bristol Channel. Fields and woods fan out on either side.

It's pissing down when I cross. I must bear it, I tell myself. Acceptance of rain is a key ability in the Welsh skill set. Acceptance of chill is something the monks have learned too. Caldey is a Norse name gifted by marauding Vikings: Cold Island. The brothers wear a lot of layers under those white robes.

I set the alarm for 3.25 a.m., rise, dress and slide downstairs. Across the glassed-in cloister, figures in white drift through the darkness towards a double door in the corner. I follow, along another corridor and right into the chapel. The monks turn and bow to the altar. When in Rome, does one follow suit? I look up and note that the monks all seem to be in a private space, so I scuttle furtively past to my pew.

A thin, white-haired monk with voluminous sleeves pads over in sandals to give me a ring-bound folder, helpfully opened to the correct page. He points without speaking. I nod. 'They fashioned a calf at Horeb'. I've never so much as dipped into the psalter, but here it is in my hands, each psalm assigned to a particular day of the week at a particular service. 'Flames devoured the rebels.' They reckon to get through all 150 psalms each fortnight. Some of them are deucedly long and are diced up and parcelled out across the schedule. 'They did not destroy the peoples,' we chant. After each psalm the monks bow once more. Glory be to the Father. Then there's a reading from the monk with the sleeves. As he nears the lectern he holds his hands up to avoid being engulfed by cloth. I do my absolute level best to listen to the story of how Jonah fetched up inside a whale, and am rewarded for my tenacity. 'Jonah was asked, "Where do you come from? What is your country?"' A good question, brother, and pertinent.

We pray. Or they pray. Standing, all facing the altar. The Lord's Prayer. Some monks turn inwards to the wall, as if they dare not send private thoughts directly up the aisle towards the image of Christ fixed high on the rear wall. This manifestation of humility is intensely moving. After Psalm 66 – 'I shall offer to you burnt offerings of fat beasts' – a monk exits stage left and a bell clangs vigorously. Someone else switches off the lights. Vigils are over, officially.

It is now four o'clock in the morning, with no sign of dawn. Some monks process out, bowing; others stay, among them my uncle. Silence is absolute. They are still praying. It seems seemly to hang on and await developments. My uncle is deep in prayer. Would it be rude to go? Bed is a temptation. Ten past. No sign of my uncle shifting. He has a list of 2,500 people he prays for, he tells me. If I leave now he might see me not bowing to the altar. Am I on the list? I could just slip past. His eyes are probably closed.

Sometimes your body decides without consulting your mind. I get up and tread purposefully out of the church, through the still-dark cloister and up into the monastic guesthouse where bed beckons. Right now I could sleep through powerdrilling. I set my alarm for 5.55. Next appointment: lauds, 6 a.m. 'Little and often for us,' says Teilo. Cistercians began living like this in Wales a millennium ago. Now it's my turn.

Christmas Day began at six, or thereabouts. That's when you'd awake to the certain knowledge that an inundation of gifts was heading your way. So it was good to get an early start.

In Mount Hill we slept in a garret room, up a creaking staircase. The sloped ceiling bore down on three serried beds. My older brother had the big one nearest the door. I was in the middle one. My younger brother was exiled up to the sharp end, next to a deep dark alcove that tended to unnerve the junior mind. For years we imagined all manner of bad shit going down in that corner. We'd discuss poltergeists long after lights out. It was presumed that things lurked behind hatboxes and old leather suitcases. My younger brother grew up stoical.

It was a curious room, full of those strange things you find in grandparents' houses. Awaiting us on the bedspreads were two uncuddly toys once sent back to Wales by someone on the Australian branch of the family tree: a koala and, weirdly, a duck-billed platypus. There was a toby mug on a shelf; flowers, framed and pressed by my grandmother, hung on a wall. A door gave onto a dusty attic storeroom, where we once found wildebeest horns mounted on a board. It's how I imagine all bedrooms of visiting grandchildren should be: semi-familiar, a little bit wonderful, cluttered with random exotica.

Through the gable windows you could see little but the sloping roof. At six on Christmas morning, you couldn't see anything. The noise of footsteps on the stairs, however, would carry.

'Back to bed now, boys.' My mother would creep up from their bedroom. 'It's not time to get up yet.' We'd settle for about a

minute. Then gradually resume our uproar. Next time the footsteps would be heavier.

'Shut up, the lot of you.' My father.

'Can't we open some presents?'

'No.'

'But …'

Slam.

Eventually we'd be allowed down the stairs to where three small
piles would await us at the foot of our parents' bed. We'd rip stuff
open, marvel at it acquisitively, then cast it aside and thunder downstairs to my grandparents' bedroom. The majority of the house was a
big sort of bungalow. On the ground floor, my grandparents slept next
to the kitchen. We didn't quite burst in. My grandfather – he was
called Bert, short for Bertram – was a forbidding figure, not given to
smiling or indeed talking much. He had a thickset frame and a heavy
square head, from which white hair had receded, leaving a trim
peppery moustache to hold the fort. No one has ever looked less unim-
pressive in his pyjamas, which I imagine were silk. He was a dandy who
shone his shoes every morning and would as often as not wear plus
fours and, outside in the Christmas chill, a deerstalker. I never felt
quite comfortable in his presence, in the bedroom least of all. The
enamel chamber pot under his side of the bed was disturbing.

As part of our rounds we might barge in on our great-aunt and
-uncle, Aunt Joan and Uncle Bob, though as they had no children
of their own they tended to greet such invasions testily. Or even our
widowed great-aunt Olwen, who lived in Saundersfoot. But for the
most part I remember following my grandmother Dorothy around
on Christmas Day. She was the soul of Mount Hill, its welcoming
bosom. You never for a second had the sense that she was anything
but delighted by your company. Which in our case must have taken
some doing. I know I adored her.

At breakfast the bread singed nicely on the prongs of a toasting fork by the fire. We sat at an octagonal dining table which stood on a central leg. Amusingly it could rotate. It didn't amuse our grandfather when we tried. Outside through a tall Gothic window we'd watch chaffinches, tits and a lone robin attack the bird table raised on a black metal post, Bert and Dorothy being eager ornithologists. The lawn outside may well have been draped in white, though my memory could have borrowed that image from the hundreds of Christmas cards crowding the polished wooden surface of the mantelpieces, the Bechstein, the dark-oak Welsh dresser.

Christmas in Carmarthen was entirely irreligious. Or it was for most of us. Our uncle – not yet known as Teilo – would rush in at breakfast time, chatting without cease. It would emerge that he had been to something called Midnight Mass with Aunt Joan. Midnight seemed a sensible time to go to church, nicely tucked away in the schedule. Aunt Joan also chatted a lot, while Bob would take a leaf out of his older brother's book and keep more or less shtum. My main memory of Uncle Bob is of a grumbler. 'Shut the door!' he'd holler from the second most important armchair as we tore in and out of the living room.

And whenever you went back to shut it, whenever you pounded across the hallway, the house clanked, floorboards squeaked, and brass bits and pieces tinkled. A rich aroma of polish entwined in your nostrils with emanations from the kitchen, where my mother laboured in support of my grandmother while Aunt Joan floated about.

Meanwhile we explored: the jungly sanctum of Bert's greenhouse, the dusty old servants' quarters hidden behind a panel door on the stairs, a utility room which had once served as the kitchen. Meat hooks hung from its ceiling. A ruddy-faced old man called Mr John would come through the back door to scrub potatoes. He was always deferential, even to us. Sometimes my grandfather came down and spoke to him in an incomprehensible language which, I dimly understood, was Welsh.

On a Sunday evening in March in the walled town of Conwy, the sun has long since slipped behind the mountain, casting Edward I's bristling ramparts in darkness. Everything's closed. It's five to six and the bell of St Mary's is calling. I push through the door into a tall and, it has to be said, empty church. A very small lady in her seventies stands at the bottom of the nave.

'Are you here for the service?'

I tell her I am.

'Holy Communion is in Welsh,' she says. 'I hope that's all right.' It certainly is. All my experiences of the Church in Wales, which disestablished itself from Canterbury by Act of Parliament in 1920, have been in English – mostly Anglican weddings and funerals of members of another branch of the Rees family on the Gower. I am handed a service book and ushered towards a choir stall. Numbers being down, there's no question of bothering with pews. She joins me and two other ladies of identical size and vintage, one of whom takes her place just behind us at the organ. Being forty-four, I've brought the average age of the congregation plummeting into the sixties. They are tiny as only old Welsh ladies can be, all muffled into best coats, scarves and hats. I feel scruffy. And tall and English.

A surpliced vicar slides in from the vestry, his trimmed dome gently reflecting a low-watt gleam from overhead lights, his spectacles as thick as prayer cushions.

'Croeso,' he says, and although he continues in Welsh it is clear that he has one of those C of E larynxes which give every utterance a squashy, benevolent sheen. He announces a hymn. My diminutive neighbour helps me to the right page as the organist toots the intro. We embark, me uncertain of the tune, the ladies' soprano voices fluting but forthright, the Reverend's baritone loud and slightly metallic.

With the prayer book to guide us, we work our way through Holy Communion's ritual calls and responses. His face all but buried in the order of service, the vicar intones plangently. I am none too certain which bits of Welsh correspond with the English wording dimly recalled, but it's good pronunciation practice. The Welsh does seem blissfully formal and seductive. The Lord's Prayer has a poetic rhythm all its own. I'm especially seduced by a word that crops up often: *gogoniant*. How wonderfully Welsh it sounds. We sing again. This time even the ladies struggle a bit with an unfamiliar hymn and sternly from behind comes the instructive voice of the organist. I grasp at the lifeline. The sermon clocks in mercifully brief at perhaps eight minutes. And all of a sudden the moment comes. The Eucharist is being prepared. It'll look odd if I'm the one person out of four who stays behind. I never go up. I'm not confirmed. But hell, I'm going for total Welsh immersion here. Sod it, I'll go up. Why ever not? I go up and kneel, three little old ladies to my left now even littler on their knees at the altar rail, like chaffinches at a bird table. The vicar proceeds along the row, dispensing the body and blood of the Saviour. I make ready, look up in expectation.

'Are you confirmed?' He's guessing it's best to ask in English. The voice is kindly. He practically adds the words 'my child'. But there's no dodging the directness of the question.

'Er, no.' Not even bloody christened, Father. I can feel my body twist in discomfort. Curses. I am being judged and found wanting. He touches my head and utters a blessing in Welsh. No bread and wine for this sinner. Smarting, I make less of an effort with the last hymn. A final benediction from the vicar and Holy Communion is over.

'It's nice to see a new face.' As I'm leaving, the vicar proffers a friendly hand. 'We're a bit light on numbers this evening,' he adds. 'Some people are away.' I ask him how often he conducts services in Welsh. 'Well, this is the problem,' he says. You can hear him fight to keep resignation out of his voice. 'This is the furthest east that you'll find a Welsh-speaking congregation. Even in Llandudno there are very few. And of course the Welsh speakers are from the older generation.' What he means is the Anglicans are from the older generation. The young Welsh speakers don't go to church, or chapel. The language may be sprouting anew, but it cannot reseed belief in the Almighty.

'Diolch am y croeso,' I say. Thank you for the welcome. It suddenly hits me that *croeso* and *croes* – the Welsh words for welcome and cross – must be etymological cousins. I remember something else.

'Please could you tell me – what does *gogoniant* mean?'

'Glory,' he says, and smiles.

Gerald of Wales, also known as Giraldus Cambrensis and Gerallt Gymro, was the Archdeacon of Brecon. He granted to posterity two books on Wales and Welshness: *The Journey Through Wales* and *The Description of Wales*. The first is the more substantial: Gerald sporadically worked on three editions across more than twenty years. It recounts a tour he undertook in 1188 with Baldwin of Exeter, the Archbishop of Canterbury. Their mission was to encourage as many Welshmen as possible to take the Cross – that is, to join Richard the Lionheart on what would become the Third Crusade. Begun in Hereford and completed in Chester, the journey lasted six weeks in spring, five of them spent in South Wales, only one north of the Dyfi river, which, Gerald remarked upon crossing it, marks the dividing line between the two halves of Wales. The trip was, he reflected, 'rather exhausting'. And no wonder. They may have stayed in all the best castles with Wales's principal nabobs, but Wales presented its usual array of obstacles: rain, rivers and mountains, all negotiated on horseback. On fording the quicksands of the Nedd, Gerald's packhorse 'was almost sucked into the abyss', he recorded, and was retrieved by their servants, 'who risked their lives in doing so, and not without some damage done to my books and baggage'.

And everywhere they stopped they had to put on a show. The journal tots up the sermons preached, the conversions made, by Baldwin and Gerald himself. The author rather vaunted his own homiletic powers. In Radnor we learn that the Archbishop's address 'was explained to the Welsh by an interpreter'. There was no such requirement for the author in Haverfordwest. 'Many found it odd and some, indeed, thought it little short of miraculous that when I, the Archdeacon, preached the word of God, speaking first in Latin and then in French, those who could not understand a word of either language were just as much moved to tears as the others, rushing forward in equal numbers to receive the sign of the Cross.'

Whence came Gerald's tendency to self-promote? He had half an eye on a long literary afterlife – correctly, as it turned out, as his portrait of medieval Wales has been a priceless handbook for students of the country down the centuries. 'I hope to please generations yet unborn,' he explained. 'Having won the right to eternal fame, one will always be praised and honoured.' But it's possible to read his productions as a form of job application. He was born in, it's thought, the mid 1140s. He was tall with bushy eyebrows and, though he said so himself, was 'greatly distinguished by my handsome physique' as a young man. By 1188 he had already written *The Topography of Ireland*, 'my own far from negligible work', which we find him frequently thrusting into the hands of the great and good. He was appointed to the Archdeaconry of Brecon, where he affected to 'pass my time in a sort of happy-go-lucky mediocrity'. In fact his burning desire was to claim for himself the see of St David's, and then to restore the archiepiscopal status it had lost, so he believed, in the Age of the Celtic Saints six centuries before. He turned down two sees in Ireland, and two more in Wales, in order to make himself available for the position he coveted.

He was an odd mixture. The Welshman in him was vehemently anti-Canterbury, but he was also an ardent keeper of the flame for Thomas à Becket, martyred when Gerald was in his mid twenties. Gerald seemed to take Becket's awkward-squad king-bothering as a template. He didn't baulk at criticising Henry II or pestering his son John. Welsh royalty also got it in the neck: the marriage of Rhys ap Gruffudd, Prince of South Wales, to his fourth cousin was, Gerald noted, 'a regrettable circumstance which happens so often in this country'. When the see at St David's fell vacant in 1198, Gerald launched a five-year campaign to secure it for himself. The quest took him back and forth twice between Wales and Rome. His avowed intention to uncouple the Church in Wales made him naturally unattractive to Baldwin's successor in Canterbury, even when Gerald helpfully pointed out that the other candidates were variously illiterate, illegitimate and given to licentiousness. Gerald was summoned to Lambeth to hear the final verdict in 1203. When the bishopric went elsewhere, he promptly gave up his archdeaconry in Brecon and for the remaining twenty years of his life buried himself sulkily among his books.

In Welsh Level 1, Module 1, not everyone keeps the faith. This is a language that likes to administer a sharp slap to the chops, regularly. Sometimes you have to turn the other cheek. The grammar is impacted, the word orders higgledy-piggledy. But when push comes to shove it's probably the verbs and the mutations, operating a classic pincer movement, which contrive to scare the bejesus out of some of our number. The class size starts to dwindle slightly. For some, anglicisation proves too big a back story. Their Englishness, forced upon them by forebears who once upon a time abandoned hills and valleys to seek employment over the border, runs too deep. It shows mostly in the pronunciation of boilerplate Welsh phrases. They get fed through a voicebox converter which spews out everything with inflections of glottalised estuary or flat-packed vowels from up the M1 or, in my case, privately educated BBC RP.

'O ble dych chi'n dod?' With his marker pen James scrawls an anagram on the board, then pronounces it. The sound in *ble* and *dod* is notably elongated.

'Where are you from?' he says. 'In Welsh they say, "From where are you?"'

'What's that apostrophe *n* thingie?' someone wants to know.

'I was getting to that.' And James proceeds to explain the trickiness of the Welsh present tense. '"*Yn*" sort of means –"ing",' he suggests. 'So, for example, "dw i'n dod o Gaerdydd". "I come from Cardiff." Literally it's "do I-ing come from Cardiff."'

I look around the room. Jaws are slack with dread. The terrified woman has upgraded her status to petrified. Only Alpha Pete has the jutting chin of someone who knows he could take a Welsh verb if it came to a fight. I've spotted something.

'Erm.' Some turn to look at me, others not. 'Isn't it Caerdydd?' My voice sounds pleased with itself in that English way.

'Well, yes it is,' says James. 'Except that after *o*, which means "from", a C mutates to a G.' That explains a lot: a mutation in action, clearly and visibly.

'So is that why the road sign after the Severn Bridge says "Croeso i Gymru" and not "Cymru"?' I can feel the cold disapproval of the rest of the class. No one likes a smart alec.

'Exactly,' says James.

I start to hear conflicting advice on the mutation system. For some it is indivisible from clarity of expression and correct usage. Others say you needn't bother. James tells us about one leading Welsh politician whose speeches are a randomly generated mutation vortex. The system plays merry hell with the universe as one knows it. Let's just take the soft mutations, said to be the easy ones but also much more frequent than the aspirate and nasal variety. Where required, *t* mutates to *d*, *d* to *dd*, *c* to *g*, *p* to *b*, *ll* to *l*. These are more or less manageable. You can keep them in your eyeline. I really struggle with *b* mutating to *f*, so that *byta* (food) or *brawd* (brother), say, or *byd* (world) and *bywyd* (life), will in certain circumstances transfigure into *fyta* and *frawd*, *fyd* and *fywyd*. These are important words. You need to recognise them when they crop up. Unmutated, you know where you are with them. Mutated, they could be anything.

But this is nothing to the nasal mutation, which scrambles the actual names of places as if to hide them in low-flying fog. It occurs infrequently but its impact is devastating, a bit like the H bomb, or man flu. You can see how it happened. Much as we have long since stopped saying 'inmodest' or 'inmaterial', Welsh elides and slurs sounds for maximum convenience. Thus my grandmother grew up *ym Mhorthmadog*, went to school *yn Nolgellau*, spent her married life *yng Nghaerfyrddin*. Wherever the hell they all are.

James, forever apologising for the complexities of Welsh syntax, continues bright and breezy, like a good day on the Gower. We get up and start asking each other where we're from.

'O ble dych chi'n dod?'

'Dw i'n dod o Llundain,' I say, forgetting to mutate it to *Lundain*.

A couple of times I ring the changes. 'Dw i'n dod o Gymru' (I come from Wales). I am thoroughly pleased with this geographical riff. Alpha Pete looks at me as if I'm a Welsh verb he'd like to thump. More smart alecry from the self-appointed class swot. I can see I'm not going to make any friends in this room. It's a fallacy, of course. I don't come from any such place. Not yet.

Lauds. It's 5.58. The bell clangs in the cloister. For an hour and a half I have slept the sleep of the shriven as dawn steals up on Caldey. There are more chanted psalms. 'For you my soul is thirsting,' we sing, 'my body pines for you, like a dry weary land without water' (Psalm 63). I note an extra monk in the stall this time, bent double with age. 'Hide me from the land of the wicked,' we chant, 'from the throng of evildoers' (Psalm 64). Presumably he misses the early shift these days. 'The Lord is King, let earth rejoice' (Psalm 97). We process out and I slip back upstairs. The air is cool in the cloister. What must it be like in winter here, the spaces big and unwarmed?

Cold Island is also known in Welsh as Ynys Bŷr, after the island's first abbot, Pyro. Pyro's life was not entirely devoted to devotion. He liked a drink, presumably to keep warm, given that in the sixth century the monks lived in huts and even sea caves. One night he fell into the monastery's well and drowned. So it says in *The Life of Samson*. Samson was the next of many saints to come to Caldey when, after the Romans had gone, Celtic Christianity took root in Wales. Later came Dyfrig, whose name is notched in ogham script into the rim of a stone slab in the island's priory. He sailed to Caldey each Lent for forty days of solitude. Then there was St Illtud, St Paul of Léon and St Gildas the Wise, whose idea it was to pray to the Lord Jesus Christ to enlarge the island. There were more dramatic tides back then; it is said you could walk the mile from St

Margaret's Island to the mainland when the tide was out, but when
it was in, the fields which they farmed when they weren't praying
would be flooded. (Even now you get letters from Caldey bearing
the stamp 'Delayed by rough seas'.)

I've just settled down with a cup of tea when I hear the shiver of
the bell in my eyrie. Saints preserve us, I think, as I trudge back
through the cloister. It's like Groundhog Day here, but with the
repetition happening *every hour*. Only this time the scene is dramatically different. A riot of colour greets my entrance. The monks
are still in their white tunics, but now some are wearing a light-
green stole which hangs round the neck and down past the waist.
And one is enveloped in a rich bright-green chasuble, the colour of
classy Christmas wrapping paper. Rome's genius for design has
struck. The colours, Teilo tells me later, vary according to occasion:
green for regular days and Sundays; white for the Virgin's major
feasts, Christmas and Easter; purple for mourning. They've worn
purple a few times in recent years as older brethren have succes-
sively given up the ghost.

Holy Mass. We are spared more psalms. The church has lured
quite a crowd at this late hour (6.45 a.m.). In addition to me and
the visiting priests there are three women scattered about the pews.
I'm guessing they're islanders. One in a woolly hat operates a doll's-
house organ parked directly behind the abbot. She accompanies us
in a doleful hymn, while up front the monk in the chasuble conse-
crates the wine and the bread at the altar. The monks now sur-
round him in a wide semicircle. They raise their arms, palms held
aloft, as they sing. The Cistercian God is a theatre director, I think,
as I am wowed by this ritualistic parade of choreographed exulta-
tion. And the props are impressive too, the white wafers as big as
biscuits, the huge chalice silver and gleaming. They ingest around
the altar. Two monks too weak to stand are ministered to in their

stalls. Presumably we the congregants go up to the altar and kneel. But I shan't brave that humiliation again. Oh, but two monks are heading our way. There's no getting out of this. The wafer is proffered. I have no choice but to open my mouth to receive it. It's crumbly, tasteless. And the chalice, rim freshly wiped. The blood of Christ is thick and sweet. I sit in a state of blushing confusion. For the first time in my life, I have taken communion on the holy island where St David may very well have been a monk. How Welsh is that?

In the hallway a grandfather clock tocked and tolled towards lunch. Over the pots and pans my mother would throw in her lot. Perhaps Aunt Joan assisted with the final push to share in the glory. My uncle would offer his services, but they were always declined. He was famously incompetent in the kitchen. None of the other men would lift a finger. Towards one o'clock my grandfather would put down his pipe and rise from his armchair in the corner nearest the fire, and summon us. We gathered, three boys with bright eyes, to follow him down the corridor, carpeted in dark red, slung with long Persian rugs, towards a door at the end. Into a small sanctum we all clustered, supplicants of this forbidding figure who, we knew, was about to dispense largesse.

'Now, boys, who would like a drink?' A hint of Welsh warmth in the voice.

'Me!' The reply in triplicate would produce a stern, expectant look. 'Me, please, Grandpa.' This contritely from my older brother, who was old enough to read the signs. After a nudge, it was echoed in duplicate.

'What would you like?' A more or less rhetorical question. We all craved the same thing: ginger beer, but ginger beer that you could get nowhere else, to our certain knowledge, in the entire world. To us it was Welsh ginger beer, Carmarthen ginger beer, Mount Hill ginger beer. From a tall bottle our grandfather slowly poured a fizzing liquid into three tumblers. You wanted to get drinking straight away.

'Now, what do you say?' Glasses pulled away from mouths.

'Thank you, Grandpa.' You sipped and felt an instant rasp at the back of the throat. This stuff was toxic. In no time you'd have drained it. Through the bubbled base of the glass you could then watch people, refracted and multiplied, taking their places around the octagonal table. The back of your mouth was searing from the ginger as now trolleys rattled across the hall and into the dining room, one pushed by my grandmother, the other by Aunt Joan flagrantly doing her bit.

My grandfather now stepped up to slice the sizzling bird on a table by the door and briskly sharpened the carving knife as if preparing for something less innocent than lunch. Our grandmother bustled. Uncles and great-aunts nattered. Children chattered. Plates groaned. Even, as the years go by, mine. Until the age of seventeen I mainly consisted of ribs, but this was one meal it was worth not turning up your nose at. You couldn't argue with those crunchy potatoes. The fleshy white meat was perfectly acceptable. Even the odd vegetable from the steam-powered trolley might find a way past your line of defence. It was the gravy that sugared the pill, a rich brown gloop that seemed to have been piped up from some Welsh Middle Earth. It had the smooth consistency of thinnish cement.

It took Dorothy an age to settle. She would spring up to fetch things or to minister to others. No such mania for Bert. Methodically he sliced, silently he chewed, carefully he swallowed. My grandfather never did anything at pace. The food, he was said to believe, was too good to spoil with talk. Which left the field open to the others. Aunt Joan, a miniaturist, regaled the room with tales of the bishops and ministers, chief rabbis and archimandrites and other assorted panjandrums she'd lately (or not so lately) painted. The first and in fact only time I ever heard my grandmother express intolerance was when Aunt Joan's narrative torrent was in full flow one time.

'You aren't listening, Granny.'

'Oh, don't worry, Jasper bach,' she said, leaning in conspiratorially. 'I've heard the stories before ever so often.' She called us all *bach* – 'little one'. For years it was the only Welsh word I knew.

After lunch they used to send us to bed. Everyone, so the argument went, would have a nap. It seemed a nonsensical rule. Who wants a nap at two in the afternoon on Christmas Day of all days? So we ruckused upstairs among the bedclothes, and generally waited while engorged Welsh elders slept off their food.

After a respectable period we were suffered to come downstairs, to be greeted by tottering stacks of presents. These should have been sledded in on an overnight delivery, but we were told that Father Christmas came late to Carmarthenshire. I would rip through my pile, barely pausing to give thanks. Children are uniquely vile in that regard. I was, anyway. My ravenous consumerist maw was fed with toys, board games and militarised figurines, which emerged from their wrapping and fanned across the available carpet space. My grandmother would take an interest in these plastic acquisitions, and my uncle too. The peripheral players would purse their lips. My grandfather was lofty in his indifference to all this knick-knackery shipped down from London toyshops. When they were young in Wales such bounty did not shower down the chimney. But who cared what they all thought? Not I. I would take my stock away and lavish it with attention for many minutes. Then I would arrange it carefully in a corner and forget all about it.

Thus was a merry Christmas worshiplessly had by all in Wales. The old house chimed to a Welsh kind of merriment, warm rich smells lingering long into the early evening when pancakes smeared in salty Welsh butter made their appearance. No doubt tensions simmered over our heads: relatives were eager for the time to fly, for twitterers to shut it, children to be silenced and the relentless flow of heavy Welsh cooking to relent. I noticed none of it. To me as a child this was Wales and this was Welshness. And every year it was to be wished for – devoutly.

The list of sundry chapels in Carmarthen testifies to the grip in which Nonconformity held the Welsh population in the nineteenth century: the Priory Independent Chapel, the Penuel Baptist Chapel, the Tabernacle Baptist Chapel, the English Congregational Chapel, the Calvinistic Methodists, the Parc-y-Felfed Unitarian Chapel, the Union Street Independent Chapel.

On a damp July Sunday morning I pause outside fine black railings in Lammas Street. Overhead are grey West Wales skies, heavy with rain. A black board tells me I've got the right place: Capel Yr Annibynwyr – the Independents' Chapel (confusingly, the Independents are also known as Congregationalists). It was here in 1927 that my grandparents married. The minister, the board says, is one J. Towyn Jones, FRSA.

The tall building at the back of the courtyard is behind scaffolding. I slip through a side doorway and enter a chapel. The welcoming smiles are bright and warm. I am handed a hymnal. It seems a small room for my grandparents to have married in. A line of varnished wooden pillars and a curtained back wall intensify the sense of a womb. The other surprise is how many fill the pews. We are led to believe that the Welsh believer is an endangered species, but the streets are running with people in their Sunday best, heading for places of worship. There are maybe twenty Congregationalists in the congregation, mostly over fifty but not all. I take my place in a row halfway up the left of the aisle and await developments.

Eventually a pianist finishes noodling beatifically on an upright piano and silence descends. The minister – J. Towyn Jones, I presume – who has been sitting among us in a chair behind a lectern, rises to speak. He's wearing a raffish bow tie, which somehow matches the kindly contours of his face and the donnish waves of white hair. We are welcomed in Welsh. We sing hymns in Welsh – 'Wel dyma'r Ceidwad', 'Cof am y cyfiawn Iesu' – not so very tunefully, but lustily. We pray in Welsh. The minister addresses us in Welsh, tells jokes. People laugh. It's all extremely benign. He has a lovely soft manner. There are hints of the avuncular entertainer. I notice all sorts of Welsh words, even understanding parts of the sentences. When we sing again, trays of tiny glass goblets with a glistening red liquid are brought out, also a bowl. This time I really shall stay put. Two deacons have picked up the trays by a handle. The glasses clink as they bring the body and blood of Christ to the people. We don't even have to leave our pews. I select a slender glass and knock it back. The wine is superior to the Catholic stuff.

A final benediction is said and the congregation rises. I am slightly wondering where to put myself when I see the minister bearing down on me.

'Croeso!' he says, thrusting out a hand. 'Towyn Jones.'

'Diolch yn fawr!' (Thank you very much!) I reply. 'Jasper Rees.' In these situations I am ever grateful for the Welsh surname.

'Mae'n braf iawn gweld wyneb newydd,' he says. (It's very nice to see a new face.) I shuffle out into the aisle. People file past, some nodding at the newcomer. Towyn Jones ignores them. I explain, in English, that my Welsh is not quite up to proper conversation. But that my grandparents married in the chapel here in 1927.

'Really?!' says Towyn Jones. 'Would you like to have a look at the marriage register? I could show you the chapel.'

'You mean this isn't it?'

'Oh goodness me, no. This is the vestry. The chapel is under restoration.' I *thought* this room looked a bit small. I hang around as he bids farewell to his congregation. Then when the minister shows me through a door in the corner of the vestry I am greeted by a remarkable sight. The chapel is spectacularly vast. Much of it is under plastic sheets and tall windows have been darkened, but a huge four-square ground floor and gallery are both tightly packed with gated pews. I wander in. Around the sides are plaques raised in memory of departed ministers going back to the late eighteenth century. One refers to a man born in 1645 during the English Civil War. There is stained glass, including two very comely Italianate figurines in ogee-shaped rear windows.

The chapel built on this site by the Independents in 1726 was the first in Carmarthen. William Owen of Haverfordwest, who must have been immensely rich, spent £2,582 rebuilding it a century later. It has seating for a thousand. This is more like it. I can see my grandparents marrying here and not remotely filling it. But then whose wedding would?

'I meant to ask,' Towyn Jones asks. 'Who were your grandparents?' I tell him. 'Bertram Rees the dentist?' he says. I nod. 'Well I never.' He looks at me over his half-moons. 'Well I never.'

I in turn ask Towyn how long he's been minister. He explains that he nearly went to art school until a charismatic man of the cloth in Newcastle Emlyn swayed him. 'He gave the impression to any boy,' says Towyn, 'that there was no honour on earth like being a minister. It might be OK being a prime minister, but being a minister you'd be a prince of the church.' He took over a rural ministry close to the Pembrokeshire border in 1964, and ten years later the call was extended by Lammas Street. He has been there ever since.

I ask him what makes the Independents so independent. There's not much to split them from the Baptists beyond timing, Towyn explains. The Baptists allow believers to choose the moment of their baptising. The Independents are so called because they answer to no central authority, which sounds like Towyn to a tee. He is the jauntiest man of God I've ever met, a far cry from the image of the finger-wagging teetotaller steeped in the Nonconformist ways of denial and doom.

'Religion isn't a big deal for me,' he says. 'It's a way of life. It's natural. I can't imagine the point of living without it. I'm not particularly interested in theology. I know much more about folklore and art. But I do believe in the Resurrection.' And with that he disappears down some stairs and re-emerges brandishing a thin volume bound in dark-green leather.

I flick eagerly through the pages to 1927 and there, on 20 September, it records the wedding of Edward Bertram Rees, twenty-six years, bachelor and dental surgeon, to Dorothy Owen, twenty-five years, spinster. The document tells several life stories. Bert was the son of Thomas Rees (deceased), Dorothy the daughter of D. G. Owen. 'Rank or Profession of Father' is listed in Bert's case as farmer, in Dorothy's as bank manager. Dorothy's only sister was her witness. Bert's was Percy Rees, one of his seven brothers.

The farming Reeses conformed. The banking Owens did not. They were Congregationalists or Independents (or Annibynwyr). So it was a mixed wedding in Lammas Street. The register says it was presided over by the minister John Dyfnallt Owen in the presence of B. Davies, vicar of St David's. Church was keeping an eye on chapel.

As Towyn and I stand in the room where this momentous

prequel to my own existence took place, I am struck by a question about religious procedure. I want to know why in his chapel I was allowed to take communion, when the Church in Wales in Conwy refused. 'We welcome anybody no matter who he may be to take part in this communion,' Towyn says, 'because this table is not ours: it belongs to Christ, so we are offering it in his name.' He looks at me, bow-tied and dapper, owlish specs glinting. 'I wouldn't dream of refusing communion to anybody.'

'Absolutely no talking,' whispers my uncle in the cloister as we line up for lunch. We've come straight from sext, a short dash through a few more psalms at 12.15, preceded by terce at 8.50. Teilo and I fill the gap by packing shortbread. The abbey sells the stuff as fast as it can bake, box and ferry it to its shop in Tenby. Shortbread packing is one of his monastic duties, along with sending the daily rainfall measurements off to the Met Office and working in the archives. They have wisely kept him from the kitchen. Brother Benedict, a wry, worldly monk from Middlesbrough who is the abbey's chef, wheels in a tall trolley of newly baked biscuits, still warm from the oven. There are sugared trays of them galore. Teilo points me to an immensely complex set of instructions he's produced in minuscule handwriting for anyone having to do the job in his stead. I take one look at it.

'Just tell me what to do, Teilo.'

I stack. He packs. Our through-put is impressive. In forty minutes we've bagged and cellophaned thirty boxes, each containing a dozen biscuits. A new monastic record, I fancy. And meanwhile we talk – copiously.

A silent order strikes me as an odd choice for a man of many words. Teilo is very Welsh in that sense. When as a young man he first thought of walling himself up in here, he recalls that his mother took to her bed for a fortnight and he thought better of it. In fact the Cistercians gave up on the life of unadulterated contemplation a while back. When Teilo first came here in 1954, no one uttered a word. The second Vatican Council in 1965 concentrated on updating the general life of the Catholic Church. 'Religious orders were encouraged to consider their way of life and rules and practices,' he tells me as he grapples with a gizmo which fastens the shortbread into its cellophane wrapping, 'and go back to the spirit of the founders and remove accretions. Silence,' he explains, 'was a very positive value, but strict silence using sign language was deemed to be unnecessary.' The order considered a revision of its constitution across its 170 monasteries. 'We had about twenty-five years to think about it,' Teilo adds. Eventually, in the early 1990s, the brothers of Caldey began to talk.

Still, there is no talking in the refectory. Unless it's by Father Daniel, who takes his lunch late so that he can read to the brothers as they eat. The choice of literature is not necessarily devotional. Today's is from a book about the Open University or the World Service or some such. Spoken into a microphone, Father Daniel's kindly Dutch voice booms across the long tall room via an over-amplified sound system. The other top monks are parked at a top table: Brother Luca, a short bald Italian from Port Talbot, and Brother Gildas, a tall and stupendously white-bearded figure. The rest of us sit along tables lining either wall of the refectory. I am sitting very much below the salt – below the psalt, if you will – beyond the last table leg of the last table.

A trolley enters from a door to the kitchen in the far corner, pushed by slow-strolling monks in sandals. The monks look well fed on this simple food: soup, cheese, bread, a rather splendid tortilla with salad. (In one or two cases, they look very well fed.) I go up to the trolley and take a hefty plateful. Father Daniel's lowland

vowels clang off the high walls. We masticate quietly. It's none next.
More psalms. Terce, sext, none: the daylight hours codified in cod
Latin. The contemplative life is entirely knackering, I think, as I get
up and take my things through to the swing door. On the other side
a bunch of beaming monks from this formerly silent order, their
hands dipped in suds or wielding tea towels, are all yakking their
heads off.

After lunch, none comes and goes. As does vespers, after which
we embark on fifteen minutes of contemplation, of which I have
been forewarned by my uncle. I sit and do not pray, though I
attempt a sort of agnostic equivalent. The day-trippers flocking
across the sound from Tenby have flocked off again to the mainland
in a flotilla of vessels. As my Cistercian immersion draws to a close,
the heavens have opened. Through tall narrow chapel windows
rain splashes on full green leaves, drips insistently from a leaking
gutter. It feels as if I have rifled through the entire Book of Psalms.
Supper passes too. The Lord has been my shepherd and I have not
wanted for quite a nice paella, a leftover from a feast day. And now
compline, the final service of the livelong day. 'Before the light of
evening fades we pray, O Lord of all,' intones Brother Titus from
The Hague, 'that by your love we may be saved from ev'ry grievous
fall.' I am a convert to monastic ritual, nodding to the altar without
a second thought now. And it's become second nature to bow with
every 'Glory be to the Father' in – for the record – Psalms 4, 90 and
133. I feel quite embedded. The visiting priests have taken their
slightly suffocating piety and nocturnal noise pollution back to the
mainland. I am alone with the monks of the abbey on this holy
island where Welshmen of yore once did much to establish Christianity in Britain.

We sing the Nunc Dimittis very, very slowly. The atmospherics
are spot on: tonally calming, hypnotic, suffusing one's frantic

restless grasshopper mind with a sensation of great peace. The bell in the tower is clanged. Most of Wales, land of monasteries and chapels, no longer worships. It has journeyed from faith through doubt to disbelief. St Mary's in Conwy was empty but for me and three short elderly ladies. The Capel Yr Annibynwyr where my grandparents married has room for a thousand believers. Where are they now? 'I wish one Sunday everyone would come at once,' Towyn says of his scattered flock. God is not in my life either, however much I may wander about Wales looking for Him. The last Rees who believes is Teilo, born and raised in Carmarthen, sent into England and now, after sixty years away, home again. It's an extreme form of repatriation. Tomorrow morning he will stand and wave on the quay. And I, the only passenger on the chugging boat, will wave back at a receding figure with cropped white hair, head hunched into bony shoulders, elderly and stooping but somehow miraculously rejuvenated at nearly eighty on this rock first occupied by saintly Welshmen fifteen centuries ago.

3

Gweithio = Work

'The miner's employment is laborious, and dangerous; and his profits uncertain. Frequent injuries happen to him in blasting the rock, and digging the ore; and cold, damp, and vapour, united in destroying his health, and shortening his life …'

Revd Richard Warner, *A Walk Through Wales in August 1797* (1798)

SWITCH ON LAMP. Tighten helmet. Check belt with battery and self-rescuer. Enter hole in side of hill.

If you're looking for Welshness, sooner or later you will be heading underground. In this case, the way leads into an arched tunnel maybe fifteen feet wide. The left half of the space is taken up by a raised conveyor belt which thrums along at a fair lick, carrying grainy black lumps up towards the light. The earth underneath is rutted and uneven, here hard, there powdery.

'Best keep your lamp on the floor,' says Brian as the gradient steepens and we start to plummet.

For one shift only, I am becoming a miner. OK, perhaps too self-aggrandising a claim. I am being shown into the clandestine underworld where that Welshest of activities has always taken place with nobody to watch: the mining of the coal which, once upon a time, powered the British Empire's trains and ships and industrial furnaces. There were always other pits in the United Kingdom, other coalfields. But in the world's imagination, nowhere is as indissolubly associated with coal as the South Wales Valleys have been for two centuries.

Not that there are many mines left anywhere in Britain, of course. The national tally of big pits is currently down to seven. Wales has two of them and they sit on opposite sides of the A465 – the Heads of the Valleys Road – as it hastens through the Vale of Neath. Over the way is Aberpergwm. I've come to the Unity mine in Cwmgwrach.

The valley is one of the least populated in the South Wales coalfield, which stretches from Llanelli to Pontypool. Cwm Rhondda, just over the mountain, is known as the Long Street. But here are no terraced villages running for miles along a deep narrow gulley carved by a river. When George Borrow walked through the Vale of Neath on his way to Merthyr Tydfil, he noted the valley 'soon became exceedingly beautiful; hills covered with woods on the tops were on either side of the dale'. Pleasing emblems of the local status quo included a passing pack of hunting hounds and, across the valley, 'a very fit mansion for a Glamorganshire squire'. There was only one breach of the peace: 'one of those detestable contrivances a railroad was on the farther side – along which trains were passing, rumbling and screaming.'

The railroad has gone. From the road, flanked on either side by mournful coniferous hills, you'd barely suspect that the embers of the old industry still burn.

I feel entirely fraudulent. I have never knowingly got my hands dirty in the course of work, let alone my face. I don't suppose they see many Jaspers at the coalface. Some Reeses, doubtless. There are no miners in my lineage that I'm aware of, though statistically it's likely that someone on my grandmother's side must once have quarried slate in the north, or on my grandfather's dug for coal in the south.

My guide underground is Brian Lewis, under-manager at Unity. In his smart blue shirt and formal trousers he has the look of someone whom office life hasn't quite succeeded in taming. He can talk the talk of business, figures, productivity, but that frame looks built for a more physical life. He's a sizeable unit is Brian; as a young man he played at centre three-quarter for Aberavon and was offered a signing-on fee to go and play league up country. Employment opportunities in Welsh mining have shrunk to almost nothing, but he has never been out of work since joining the industry in 1976 as an eighteen-year-old. 'I signed on behind my father's back,' he says. 'He wasn't happy, but I could make £22 a week instead of £11.' He started as a face worker at Blaenant, but was offered the chance to train as a mine deputy in Swansea, then, having some O levels, as a mining engineer in Pontypridd. While on strike in 1984–5, he was allowed by the union to attend college. He has since worked mostly at the western end of the coalfield – at Abernant near Pontardawe, Betws near Ammanford, Penallta near Ystrad Mynach. But much of his working life was spent at Tower colliery in Hirwaun. Until 1993, when coal prices dropped through the floor and the pit was deemed uneconomical, it was just another struggling mine. It acquired notoriety when it reopened as a workers' buyout. Brian stayed there till it finally closed in early 2008 and after a brief spell in small mines he came to Cwmgwrach.

The first portal to the underworld is the pithead baths. It's full of row upon row of three-tier numbered metal lockers – far more than is needed for a mine that employs around one hundred men. I change into bright-orange trousers, bright-orange shirt, bright-orange jacket with white luminous strips, bright-orange shin-guards and black lace-up boots. The trousers would be a snug fit for a plumper midriff. As I transmogrify myself from civilian to collier, I think of Big Pit, the museum at Blaenavon which memorialises a decimated industry. The locker doors there are decorated with images of famous mining men. Idris Davies, b. 1905, the collier's boy who became the people's poet for inter-war industrial Wales. A. J. Cook, b. 1884, the miners' leader who during the General Strike coined the phrase 'Not a penny off the pay, not a second on the day'. Bert Coombes, b. 1897, author of the collier's autobiography *These Poor Hands*. 'Slogger Bill', b. 1921, who cut 234 tons of coal in six shifts from a six-foot seam, and turned down an MBE.

I stumble out into the bright morning light, barrel down one of those metal-grill stairwells that sing with each tread, then cross the yard. There is a pile of coal as tall as a house and as long as four. It must weigh thousands of tons. Beyond it we enter the hole in the flank of the hill. This is a drift mine. Unlike a deep-shaft pit, fed by lifts sunk hundreds of metres into the netherworld, in a drift mine you descend to the coal seam on foot (though at the start of the shift the men travel down on the belt).

Brian walks about four miles a day. In previous jobs it was up to twelve. He moves with a burly stride, booted feet wide apart. I stumble along like an eager child, trying hard to feel manly. I am intensely conscious of the signals I must give out: privileged, metropolitan, puny. These are the badges of my white-collar life. They are only partly shrouded by the luminous gear I've been issued with. At least in the darkness everyone else sticks out like a sore thumb too. After reaching a point where we have to clamber over the conveyor belt and dip through a gap, we come to a junction. Down to the right is one of the two roads Unity has been driving into the earth to reach the seam. But we take the left fork and keep walking. Overhead on the left is a huge cylindrical fan pumping air down towards the coalface. We follow it for nearly half a mile, the slope keeping to a constant gradient of one in seven. Every so often there are man-sized holes dug into the corrugated walling – for colliers to squeeze into when machinery passes. I'm wondering what on earth could be big enough to force a man into the fabric of the wall.

A few minutes later I have my answer. A hundred metres off I can see lights and white strips looming; cap lamps are milling around a huge solid presence squatting on the arched roadway. It glowers ominously as we approach, a brontosaurian vehicular hulk. It's as long as a pantechnicon, as low as a Land Cruiser, an unspeakable mechanised apparition. As we pass its flank I can see tank tracks under its skirts.

And here suddenly the corrugated tunnel runs out. After just over a mile of walking downhill we have come to the end of the road. Above us are 550 metres of solid earth. In front is only wall – wall which, by some miracle, broils with fretful life. It convulses in angry reaction to the advance of man and machine. A cluster of miners, faces entirely blackened with coal dust, stand and watch as clumps of rock and rubble detach themselves from the ceiling to thump and scatter cussedly onto the floor, puffing up clouds of particles. A man leaps onto the back of the machine, guns the engine and grapples with the gearstick. The beast jerks and nudges slowly forwards, tank tracks a-growl. And there, mounted on its front and edging towards the coalface, is the most fearsome drill I have ever seen.

One year, to test a much floated family boast that our grandfather was so well-known a figure in South Wales that even the Post Office knew where he lived, my younger brother wrote a letter. On the envelope were the following words:

Bertram
Carmarthen

It took its time but the letter, stamped and franked, found its way to Mount Hill. The postman knocked on the black-and-white front door and asked my grandfather to ensure that next time his correspondent provide them with a little more information to go on. But the barest amount, excluding even his surname, had on this occasion proved sufficient. Bertram Rees was not just any old dentist.

Bert was born in 1901 and grew up on a small farm in Meidrim, a village ten or so miles west of Carmarthen. There were six siblings above him, two below. As in many a home in Wales, education and self-improvement were valued. The four oldest sons went into farming. The only daughter, who was the middle child, married a farmer. The next four sons all qualified as doctors and dentists.

As a young man Bert went up to London to train at Guy's Hospital. On his return to Wales he established himself in Lammas Street in Carmarthen and by 1936 he had managed to buy Mount Hill. Built in the late 1700s in the style of a pavilion in India, it was a prestigious local property which had been in the possession of the family of the Soviet spy Donald Maclean. It cost £2,000. Among his patients was Dylan Thomas, who would come into town from Laugharne and leave without ever, apparently, settling his bill.

My grandfather did not have that difficulty with most of his clients. When the National Health Service was created after the war, the farmers came down from the rolling Carmarthenshire hills and the miners came up from the valleys of the western coalfield and they queued in Lammas Street to have, for the first time in their lives, free dental care – probably, in most cases, their first dental care of any kind at all. The state reimbursed my grandfather handsomely. His compatriot Aneurin Bevan, the member for Ebbw Vale and architect of the NHS, perhaps did not anticipate that free dentistry for the disenfranchised would entail enriching a few practitioners. So prolific was my grandfather's practice, so assiduous his throughput, that in the House of Commons he was held up as an example of dentists milking the system. That's what we were always told, anyway. By the time Bert retired in his seventies, his practice had the records of 70,000 patients, their names and addresses all entered on individual cards. His sons and grandsons went to Harrow. He himself became a name in Lloyds. He was a pillar of the community, so much so that in 1959 he was appointed High Sheriff of Carmarthenshire and ten years later was president of the Three Counties Argricultural Show, in which capacity he took the salute of the Household Cavalry when that summer – I remember this distinctly – they came down to perform a disappointingly squelchy tattoo at the county show under laden summer skies. For the seventh child of a farmer from Meidrim, it was quite a journey.

Teach yourself Welsh. The time has come. My City Lit course is all very well, but we are learning an average of two and a half useful phrases a week, plus approximately twelve new words. At this rate I will be able to hold a conversation shortly before I retire. So I go to a language bookshop in London and invest in a Teach Yourself Welsh book with a pair of CDs.

I've never taught myself a language before. The emphasis is on listening first, and using the book only as a second line of defence. I click the play button. There's a demo of how to pronounce the various letters. The hard *ch*. I know all this, I think contentedly. The salivating *ll*. I am very much ahead of the curve. The windy *rh*. Maybe I should just skip the first chapter. But hold on. 'Jayne, Tom and Matthew,' says the CD, 'have enrolled on a residential Welsh course in Lampeter.' That's actually not a bad idea. 'Matthew has been learning Welsh on his own for a few months. On the first morning he is wandering around the college when he meets someone.'

I listen to the dialogue – *y deialog* – between Matthew and his tutor, Elen. After the initial greeting ('Bore da.' 'Bore da, pwy dych chi?') I fail to understand a single word. I listen again. No. And again. Nope. This is quite upsetting. On about the fifth go I start to make out indistinct sonic patterns, although none that I recognise. After the sixth I check the transcript in the book and it becomes clear that they are indeed, although you could have entirely fooled me, speaking Welsh.

There seems little choice but to clamber onto the snake and slither back down to square one. And so I start all over again, listening, not comprehending, listening, half comprehending, listening, slightly comprehending. I establish that Matthew is by his own admission nervous (*nerfus*). Elen advises him to chillax (*paid a becso* = don't worry).

The sessions are not all about Matthew. There are exercises. How would you greet someone at (a) 10 a.m., (b) 3.20 p.m., (c) 7 p.m.? Answers: *bore da / prynhawn da / noswaith dda* (soft mutation). We are introduced to the concept of the formal (*chi*) and informal (*ti*) mode of address: which would you use with (a) your grandmother, (b) your best friend, (c) the vicar, (d) the little boy from across the road? The answer to (a), incidentally, is *chi*: in Wales there is respect for grandmothers. We move on to *deialog* 2. Jayne, also on the course in Lampeter, claims to be from Ohio ('Americanes dw i'). A likely story. More improbably still, every learner at this fictive Lampeter seems to be already fluent. 'Don't forget to mutate!' says exercise five. These model students never forget to mutate. By *deialog* 5 they've had their first coffee break, Matthew is no longer nervous and they are thickening their arteries in the canteen. Matthew orders coffee and chips, which seems a strange combination. Jayne – presumably a lardbucket Midwesterner – is on a diet (*ar ddeiet*). As they chat with Elen the tutor, I come across my first idiom: steady tapping breaks the stone. Persevere, in other words.

From now on I find a corner of every day to teach myself Welsh. I work through a lesson a week. We get on to numbers, addresses, jobs, family trees, age, marital status, shopping habits, likes, dislikes and preferences. Basically it's a dating manual. In Lesson 2 it emerges that the characters are not only excellent Welsh speakers, they are also proficient in a whole panoply of languages. Nor just the regular ones I've had a crack at myself. Jayne claims to speak Irish fluently. Another likely story. Matthew pipes up that he'd like to learn Irish too. I suspect he fancies her, although learning Irish seems an odd route to the heart of a large woman from Ohio. By Lesson 4 I find I can take no further interest in the lives of these characters when the actors voicing them all seem to be the wrong age. Matthew is clearly in his twenties but played by someone who sounds like my great-uncle Bob. I keep on expecting him to holler, 'Shut the door!' So I just learn the Welsh instead.

By the end of one term of Welsh 1, Module 1, I duck out of the City Lit course. Others have preceded me through the exit, but not for the same reason: they can't stand the heat. I'm so far in front I'm actually in the future, in that thanks to DIY Welsh I can now say how I will do something as well as how I have done it, not to mention how I was doing something and how I did it. Do something (and that's an order): all is being covered in my afternoon study. I no longer exist in the continuous present of the entry-level learner. I have shown a clean pair of heels to Alpha Pete and to the rest of the class who never liked me anyway.

Vocabulary intake is now officially a compulsion. I know the Welsh words for the parts of the body, the weather, the professions. If I meet a lawyer with a thick moustache on a windy afternoon, I am now equipped to report back in Welsh. I start to make regular visits to the BBC Cymru website, where there's a handy button you can turn on (*troi ymlaen*) and suddenly have tricky words highlighted. If you hover the cursor over them, a translation will ping up on the screen. It's a rich new seam to mine. As well as learning the clichés of news (*newyddion*) and sport (*chwaraeon*) in Welsh, there are articles on Welsh culture and heritage full of handy buzz phrases that I'm going to need as I make my way towards Welshness – things like coal mine (*pwll glo*), National Assembly for Wales (*Cynulliad Cenedlaethol Cymru*), hospital appointment (*apwyntiad ysbyty*) and motte-and-bailey (actually I decided I don't need to know that). The website has a vocabulary page which, for someone with my pathology, is as addictive as crack.

As the pages of my red booklet fill, I come across a number of problems. The first is that, Welsh being a largely insular language, give or take the odd cross-fertilisation with Latin and, more recently, the invasion of English, words have a habit of melding. It takes a more agile and adhesive brain than mine to sift and label *llaw, llawn, llawr, llawer, llawen, llew, lle, llo, lleol, llem, lled, lles* and many more. And then there's something curious going on with a lot of the adjectives. The friendlier ones are short and manageable: *hen* = old, *braf* = nice, *gryf* = strong, etc. I'm mildly concerned about some of the longer ones: *difrifol*, for example, which means serious, or *hanfodol* (essential); or *priodol* (appropriate), *ddelfrydol* (ideal), *annhebygol* (unlikely). They all more or less merge. And they all sound like pharmaceutical applications. Rub this *difrifol* on your bunions. If you take three *priodol* a day that rash'll clear up in a trice. A spoonful of *annhebygol* ...

There's no cure for galloping mutation psychosis. The BBC Cymru website actually supplies a mutation checker, but I discover in due course that it's virtually useless because it acknowledges only one trigger for mutations. I am now making the acquaintance of some truly obnoxious rules about when and where and indeed why to deploy the mutation. I read somewhere that you use the nasal mutation for days and years if there are a certain number of them – specifically five, seven, eight, nine, ten, twelve, fifteen, eighteen, twenty, twenty-nine and one hundred.

Sometimes you get a whole conga line of mutated words, as if out on the town after a rummage in the dressing-up box. Every time I think I've got the system locked down, another rule will pop up like a fresh carbuncle. Fired by enthusiasm to approach the problem from several angles rather than learn Welsh entirely through the medium of Matthew's dysfunctional experiences in Lampeter, I invest in a book of Welsh grammar. The first chapter doesn't mince its words. No one would ever guess how many different triggers there are for the soft mutation in the Welsh language. It comes to an inconceivable tally. Thirty-one! A soft mutation can be caused in THIRTY-ONE different and separate ways. If they told you that before you started, you wouldn't start. The book even talks of how certain words 'suffer a mutation'. I know *exactly* how they feel.

'The real traveller in Wales must explore the coal valleys which stretch northward like the fingers of a hand, of which Cardiff is the palm.' Long before Bill Bryson, there was H. V. Morton. The first of the mass-appeal travel writers, the puppyish Morton leapt aboard his open-top, two-seat Bullnose Morris in 1926 to go *In Search of England* and came back with a picture of a pleasing arcadia that, even then, didn't quite exist. Books on Scotland and Ireland promptly followed, both based like their predecessor on articles for Lord Beaverbrook's *Daily Express*.

Morton had defected to the *Daily Herald* by the time *In Search of Wales* was published in 1932. It managed more than any other travel book on Wales to capture the binary nature of the country. Remote and rustic North Wales mesmerised Morton with its antiquity and foreignness. Excluded from all conversation only a few miles from the border, he began to have paranoid hallucinations in the classic English manner: 'It seemed to me that they were hatching another Glendower rebellion,' he said, as he looked at Welshmen chattering incomprehensibly all around him. 'A Roman might have felt like this in a British village.'

But Wales worked away at him. By the time he had driven to the end of the Llŷn peninsula and back he had seen and heard enough to be lecturing a Welshman in an inn in Llanberis about the shameful way the English misunderstood the Welsh. 'Too many people come to Wales, look at it and go home without the slightest idea that they have encountered an alien culture.'

The first two-thirds of *In Search of Wales* concerns itself with the north. Morton kept his gaze fixed on the Wales of old, of Merlin and Arthur, the Romans, of Llewelyn the Last's doomed resistance to Edward I, Owain Glyndŵr's heroic campaign against Henry IV ('I will stick to Shakespeare's spelling,' he said). It was only halfway through the tenth of twelve chapters that he entered what he called 'Black Wales'. Suddenly the observational journalist in Morton had a more urgent sort of spectacle dancing in front of his eyes. He visited a steel works in Llanelli, a copper works in Swansea, an oil refinery at Llandarcy, a zinc works in Llansamlet, an iron forge in Pontypridd. He also spent a blustery day on the Gower with female cockle-pickers on donkeys who hid their faces from the camera for fear of incurring bad luck. (Never mind that rather worse luck was invited by Morton himself when he and a photographer from the *Herald*, using 'a new safe-light apparatus', took the first ever flash-light picture in the potentially explosive methane-rich environment of a coal mine.)

Morton's Welsh journey concluded in the Rhondda. His compassionate portrait of dignity wrestling with poverty reads like the complex, layered climax to an epic symphony. In Heartbreak Valley, as it was known in the Great Depression, Morton found the river running black, chimneys no longer belching smoke, jobless men loitering on street corners and stoical women feeding and clothing 'insanely large families'. But when he spoke to the men of the Rhondda, whether they had work or not, he was astonished not only by their mild manners and gentleness, but by the high level of education, culture and intellectual curiosity.

And then he plunged underground. Issued with dungarees and a lamp, he stepped into a cage with a group of men for the afternoon shift and reached fifty miles an hour as they dropped half a mile into the earth. 'It roared. It rattled. It banged. I felt that my feet had left the bottom of the cage and that my ears were being pulled upwards.' It slowed to a halt, out he stepped and began walking for more than a mile towards the coalface. Overhead, steel girders had been wrenched out of shape by the weight of half a mile of terra firma. Underfoot, as he walked between rails, his boots kicked through fluffy powder. A voice hallooed from a great distance. Then another noise was heard, which grew and grew until 'it was as if the miners in the front line had released some dragon that was tearing towards us in the dark': a train of twenty-five cars laden with coal growled past, as Morton and his guide stepped into a lay-by.

Eventually he came to the coalface, where he found not only

miners but boys and a horse. He seemed to show more interest in the fate of the colliery horses than the boys, and indeed reported on the care they received at greater length than the business of working the seam. Nonetheless, Morton did marvel at the extraordinary skill with which the men attacked the face:

> You who know coal only as something in a homely fire-bucket can have no conception of its appearance deep down in the earth … A child would realise the peril of picking at this soft black stuff, with the hard rock above always in danger of falling and crushing you to death. The miners … knew exactly where to strike. They were as black as negroes. Their shirts, wet with sweat, clung to ebony bodies. There seemed something gallant and desperate every time a man tapped a great ledge of coal, gently felt it move until it seemed to tear like cloth, then – 'Stand clear!' – and down it fell in a black rush, lumps of it big enough to break your back!

He seemed to find no means of expressing his admiration for these men other than through punctuation: he littered these paragraphs with exclamation marks as he met and talked with them of music ('He was fond of Handel!') and of greyhounds ('We talked of dogs!'). The readers of the *Daily Herald* needed to be told that these miners were no worse than themselves, and possibly rather better. 'It was like finding hell inhabited by angels,' said Morton.

His imagination made a link with still-fresh memories of the trenches, a coal mine's atmospheric equivalent for camaraderie in the face of danger.

'Well, and what do you think of it?' a miner asked him as he entered the cage to be sent back up towards green grass and soft rain.

'You are always in the firing-line.'

'We get used to it. It's got to be done! I wish a few more people
would come and see us work. Cheerio!'

The DOSCO Mark IIB Roadheader bears down on the coalface,
its ferocious cutting head a-jigger. A new upgraded DOSCO would
cost in the neighbourhood of one and a half million quid, Brian
tells me. This one's forty years old. If it were a whale it would be
smothered in barnacles. Under advice, I've got my breathing mask
on.

Visible across the vertical surface is a join between the six-foot
coal seam and, above it, a mixture of sandstone and mudstone. The
miners call it muck, because it's worthless. The cutting head
engages the wall of rock and begins the work of ripping it to shreds.
As the arm swings left and right, up and down, the whole lot spits
off in an indiscriminate mix onto the floor, where it is swept into
the bowels of the machine by two huge, flat, rotating star-shaped
wheels. The roar is all-engulfing. There's no point in attempting to
talk unless you want to howl directly into someone's inner ear. I am
transfixed by the unequal battle between machine and mineral.
This, it suddenly strikes me, is modern coal-mining. Unlike their
hundreds of thousands of Welsh forerunners, fellow moles under
these mountains, the men scurrying around in luminous orange
barely touch the coal itself.

In due course the cutting head stops and a kind of peace is
restored. The road has been swept clear of dusty clumps and
mangled heaps, the coalface pushed back by perhaps a metre.
Between fifteen and eighteen tons have been sent back on the conveyor belt. In the silence a miner greets me with a handshake and
a plug of tobacco. Miners chew tobacco as an alternative to smoking,
which along with all forms of battery-powered equipment is
banned. Slung on a wire across the roof of the tunnel is a winking

gizmo designed to measure the level of flammable gas which has claimed so many local lives over the last two centuries. I've never taken so much as a single drag on a cigarette but it seems unadventurous to refuse.

'Don't swallow, mind,' he says. 'Whatever you do …'

'Why, what happens?'

'You won't feel very well is what.' Brian, who is listening in, advises that I'll be vomiting without cease if I let so much as a drop of saliva near my epiglottis. He can't stand the stuff, he adds. How they'd all chuckle if I sprayed the road with neophyte's chunder. Warily I put the plug in my mouth and bite. It feels like munching on a wet twig dipped in bitumen. Within a minute I spit it into the dust and for the next quarter-hour I'm neurotically gobbing spumes of saliva. I've failed my first underground trial.

There were 35,000 miners working in the South Wales coalfield in 1984. There are now around 1 per cent of that figure. These men down here in the bowels of the earth are survivors of an industrial holocaust. There are eight of them: a fitter, an electrician and a deputy, an apprentice engineer and three heading men. Not that you'd ever guess who does what. Everyone has a job title but, whereas miners used to have very specific roles in the days when there were thousands of them, these days everyone seems to muck in. If a job needs doing, someone does it. That's not the only reason it's hard to tell them apart. They're all in a version of the same outfit, with every head covered, every face coated in dust. It appears there is also a regular collier's size and shape too – a generous midriff, thick shoulders and a general air of stumpiness. There are no beanpoles at the coalface. In this environment, teeth become much stronger marks of identity (although in the old days of course none of them would have had many). Caught in the light of my cap lamp, feline eyes – briny blue or iridescent green-brown – blaze in the darkness.

It's time for the lunch break. I collar a man who introduces himself as Charlie – Charlie Richards. Under the coal dust he has one of those aquiline Welsh faces, quizzical and alert. He's untypical of those working down here, having started at twenty-six. 'My father was a miner,' he explains, 'and he dissuaded me from working underground because of the dangers and the dirtiness of the job. But once I got married at twenty-one he told me you have to go your own way and do what you think is right and there wasn't a lot of work about that I fancied so I started underground then.' He worked at a pit in Maesteg until it closed in 1985 and 600 lost their jobs. He then spent thirteen years working in a brickworks in Bridgend. 'It was totally different,' he says. 'Nothing compares to being a miner.' I ask him why. 'It's the type of men you're working with. Everybody watches everybody else. You're looking after everybody else's safety. You can't compare it. No mind that you're working in a dangerous place, somebody will always come out with a crack and we have a laugh. As I say, it's totally different. It's dangerous, but everybody mucks in together.'

That was what he missed. He came back to mining when jobs were going at Tower, worked there till it closed and came on to Unity. He's sixty-one now. I ask him if he still looks forward to work. There's no hesitation. 'Yeah, I do, funnily enough. A lot of the boys I know say, "Oh, why do you work there? Stinking dirty dangerous hole." Unless you've been underground and worked with the men I work with you can't say that. You don't know what it's about.' The sentiment is echoed by Wayne Morris from Ystrad Mynach, a wide-faced man who leans in so close that I can see the coal dust dotting the pores on his broad nose.

'The atmosphere underground and all the camaraderie and the boys and that,' he says in a looping accent, 'it's something that you will never get outside.' When I ask around, it seems that everyone at the face comes from a mining background. But no one has mining flowing through his veins quite as much as Wayne. He's one of twelve children, he tells me; of the five boys, three went underground. His father was one of twenty-one; of the eleven boys, nine went underground. From Wayne's class in school, twenty-four of thirty boys went underground. Wayne is the last of all of these men still to work in the Welsh coalfield. 'It's something that is born into you,' he says. Increasingly it is being bred out of men like him.

These remnants of decimation by the forces of history have come through with good humour intact. With my background I half expect to be ribbed or cut amusingly down to size or even quietly cold-shouldered, but there is none of that. The humour is laced with expletives but drained of aggression. Wayne seems to embody to an almost parodic extent a spirit of optimism and jaunty warmth that exists at the coalface. He tells me a tale he must have repeated a thousand times. 'There were six girls in my family before there was one boy. Up until the age of sixteen when we used to have hand-me-downs I was in a skirt!'

At sixteen he went underground at Penallta. It was 1979. What does he remember of his first day of work? 'Frightening,' he says. 'Standing in that cage and being dropped into the bowels of the earth. The colliery that I did work in was the deepest sunken shaft in South Wales: 998 metres. It was like you was freefalling.' He didn't anticipate that the entire industry was freefalling too. He chose mining over factory work 'because there was more money there like and more of a future'. It was a fair assumption: the Rhymney Valley where he grew up boasted fifty-six pits at the time. Twelve years later he was one of 360 men who lost their jobs when the last of them closed. Wayne managed to find work, mostly at Tower until it too closed. A week later he started at Unity.

Wayne is forty-eight, a grandfather five times over. Despite the

growth in demand for coal, and the rise in price that has allowed
two neighbouring mines to open in the Vale of Neath, there's no
sign that the industry is investing in a long-term future. He and
Charlie both express anxiety that young men are not being taken
on and trained as miners. 'We are the last of a dying breed,' says
Wayne. There is one boy down here, a diffident apprentice engineer
called Nathan from Merthyr who signed up because his father
mined and all his friends with degrees now work in Tesco. He's
twenty. After qualifying he'll do ten years underground, he tells me,
and then he'll get out. By then, most of these men will have retired
and the world-renowned breed of Welsh miners that stretches back
to the eighteenth century and beyond will be all but extinct.

In Welsh phonebooks and Welsh graveyards you are reminded how
hard it is to track Welsh people down. It's no mystery why the
Welsh use nicknames like Dai the Post and Dai the Brick: to dis-
tinguish between two of the countless Dai Joneses in any given
village. It's more of a mystery why those names never eventually
mutated into surnames, the way Farmer and Cook, Baker and
Taylor did over the border. There are few indigenous surnames and
only a small pool of patronymics – Jones, Williams and Phillips,
etc. Even the ones that look like real surnames – Pritchard and
Bevan, Bowen, Powell and Price – are corruptions of ap Richard,
ap Evan, ap Owen, ap Hywel, ap Rhys. *Ap* means 'son of '.

On the other hand it must have made marriage much less com-
plicated. In Wales, the statistical likelihood of finding a husband of
the same name meant that many brides could go from Miss Jones
to Mrs Jones without any mental adjustment. It nearly happened
with my great-grandmother, known to all as Nain. Nearly, but not
quite. When she met and married her husband David Goronwy
Owens in 1901, convention required her to make only a small

alteration, from Owen to Owens. The story goes that she didn't fancy that extra s, and invited her new husband to drop the final letter from his surname. It's hard to imagine how castrating that must have been for a young man employed in the bank during the last gasp of the Victorian age, how much shaking of heads and elbowing of ribs it must have provoked.

The yew-fringed graveyard at Meidrim is teeming with Hywels and Evanses. I'm looking for Reeses. Two in particular. Teilo has told me that Bert's parents – my great-grandparents – are both buried there. I know very little of them beyond their names – Thomas and Eliza Rees.

I am wearing my Welsh rugby shirt for the occasion. It's a bright warm morning. The thick grass on either side of the path is crowded with graves, some of the garish marble headstones relatively new, the masonry of others withered and illegible with age. I decide to work through them meticulously. There are hundreds of names, some going back to the eighteenth century, many of the dead fondly remembered in Welsh.

When Borrow was nosing around a church in Llandovery, else-where in Carmarthenshire, he noted 'no remarkable tombs'. 'I was pleased, however, to observe upon one or two of the monuments the name of Ryce, the appellation of the great clan …; of old the regal race of South Wales.' It's nice to know one is of Welsh royalty, but there are only a couple of Reeses that I can find in Meidrim and none of them the right ones. I scour the whole graveyard, all the way down the slope beyond the apse. Nothing. Perhaps Teilo was wrong, I think. I'm just finishing my circuit when I hear a voice.

'You playing for Wales, are you?' I look up and see a short old man wielding a bristly broom. He's noticed my shirt.

'I'm waiting for selection,' I reply. He laughs.

'Looking for any grave in particular?' He has a round, open

countenance and wears a cheerful grin, as well as a dark-blue Carmarthenshire County Council shirt. I tell him I'm looking for my great-grandparents, and mention their names.

'There are a couple of Reeses over there,' he says, indicating one flank of the graveyard, 'and another one down by there,' pointing down the side of the church.

'That's not them though,' I say. 'Maybe they're not here after all.' I ask how long he's lived in Meidrim. All his life, he says. 'Born in 1932, I was. I was helping my grandfather in 1938, '9, giving him a hand. He was cutting the churchyard with a scythe or a hook. No mowers then.' He has a Welsh accent from another age, thick, musical and almost folkishly rural. I ask him his name.

'Les,' he says. 'What did you say your name was again?'

'Rees,' I say. I leave my first name unspoken. Then out of the blue he says something extraordinary.

'Did you know Bertram Rees?'

'As a matter of fact he was my grandfather.'

'Was he now?' Les giggles. 'Oh, I remember him. Dentist, wasn't he?'

'He was. Was he yours?'

'Yes, he was.'

'And what was your memory of him?'

'He was a fucking butcher!' The only reaction I can think of is to laugh. Les warms to his theme. 'All of my family was with him having teeth out.'

'Really?'

'My father was the first person who had a tooth out by him. He was an apprentice then. My father had his teeth out no bother at all and then he went to the pub straight. Well, I couldn't do that. Different type of teeth, you know, because I had big roots on 'em.' He shakes his head. 'I had bad teeth. He couldn't help it anyway.'

Les is embarrassed that he might have gone too far. We stand in the middle of a churchyard, him remembering and me imagining an event that must have taken place sixty-five years ago.

'I know I laugh now, but I was crying in them days. Oh, he was very strong. Big 'ands, you know.'

'He was missing two fingers,' I remind Les.

'Yes, I know. But I think he had more strength in the hand then. Because he nearly pulled my bloody 'ead off.'

I've been learning Welsh for a few months now, but I've yet to have a conversation in Welsh in Wales. Something is holding me back. It's not just common-or-garden self-consciousness, a perfectly reasonable phobia of looking thick as pigshit in front of strangers. There's a political dimension to my anxiety too. The overarching fear is that you summon up the courage to ask a question in Welsh, spend an age building the sentence in the language lab in your head, tinkering with it, probing it for structural weaknesses, and then you go and waste it on a very Welsh-looking person who is *di-Gymraeg*: a Welsh non-Welsh speaker. In the minefield of the two Waleses, you can very easily cause offence.

However, I'm learning to play the percentages. There are parts of Wales where you can be fairly certain of not being understood. The closer you are to England, for example, the lower the ratio of Welsh speakers per capita. Gwent for that reason is not a good place to try your Welsh on people. In a Black Mountains pub I meet a chirpy old waitress from Pontypool who chats with classical Welsh abandon about her health. I mention I'm learning Welsh. It's as if I've slapped her violently across the face, then spat in her eyes. 'Oh, are you?' she sniffs peremptorily, turning her back on me. 'Nobody speaks Welsh around here,' she says over her shoulder as she struts out. Her implication is clear: if I were you I wouldn't bother.

But I am bothering. I've rented a cottage in Carmarthenshire for a week on my own. One day I take the bus into Lampeter and head for the smallest university in Britain. I am following in Matthew's daring footsteps and seeking information about a residential Welsh language course. I am directed from the front desk towards a room in the corner of the quadrangle where I knock on a door and hear a sing-song female voice.

'Dewch i mewn.' Come in (and that's an order). I push open the door and am confronted with a terrifying sight. The situation could not be more dire. I have to have my first conversation in Welsh in Wales in front of two people, and emasculatingly, two female people. One smiles up at me from behind the desk.

'Gaf i'ch helpu chi?' May she help me?

'Er …' Two not unfriendly faces look at me expectantly.

'Dw i'n dysgu Cymraeg,' I manage.

'O da iawn,' says the one behind the desk. 'Ble?'

'Yn Lundain …' An uncalled-for mutation. I am struggling. I can't say the next bit in Welsh. 'I can't say the next bit in Welsh.' She says something I don't understand.

'Dw i ddim yn deall,' I say. I haven't got a clue what she's just said.

'Try.'

I try. No wonder Matthew was nervous. They're content to let you wriggle on a spit in Lampeter. And there is no oxygen anywhere near my head. It's hideously warm in here. Welsh is making me faint. This might as well be the doctor's surgery. I might as well be having to undress. It would be so very easy to slip into one's mother tongue. But no. Tap tap. I trip and stumble, with much bumping into obstacles and patient nursing over hurdles from the two women, towards a request for information about a residential course in Welsh in Lampeter. I sound like the utterest moron, all tongue-tied blushes and self-recrimination. The woman behind the desk takes my email address and I make my sheepish exit. As I pull the door to I can feel my shirt clinging fast to my back.

That afternoon, to recover from my humiliation, I set out on a walk to the pub over the hill near Pumsaint, where the Romans came to mine gold. This is a more tumultuous Carmarthenshire than the smooth pastoral hummocks around Carmarthen I'm used to. A few miles to the north the road slopes up into the full-blown Cambrian Mountains of Mid Wales, many of whose valleys were flooded to provide water, like so many other Welsh dams, for England. There's absolutely no one about, even on a sunny warm afternoon. Most of the land seems to be private, with few public footpaths to choose from, so I just turn off the road and head up a randomly selected track. I rise and rise until the narrow Cwm Cothi fans out below in a pretty patchwork. Eventually the rutted path bisects a farmyard. A dog of indeterminate breed sets off a racket behind the gate of a house. I hurry on for thirty yards or so only to hear voices. I turn round and spot two people staring up at me, a couple in their sixties. They don't look friendly. I deem it best to walk back down.

'Am I trespassing?' I call. I'm still fifteen yards off, but can see two faces set hard. I definitely am trespassing, and in a posh English accent.

'Where are you going?' It's the hunched figure of the farmer who calls back. He's come out of the barn.

'Over the hill to Caio.'

'This is private land here.'

'I'm very sorry. I didn't realise.' If I'm honest I did realise.

'But if you keep on up you get to the path by there.' He points begrudgingly up the hill, not quite having the heart to send me all the way down into the valley and round. I don't know how it happens, but the permission kicks a tripwire in my brain.

'Diolch yn fawr iawn,' I say. Thank you very much indeed. The farmer's wife pipes up.

'Dych chi'n siarad Cymraeg?' She wants to know if I speak Welsh.

'Dw i'n dysgu ar hyn o bryd.' I'm learning at the moment. Then something marvellous happens. Two stony weathered faces crease into the warmest, broadest smiles. It's as if these few words have raised a portcullis and I've passed through to a sunlit inner sanctum. She wants to know where I'm learning.

'Yn Llundain. Ond mae fy tad yn dod o Gaerfyrddin.' I cock up the nasal mutation of *tad*, but the important thing is to tell them that I belong to this part of the world, at least ancestrally: my father comes from Carmarthen. She then says something else which I don't remotely understand and we revert to English to establish the precise route up the hill. But it doesn't matter. I suddenly feel I've cracked it. I am on the right path.

'I worked 'eadings five years, then I moved to …' 'I started off as an apprentice then went to 'eadings.' I have no idea what they're talking about and am too embarrassed to ask. Headings? What are headings? Then it dawns on me. With every fresh metre hewn away, every length added to the tunnel, the walls and ceiling have to be secured. Otherwise, the whole place could collapse. This is what the men mean by working on headings. They are building the tunnel that will prevent the world falling on their heads.

For mile upon mile the tunnel is held in place by steel arches placed a metre apart. Between the arches is corrugated sheeting. It takes a shift to move forwards two to three metres. It seems slow work, but the surprise down here is the speed at which the men move. The energy is frenetic. Two men lift a curved steel girder and place it upright at the flank of the tunnel. A longer piece is lifted by the DOSCO and suspended just under the roof. The two pieces are then bolted swiftly together using a clamp, the same for the girder on the other flank. To reach the roof a gantry platform is fixed to the extendable arm of the DOSCO so that two men can whack the corrugated sheets behind the girders. The sound of banging mingles with monosyllabic shouts, coded communications that are meaningless to my virgin ears but seem to indicate stop, start, lift, drop, pass, left, right. It's neither English nor Welsh but almost pre-verbal.

I feel a bit spare. Charlie is carrying sacks from further down the tunnel and bringing them to the face. It's a feeble token of goodwill, but rather than watch him I might as well join in. Then there are some thick, square, four-by-four lengths of wood to lug too. I do a bit of that as well. No sooner delivered than they are hauled onto the gantry and shoved as packing into the gap between the heading roof and the tunnel ceiling. Another metre, another bit of the Welsh underground has been claimed by these men, dug out and sent up to be sold as it has been for centuries.

It's hardly participation Welshness. Manual labour and me are not, historically, a comfortable fit. I feel frustrated that, owing to health and safety, industrial rules and lack of insurance, I can't get my hands dirty. I speak metaphorically of course. My hands are filthy. But it is a privilege, when fewer and fewer Welshmen can claim first-hand knowledge of the dust and the heat, at least to visit a secret sphere so linked with Wales's national identity. The DOSCO Mark IIB chokes into life. Men clear out of its path. The gantry has been removed; the arm of the cutting head is ready to scour more coal from the seam. How many more metres will these men cut? How many more miles of tunnel excavated under these hills? There are many millions of tons of coal still there – an inexhaustible resource. But the men to do the job will not be here for ever. I shake all their hands, and those teeth and eyes glint once more in the beam of my cap lamp. 'So long, Jas,' they say; 'Thanks for coming down, Jasper,' my unWelsh name shouted above the bellow of the engine.

Turning away from the coalface I accompany Brian back up the slope. It's hard work walking uphill for half a mile, and when eventually we reach the junction I'm relieved that Brian says we can travel on the conveyor belt. I lie face down on a bed of coal and am spirited back towards the light, towards the Wales the world knows. Only when we emerge into the sunshine there is something new I hadn't noticed before. Just over the brow of the hill on the other side of the Vale of Neath is a monstrous white wind turbine looking imperiously down at the Unity mine and its black tip of coal. The future confronts the past.

I head back to the pithead baths. In a mirror my face has been impressively rebranded. It looks a bit like theatre make-up, wispy and too tasteful, but I'm thrilled with my new look. With reluctance I peel off my orange pelt and head for the shower. As they have for decades, Brian and two other miners are washing the black dust from their pores, reminiscing about the days when you had to catch the bus home and leap into a tin bath. I scrub too, but with less commitment. Like a fan who doesn't wash the bit of their cheek kissed by a pin-up, I want to keep some of the grime about my person. I want these Welsh particles to seep into my skin until there is no scrubbing them away.

4

Canu = Sing

'When it is remembered that this chorus is almost entirely drawn from the labouring classes of the Principality, miners, colliers, etc., their wives, daughter and relatives, we cannot but wonder at the excellence they have attained.'

The Times (1872)

MY FIRST FIRST-HAND EXPERIENCE of Welsh choralism is in the Millennium Stadium. The occasion is another battering from the All Blacks. I stand to attention more or less in the back row. It's as if I'm at the top of a small Welsh mountain and looking down a seething slope to the foot of the hill. A flat rectangular field is peopled with matchstick figurines: one line of microscopic beef-cakes in black, another in red. Perched on a box is a minuscule conductor who swishes a baton as a military ensemble of tiny bandsmen strike up the famous opening chords. I spy a long male choir, twenty-five wide and four deep, who lend support to the noise which now swirls and booms around this secular cathedral like no other musical sound on earth. There is not the vocabulary to encompass the sensation of hearing for the first time 'Hen Wlad Fy Nhadau' sung by 75,000 voices. The most expansive superlatives shrivel into inadequacy.

Regrettably, so do I. I know the tune. I do not know the words. Result: I cannot join in. There is nothing for it, while all Wales fills its Welsh lungs and sings, but to stand – uselessly, space-wastingly – in limp-dicked, shaming silence. I feel ever so grimly in sync with that most abominably unWelsh of figures: John Redwood. As a Secretary of State for Wales foisted on the Principality in the 1990s, Mr Redwood did not spend a single night in Wales. He was once caught off-guard by the camera, miming a version of the words to the anthem. It looked like he'd been dubbed from Bulgarian. He bobbled his head from side to side as if trying to cover his blushes with boyish enthusiasm while a pair of darting eyes betrayed his fear of discovery. How Wales howled.

I need to work on this core Welsh skill as a matter of urgency.

'I now propose to describe the Welsh people, who are so very different from other nations.' In *The Description of Wales*, Gerald took the long historical view that the Welsh, who were the original Britons, derived their name from Brutus, whose people fled Troy and tarried in Greece. They might still be in Troy, he argued, were it not for their moral weaknesses. 'It was because of their sins, and more particularly the wicked and detestable vice of homosexuality, that the Welsh were punished by God and so lost first Troy and then Britain.' Without Welsh vices, according to this reading of mythology, Aeneas would have never left to found Rome and the word 'odyssey' would not exist.

This comes in a section ominously called 'The Less Good Points'. The list is carefully demarcated into chapters with such unpromising titles as 'They live on plunder and have no regard for the ties of peace and friendship' and 'Their weakness in battle: how shamefully and ignobly they run away'. The Welsh, we learn, are greedy, inconstant and far too keen on incest. Gerald incorporated advice to the English on how the Welsh can be conquered and governed, before even-handedly offering some tips to the Welsh on resistance. 'I myself am descended from both peoples,' he reasoned, 'and it seems only fair.'

Perhaps Edward I had read it with interest by the summer of 1277 when he marched into Wales with a 15,500-strong army (more than half of whom were Welsh) and, having subordinated it, turned it into a principality. But even the king who encircled unruly Wales with castles stopped short of following Gerald's recommendation to the letter. 'It may well be thought preferable,' mused the man who yearned to become Archbishop of St David's, 'to eject the entire population which lives there now, so that Wales can be colonised anew. The present inhabitants are virtually ungovernable, and there are some who think that it would be far safer and more sensible to turn this rough and impenetrable country into an unpopulated forest area and game preserve.' Even the most rabid Englishman might struggle to acquiesce to ethnic cleansing.

But Gerald also praised the agility and courage of the Welsh, their frugality, hospitality and intelligence: 'they are quicker-witted and more shrewd than any other Western people' (by which he meant the Celts). Their respect for genealogy earned his approval, and of course their piety. He also had the highest praise for their cultural attainments, and one of them in particular:

> When they come together to make music, the Welsh sing their traditional songs, not in unison, as is done elsewhere, but in parts, in many modes and modulations. When a choir gathers to sing, which happens often in this country, you will hear as many different parts and voices as there are performers, all joining together in the end to produce a single organic harmony and melody in the soft sweetness of B-flat.

I've never been to the Rhondda Valley. It's about time. I send an email out into the ether. A few days later I get a phone call. A chirpy voice invites me to come along any time. Visitors are always welcome. I'm told to make my way to Tylorstown between Porth and Maerdy. For anyone who has dipped a toe in the narrative of Wales after the Industrial Revolution, these place names are rich with history.

As I drive up the Taf Valley one evening and enter the mouth of the Rhondda Fach, I have an almost tangible sense that I am heading into the Wales that everyone has heard of but no outsider ever visits. Pendyrus Male Choir meets twice a week in a sports centre near the floor of the valley. Several senior gents carrying briefcases flow towards an entrance. I am greeted by a smile from a short man in his sixties. And another with a big grey beard. They urge me to follow with a knowing jaunty air. Through a big window the odd swimmer is splashing in a pool. Other young and spry types loiter in reception, either on their way to the gym, or freshly returned. The same cannot be said for the seventy or so men gathered in a room down a long corridor whose average age is certainly sixty, possibly older. Unless I'm much mistaken everyone seems to be chuckling. I seek out the Pendyrus secretary Graham, who turns out to be a benign bruiser with shiny blue eyes and a pinkish face behind wire-rimmed specs.

'Glad you could make it, Jasper,' he booms. Graham, I sense, is an extrovert. 'The question is where do we put you?' I give him a blank look. 'Your voice. You fancy singing with the tops or down with me in the basses?'

'Ah. Not too high and not too low,' I say. 'If that's OK. Sort of in the middle.'

'Sounds to me like you're a second tenor. You'd best sit by here.' 'By here' is pronounced to sound like a famous Norman tapestry.

'Got room in there for one more, boys?' Two men, also in their sixties, stand and usher me to a seat in the third row with extravagant friendliness. They introduce themselves as Alan and Mal. Alan has a full head of curling white hair and a look of wry amusement. Mal, tanned and poker-faced, is dapper with a generous girth. Around me other singers turn to nod and smile or shake my hand.

'Good evening, gentlemen.' The hubbub suddenly pipes down. A tall man is standing out front behind a music stand: Pendyrus's conductor, Stewart Roberts. Tall, with a fresh open face and neatly parted hair, he has the confident manner of a teacher who knows that his class's attention may wander but can be effortlessly controlled with a well-placed word. In his mid thirties, he is half the age of half the room.

'Now then, gentlemen, since we're performing at the international swimming gala in Swansea quite soon, why don't we warm up with the European anthem?'

Seventy men rummage in briefcases and produce sheets of music. Mal indicates that I can share with him. Our conductor counts us in and away we go. And so the first song I sing in the first of many practices with Pendyrus Male Choir is Beethoven's 'Ode to Joy', adopted by the European Union as its anthem. It's all highly apposite. The tradition of the Welsh male-voice choir has its roots in this and adjacent valleys when men came out of the pit and the foundry and, deprived of other communal entertainment as the temperance movement kept them increasingly from the tavern, joined choirs. Without much in the way of musical training, they learned to sing in four-part harmony. The repertoire consisted of stirring, lyrical tunes composed by Welshmen and sung in Welsh, but also of music in the German oratorio tradition.

The Welsh gift for choral singing came to international attention in 1872 when the South Wales Choral Union, a 350-strong

ensemble gathered from all over the Valleys, travelled up to compete
in the Crystal Palace. They performed choruses from Bach's 'St
Matthew Passion', Handel's *Samson* and Mendelssohn's 'Hymn of
Praise' and returned triumphantly to Wales with the Challenge
Cup and the praise of *The Times* ringing in their ears. Their conductor was Griffith Rhys Jones, a blacksmith turned breweries'
director known by his bardic name of Caradog. It was Caradog who
coined the phrase that has resonated across the years: the Land of
Song. The South Wales Choral Union went back to London the
following year and won the Challenge Cup again.

It's hard, in the midst of the second tenors, to appreciate the
richness of the four-part sound. I concentrate on my Beethovenian
line, while the familiar high tune is taken by the first tenors on my
right – 'the girls', Mal calls them. Chuntering some way off to my
left are rumbles and growls from the baritones and basses. After
one sing-through our conductor gets under the bonnet and starts
to work on individual parts.

The atmosphere could not be cheerier. Banter pings around the
room. For someone who spends his working life alone, it is a strange
feeling to move seamlessly into an atmosphere that ought by rights
to be swilling in testosterone but has somehow had the edge of
male assertion syringed away.

'Now then, second tenors.' Stewart asks us to sing our line. 'The
cream of the choir,' he adds. From the rest of the choir comes a
sforzando of mock disapproval, an uproar of hissing and tutting.
Around me the sixteen or so second tenors puff out their chests
with an air of casual entitlement. Stewart, his hands raised to beat
us in, wears the chirpy grin of someone who knew he would provoke
that reaction. It's as if he has at his beck and call the vocal services
of seventy sixty-year-olds in short trousers.

We're on to the German national anthem now, the swimming

gala being Great Britain against Germany. Mal says they've sung all sorts: the Canadian and American when they go there on tour, various European anthems, even the Japanese. The harmonic line has a beautiful Teutonic certainty about it, and I am kept afloat by the singers around me. It would be nice, I think, as we are invited after ten minutes' rehearsal to stand and belt out 'Deutschland Über Alles' in unison, to sing something in Welsh. No sooner is the German anthem done and dusted than I have my wish.

'Excellent, gentlemen. Now I think it might be an idea to have a look at "Heriwn, Wynebwn y Wawr".' More rummaging in brief-cases, and suddenly I'm trying to sight-read fiendish music in Welsh. On an electric upright an accompanist spatters out aggres-sive dissonant chords. Our conductor mouths the words back at us as we sing. 'Gloyw fo'n llygaid a'n gobaith yn fflam!' I have no idea what much of this means, there being no time to peruse the over-poeticised English translation. *Llygaid* = eyes. *Gobaith* = hope. *Fflam* (presumably) = flame. The music is clearly eager to excite passion and incite fervour in a Welsh breast, with stabs of staccato and dotted power surges. On *fflam* the second tenors hold a screech-ingly high note, then veer up a tone, then clamber up again. For a male choir novice, this is voicebox boot camp. Next to me I can hear Mal soaring effortlessly, but for me the second tenor line slips up into the clouds, past the top of my range, and I feel my enfee-bled throat squawk and squeal in protest. Just in time the tune plummets vertically south. 'Mae'r dyfodol yn dechrau,' we sing, quick and fast, repeating and varying the phrase urgently until it fans out into a closing climactic four-voice chord. 'Mae'r dyfodol yn dechrau … yn awr!' The future is beginning … now!

'Very good, gentlemen. Now, baritones …' Stewart is back under the bonnet. As he tinkers, I mop my brow.

'Popeth yn iawn?' says Mal. Everything OK?

'Ddim yn siwr, Mal.' I'm not sure. I cough hesitantly.

'Paid a becso, bychan.' Don't worry. He's called me *bychan* (lit. little one). I suppose in this room, unlike any other, the diminutive is legitimate. There are a couple of teenagers, but apart from them Stewart seems to be the only one younger than me.

Eventually, after two strenuous hours of pushing lungs and larynx, the choir's chairman stands up and makes an announcement or two. The arrangements for travelling by coach down to the gala in Swansea are discussed – times, dress code and so forth. The chairman passes on the news with regret that someone's wife is unwell – the whole room in unison voices deep concern – but that recovery is hoped for. Then something happens that I'm not expecting.

'We'd like to welcome a visitor from London – Jasper Rees – who has come along to sing with us tonight.' I can feel myself itching to shrink from the attention, only for spontaneous applause to swell. I am being clapped for turning up in this wide room in the Rhondda Fach full of full-bodied men with honeyed voices. Alan pats me on the shoulder. As the applause fades, Mal hollers out a welcome.

'Give him a jacket!'

It's music to my ears.

'We had heard much of Welsh hospitality,' wrote the Revd Richard Warner upon arriving at an inn near Abergavenny, after a long day's slog in 1797; 'it gave us … no little pleasure to find it exemplified towards ourselves.' In 1854 George Borrow found the Welsh welcome in robust health in Llanfair on Anglesey, where he entered the home of a poor miller who shared his enthusiasm for a long-dead bard. 'My eyes filled with tears,' he recalled, 'for in the whole course of my life I had never experienced so much genuine hospitality.' Shame on the Saxon, he added, for his 'uncouth and ungracious' ways. In 1870 the curate Francis Kilvert, wandering

the parish of Clyro in Radnorshire, was similarly overwhelmed in
the house of another miller. 'Oh these kindly hospitable houses
about these hospitable hills!' he exclaimed at the memory of tea,
bread, butter and preserves brought to him by the fireside. 'I
believe I might wander about these hills all my life and never want
a kindly welcome, a meal, or a seat by the fireside.'

My grandparents believed in the Welsh welcome. Before or after
Christmas, the house would jostle with guests – old friends and
colleagues, neighbours, people they'd known for decades. The
entertainment mostly took a musical form. As a girl at school in
Dolgellau, Dorothy was a proficient enough pianist to gain a place
at the Royal Academy of Music in London. She won a gold medal
there and returned to Wales to teach 'but *hated* it', Teilo tells me.
'The pupils were so unenthusiastic about music and reluctant to
learn.' Her mother succumbed to diabetes in the early 1920s and
Dorothy had her excuse to give up teaching piano. She gave charity
recitals in Carmarthen. Bert saw her performing at one and determined there and then to marry her.

At Mount Hill there was a Bechstein baby grand in a room we
rarely visited, just inside the front door on the left. The drawing
room had a feminine ambience: whereas everywhere else the house
had rich red carpets and polished wood, here were white walls and
a light-green carpet; dainty porcelain knick-knacks covered low
shelving. Only the piano came from another part of the colour
chart: the wood was stained stark black. I remember the shock one
afternoon of hearing rambunctious, fiery music detonating out of
the drawing room. I slipped in and discovered my grandmother,
whose extremely benign disposition was a matter of fact, thrashing
and lashing the keys. Soon enough she noticed me standing next to
her, lifted her fingers away from the piano, turned and smiled, as if
she'd been caught.

'I didn't know you could play the piano that well, Granny.'

'Oh, I'm not very good, bach,' she said. 'I can't get my silly fingers to move any more!' Her sing-song voice was full of self-remonstration. I remember asking her what she was playing and she said it was the 'Moonlight' Sonata by Beethoven. She played a bit more, her hands ripping through angry upward scales. Away from the piano that side of her was invisible.

The singer in the family was my father. As head chorister at St George's in Windsor, he wasn't allowed to leave – so the story goes – until his voice broke belatedly at fourteen. Once he'd dispensed with his Welshness, the umbilical which alone seemed to connect him to his mother was music. She would accompany; he would sing a repertoire that included Gilbert and Sullivan and other flavoursome tunes of the era. The welcome guests would be ranged about the room, perched on the arms of chairs, a sofa, on stools and dining chairs carried in for the occasion. They would listen politely, some beaming, some tapping and all, on cue, clapping. There was also a local soprano my grandmother had befriended who would stand by the Bechstein and shatter the peace with mighty warbling from lively arias I did not then recognise. We didn't like warbling in our family.

There was a moment, always hideous, when the grandsons were prodded to the fore to show what they could do. We'd hammer out tunes learned back at home in England, loamy celebrations of Englishness like 'Glorious Devon' and 'The Floral Dance'. Although not yet old enough to board at Harrow-on-the-Hill, we'd obediently parade our familiarity with the school's rumpty-tumpty Victorian songbook. Dorothy would sight-read while her son would lead us in bovine choral unison. It was only out of respect for our grandparents, I'm guessing, that the guests would tolerate this anglophone lowering of the tone.

But the real nadir would involve me on my own. As neither of my brothers could sing much, the solo duties landed in my lap. Before my voice went south, this meant delivering weedy renditions from the treble's classic repertoire – 'O For the Wings of a Dove', Mozart's 'Ave Verum'. Many of them must have heard my father singing the same tunes much, much better than me. Thus is talent thinned out across generations.

Once, when I stayed in Wales on my own for several days, I remember refusing to sing for my grandparents. This would have been a counter-intuitive bid for attention. My grandmother reacted with a rare display of coldness. If I would not sing for her, she would not speak to me. And she didn't. I was being punished for my unWelshness.

'Helo, Jasper, sut wyt ti?' It's a simple question.

'Er …' Requiring a simple answer. 'Bit nervous actually.' A simple answer in Welsh. 'Nerfus,' I add.

'Paid a becso.' Easy for him to say. I'll worry if I want to.

Halfway along Gray's Inn Road, between Chancery Lane and St Pancras in the very heart of London, a Welsh flag hangs limply from a pole. The red dragon – *y ddraig goch* – on its white and green background welcomes visitors to the London Welsh Centre, or Canolfan Cymry Llundain. Upstairs in the bar James, the teacher of Welsh Level 1, Module 1, sits at a table. It's a long, lived-in room flanked on the street side by mock-Tudor windows. Lest we forget, the Tudors were Welsh. I've always been faintly grateful that Henry VII's great-uncle was Jasper Tudor, though one suspects it was his French mother, the widow of Henry V who married Owen Tudor, who chose his name.

Having learned a lot of words, the time has come to stop being afraid to use them. There is only one option. To pay someone to hold a weekly conversation with me in Welsh at an hourly rate. I know only one Welsh teacher and that is James. He nominates a time and a place – six o'clock on Tuesday evenings at the London Welsh Centre in the hour before he goes into choir practice.

No sooner have we settled, each with a pint of beer (*cwrw*), than I am required to explain what I have done this week. Into the past tense I have been summoned. I consider my options and plump for the obvious.

'Dw i wedi gweithio.' I have worked/been working (Welsh seems to make no distinction).

And what do I do for work?

'Ysgrifennwr dw i.' I have been using this formulation for a while now. I want to say I am a journalist but I've not got round to learning the word, so I stick with 'writer'. It's definitely one of the reasons they didn't like me in Welsh Level 1, Module 1. 'I am a writer' oozes self-importance.

And why, he asks, do I want to learn Welsh? The important question. I mention Welsh roots – *wreiddiau* – and Welsh family – *teulu*. I attempt explanations. I learn the word for 'uncle' (*ewythr*), 'monk' (*mynach*) and 'monastery' (*mynachdy*). Every time something comes up, down it goes in the red book. It's one of the slowest hours of my life, punctuated by long silences from me and puzzled looks from James. My problem is not so much in formulating sentences. This I can manage if I apply myself to a meticulous step-by-step process. If I want to construct a sentence, I'm going to need this noun, that verb, an adjective or two and maybe a preposition or conjunction, depending on the level of complexity I'm after. It feels like a visit to the word larder, but one subject to strict rationing: the shelves are post-apocalyptically bare. Therefore the range and subtlety of my conversation is limited. Forget about subsidiary clauses and pleasing parenthetical asides. Abandon complexity and sophistication, all ye who enter into Welsh conversation here. Abandon nuance and irony. Abandon, in effect, adulthood. If my on-board translator is correct, James teaches children with learning difficulties. And now, for one hour only, a middle-aged man answering to the same description. I find I have the speech skills of a six-year-old introvert.

But my speech skills are at PhD level compared to my listening skills. James will ask a simple boilerplate question. I will reply in the following manner: 'Dw i ddim yn deall' (I do not understand). He will repeat the question. I will give him a vacant look. He will repeat the question very slowly. I will ask for a translation of at least one of the words. It will turn out to be a word I already know but do not recognise in an oral context. I will slap my forehead in self-reproach. Eventually, after this long rite has been completed, I will go to my word larder and, from the paucity of provisions available, start piecing together an answer.

We move in super-slo-mo. Paint has dried in less time than it takes me to decipher a perfectly ordinary sentence. By the end of the first hour I have made no perceptible improvement in the Welsh language. It is plain to me that my depleting brain is not set up for this sort of mental agility any more. It can no longer touch its toes. It cannot learn new tricks.

But I also think I'm hard of hearing. Not clinically – it's not as if I have a physiological defect, more that stuff doesn't go in because I simply won't let it. I hear, but I don't want to listen. In English I've been noticing I interrupt a lot (in fact my daughters tell me). Or someone is about to talk and I'll be overcome by the need to talk over them. There is no alternative conclusion: I like the sound of my own voice. I am constitutionally deficient when I am required to take in the point of view of others. It must explain why with other languages I have always got so far and no further. I have imposed my own ceiling by refusing to learn to listen more than is strictly necessary. And now when I really need the skill, it is in a state of semi-development. It is extremely tempting to blame England and Englishness, specifically that part which my backgrounds represents: public school, privilege, lack of struggle. It could be argued that the English majority cannot or will not learn languages because, at a pre-conscious level imposed by history and embedded in the culture, they lack empathy. To learn to speak Welsh with any level of competence, I am going to have to do nothing less than take up arms against my inner Englishman. Let battle commence. Or recommence same time, same place next week.

I hand James thirty quid and slip out of the London Welsh Centre. Above me on the doorstep the dragon moves in the breeze.

Côr Meibion Pendyrus is one of the great choirs in Wales. It was founded in 1924 by two of Tylorstown's out-of-work miners. These were grim years in the industry, when the workers were either striking for better wages and conditions ('Not a penny off the pay, not a second on the day') or the owners were locking them out.

Welsh choralism had already been flourishing for more than fifty years, and choirs had sprung up all over South Wales and beyond, fired by the rise of Nonconformity and the temperance movement. But singing came relatively late to the Rhondda Fach. The smaller of the two Rhondda valleys had its first mineshafts sunk in 1872. Before that, the valley was home only to hill farmers and sheep. Like many other mine owners, Alfred Tylor gave his own name to the community which sprouted around the pits. He may also by extension have given it to the choir but for an accident on the night the inaugural members first convened. A fire destroyed the power station in the valley. As the men gathered outside to watch the flames, they noticed, written on a railway signal box and presumably illuminated by the fire, the word *Pendyris*, itself named after a local farm. Having much more of a Welsh ring they took it, with a minor spelling change, for the name of the nascent choir. It has since travelled around the world, from the far side of Canada to Australia, most recently the Baltic. A street in Pennsylvania – one of the American states which received the Welsh Diaspora – took the name of Pendyrus in honour of a visit in 1989.

The choir soon accrued 150 members, most of them miners, most of them young from the evidence of a 1928 photograph of row upon row of callow youths with bony cheeks and full dark moustaches. In only its fourth year the choir was invited to perform in Cardiff Castle, the splendour of which will have intimidated some choristers and enraged others: the Bute family's immense wealth derived from the coalfield. In 1930 Pendyrus's founding conductor, Arthur Duggan, briefly stepped aside so they could have the privilege of singing for Sir Henry Wood, founder of the Proms. They won their first National Eisteddfod in 1935 in the presence of Lloyd George, and two years later performed with the great Russian bass Chaliapin. These triumphs all came in a decade which found more than half of the choir jobless. Duggan continued until 1960 when, suffering from ill health, he reluctantly accepted a recommendation to retire. By that time, one or two members of the current choir had already joined.

One night after practice I sit in a club just down the valley in Wattstown, another mining village named after a Victorian owner. There are a dozen men round the table, including Jakey, a short man in his late sixties with a knowing glint in his eye and miraculously dark hair. I'm guessing he used to play scrum half: he has some of that birdlike awareness, and a prodigious bow in his legs. Jakey has been a second tenor with Pendyrus for forty-nine years. For most of that time the choir was under the baton of another hugely significant figure in Welsh choral music: Glynne Jones. 'There must have been twenty boys around about twenty years of age who joined at the same time,' Jakey tells me. 'At the time we had a new conductor who was a breath of fresh air. He was lucky because he had all these young voices.'

Jones was by all accounts a figure of terrific flamboyance – and the choristers around the table nursing their pints leave little room for doubt about what they mean by flamboyance. He'd wear a cape and sip pink gin. Photographs show a man with a long face, small eyes and a goatee beard. In order to tell his choristers apart, Jones allocated nicknames, many of them acquired thanks to their professions: Puffing Billy worked on the railways, Granada was a television engineer, Dai Sausage had once been the accountant to a butcher. Other handles were often a product of convoluted word association – Tokyo was inscrutable; Sickies did not take well to his first curry; Starsky and Hutch were a pair of new young blades. Keith, a voluble and bearded upholsterer, tells me he was known as Buttons. Barry, an extremely vigorous first tenor who briefly dabbled in his youth in a musical instrument, has for decades been called French Horn.

Glynne Jones's individualism extended to repertoire. Alongside the traditional array of Welsh compositions and nineteenth-century oratorios and masses, he introduced choir and audiences to the music of the sixteenth century. Unlike other famous Welsh choirs – Treorchy in the Rhondda Fawr and Morriston in Swansea – performing challenging new Welsh work has been Pendyrus's life-blood and mainstay. 'I don't think I'd listen to them myself,' says Jakey, pulling a face, 'but in the saloon bar you really felt you'd done something. Discordant is not the word.'

Their fame rose and rose. When the Aberfan disaster claimed the lives of 118 children and 26 adults in 1966, it was Pendyrus who were invited up to London to appear in ITV's special commemorative programme. The choir continued to compete in the National Eisteddfod but there came a time when Jones refused to submit to adjudication he regarded as wrong-headed. In 1968 they performed a dissonant piece of modern music and the judges marked them down. 'Glynne in his mind thought we were the best choir,' says Jakey. 'He said, "It's not you guys, it's me. They didn't adjudicate Pendyrus; they adjudicated Glynne Jones."' Choral competition is in the marrow of Welsh culture, but while Pendyrus Male Choir has sung all over the world, been broadcast countless times on Welsh television and radio and performed with sundry great orchestras, it has never competed since.

What does it take to be a Welsh male chorister? 'You need a very understanding wife,' suggests one of them, to general nodding. Several members of the choir I meet are widowers, including Mal and Alan, the second tenors who nursed me through my first rehearsal. Roy, a wiry second tenor who joined even later than me, was persuaded to sign up after losing his wife. 'I was spending all my time staring at the big black box in the corner,' he says. Pendyrus has given him a new lease of life. There are two rehearsals a week, on Mondays and Wednesdays, and up to twenty-five concerts a year. And then there are marriages and funerals to sing at, usually the latter. Illness and infirmity are a constant shadow. At the end of at least half the rehearsals I attend the chairman asks how many choristers are available on a weekday morning a few days hence to sing a chorister's wife or other relative to their rest. They will all presumably sing at one another's funerals.

Many of the choristers have been with Pendyrus for many years. Mal joined twenty-one years ago. It sounds like a long time. 'I'm just starting to speak up now,' he says with a straight face. He regrets not having joined much earlier. 'The choir was something that you wanted to do when you retired. But we're all of the same mind. When we joined the choir we all wished we'd joined twenty years previous to that.'

Glynne Jones conducted Pendryrus for the last time in December 2000 and died on Christmas Eve. A distinguished new conductor was appointed but the consensus around the table is that it was not a happy union. Stewart Roberts, a young music teacher in the Rhondda and a professional concert pianist, was invited to take over in 2009 and with him have come young singers scoured from local schools, who in turn have even brought their fathers along. The older members acknowledge that without that renewal this magnificent Welsh tradition will follow them all to the grave. The men around the table seem unanimous that after long years of stagnation Pendryrus sounds better than it ever has.

Stewart has decided to test that claim. For the first time in more than forty years, he is entering them in a competition. The target is the prestigious local eisteddfod in Cardigan, where the earliest recorded eisteddfod – literally a sitting – took place in Cardigan in 1176 at the invitation of Lord Rhys. What's more, after discussion of the pros and cons, Graham and the committee have invited me to compete with them. Pendryrus are offering total Welsh immersion: I am to become a member of one of the oldest choirs in Wales.

I've been given dispensation not to attend every rehearsal, but nor will they contemplate carrying a passenger. There seems little for it but to spend a lot of time on the M4. The drive to and from choir practice is 320 miles. I usually leave at half three in the afternoon, stop off at Mal's for a bite in Penrhiwceibr, a pit village in the Cynon Valley where several of the choir live, take the spectacular route over the ridge and down into the Rhondda Fach, attend two hours' intense practice in the sports centre in Tylorstown, get back in the car, drive slowly home and flop into bed back in London at, if I'm lucky, half past midnight. It's a long way to go for a sing-song.

Practices have a regular shape. We sing something to warm up, then Stewart will go through a musical line with each section. As a result there's not a lot of singing for the second tenors, who are, it seems, the most musically able section in the choir. The top tenors, required to send largely ageing voices into the rooftops, are the ones most regularly subjected to forensic examination of technique. 'Top tenors, you've had an easy night,' Stewart will say. 'Now stand up and sing like Caruso.' The basses do a lot of heavy lifting. 'The further away I am from them,' suggests Stewart, 'the better they sound.' Once the pieces have been put together we'll sing in unison and, prompted by a motion from Stewart's hands, stand and deliver a rendition.

I shift around the second tenors depending on where a seat is available. Colin is the spryest of them, a barely suppressed sixteen-year-old in a sixty-year-old's body. Dai gives avuncular advice on breathing technique. I often find myself next to a serious man known as the Prof, whom I daren't call anything but Gareth. It turns out he really is a professor of history at the University of West Glamorgan and has written the definitive history of Welsh choralism. The first time I try to engage him in conversation I am promptly given to understand that it's not done to talk on these occasions. The Prof does a lot of shushing.

His more official duty is advice on Welsh pronunciation. Stewart is a Welsh learner and several of the choristers have taken up Welsh after retiring, but being of the generation before the language revival when Welsh was barely present in the Valleys, most of the choristers learn Welsh lyrics by rote. Welsh pronunciation is important. 'Heriwn, Wynebwn y Wawr' will be judged not only on musicality. It's Buttons who articulates a pervasive anxiety. 'We've got to

learn the piece fluently. Now I'm not a Welsh speaker and I find it
a bit hard – I'll put my cards on the table, you know. If you don't
get the pronunciation right, you're not going to win.' And Pendyrus
has not re-entered competition after four decades in order to make
up the numbers.

One evening at the London Welsh Centre I buy a ticket to a
concert given by Dafydd Iwan. Being a provisional Welshman, I
can't say I've ever heard of him, but am assured by a Welsh-speaking friend that he's the musical heartbeat of Cymry Cymraeg, the
people of Welsh Wales. The long room where James and I have
weekly conversations is now heaving, the bar shifting barrels of
cwrw da (good beer). A stocky man in his sixties with a jocular face
and an acoustic guitar takes to the makeshift stage at one end and,
in a rough-hewn voice, works his way through a folkish songbook
that is entirely familiar to everyone else in the room. They sing
along, a wistful, middle-distant look in expat eyes. There are hoots
of laughter as he performs 'Carlo', a song about a young Englishman becoming Prince of Wales. I get that lonely feeling again – the
barred door, the inaccessible sanctum.

My Welsh isn't good enough to understand his amplified speech
between songs. On one occasion breaking into English, he tells a
lovely joke about mutations. They were invented, he suggests, to
'keep the numbers down. We don't want every Tom, Dick and
Harry speaking Welsh, so we make it difficult.' Everyone laughs,
although not as hollowly as me. In the interval, in faltering Welsh,
I go and introduce myself to the evidently great man. I buy a CD,
which he signs. I also ask if we can meet. He hands me his bilingual
card. On it are written the words 'President, Plaid Cymru'. He's an
even bigger cheese than I thought.

A month or so later, one evening in late winter, I drive up

winding Gwynedd lanes into the countryside and soon I am installed in the spacious kitchen of Dafydd Iwan. His real surname is Jones of course. He comes from a formidable clan brought up in Brynaman in Carmarthenshire by fiercely nationalist parents who insisted their sons sit the Eleven Plus exam in Welsh. 'A non-Welsh speaker was something of an oddity,' he tells me. 'I have vivid memories of coming across this other language – I was probably six or seven – running to school late one morning when the mother of one of my friends who was non-Welsh-speaking said, "You're late, you're late!" And I didn't understand what it meant.' His older brother, the actor Huw Ceredig, was a mainstay for years of the BBC's longest-running soap, *Pobol y Cwm*. His younger brother, the politician Alun Ffred Jones, is Minister for Culture in the Welsh government. Dafydd Iwan has hovered somewhere between music and politics for more than forty years.

He first attracted attention across the border on 1 January 1969 in Betws-y-Coed. He was chairman of Cymdeithas yr Iaith Gymraeg at the time – the Welsh Language Society – which had convened a large crowd to make a symbolic protest against the English-only road signs by painting over them. The movement chose the heart of Snowdonia because it was close to Tŷ Mawr, the home of Bishop William Morgan. It was Bishop Morgan who was granted permission by Elizabeth I to translate the Bible into Welsh. The Welsh Bible, used for centuries as a manual for teaching literacy, is credited with saving Welsh as a written language. Now it needed saving as a spoken language. The campaign to restore Welsh to its place in Welsh national life got eye-catchingly underway when Dafydd Iwan painted out the word *police* on the door of the local constabulary, was arrested, duly fined and eventually imprisoned for non-payment. Others were arrested too, but the campaign's focus was tightly on this pugnacious, guitar-strumming nationalist.

'We were talking pretty historic stuff,' he tells me. 'We knew we were part of a big change in the history of Wales and we were quite confident we were right.' If they needed proof of that, it came in the tacit collusion of the police throughout their non-violent campaign. The Archbishop of Wales visited him in Cardiff prison. 'When you're in there for a cause the other prisoners think you're barmy. "Could you have paid the fine?" "Yes." "You must be bloody mad."'

So the campaign to save Welsh must have appeared to many at the time. I remember my grandmother voicing her disapproval of Plaid Cymru, the Party of Wales, which won Carmarthen as its first ever constituency. But the concessions to the language and by extension to the individualism of Welsh identity were gradually made: bilingual road signs, a Welsh-language radio station, a Welsh-language television channel, devolution, a Welsh Assembly, Plaid Cymru in coalition government and now an independent commissioner for the Welsh language. And throughout this long struggle, Dafydd Iwan's songs have been the soundtrack. In particular 'Yma o Hyd' – which translates as 'still here' – is a paean to the sheer bloody-minded durability of Welsh Wales, its people, customs, language. 'I don't look at myself as a musician,' he says. 'My musicianship is always a bit of a joke, but what I really am is a songwriter. My songs are my main medium of communication. I can tone down the politics to fit the occasion, but wherever I go in the end I hope I communicate a similar kind of message.'

The new inclusive message is that Wales is for all who sail in her. The president of Plaid Cymru isn't interested in hating the English back. 'There is always that danger that pro-Welshness becomes anti-Englishness, and you've got to steer clear of that or it becomes blatant racism.' But he is by implication grateful to English hauteur for helping to keep the language alive. 'The survival of the Welsh language is a miracle,' he argues, 'in that it has survived so very close to the centre of the British Empire, who imposed English on so many countries to the detriment of the native language. And yet this language has survived probably to some extent because of this imperious official attitude. The Welsh language was a symbol of our refusal to give in to the landlord and the Church and the law and all these foreign-based authorities.'

I ask him what he makes of my quest to slip the bonds of my inheritance and be re-embraced by the land of my fathers. Being a politician, he doesn't want to say the wrong thing. He's met others who've looked for their Welshness, he says. 'But many of them have not included the language. "I don't have to learn the language, do I?" "No, you can be Welsh without the language." But making the language pretty central is the one sure way of opening that door to a different world and seeing the Welsh from the inside. If you want to simplify it, that quest is attainable if you attain the Welsh language.' I'm trying, I tell the moral and musical guardian of Welsh. I'm really trying.

Over the weeks the word larder is becoming better stocked, and the sentences come out more quickly and have a richer texture. Small red book in my lap, I learn words on Tube journeys: Welsh on the left, English on the right obscured by a ticket to the Millennium Stadium, then the ticket switched as I mouth the Welsh. Funny looks occasionally stray in my direction. Or I'll catch a neighbour peering over my shoulder. Who knows what they think? Who cares? At night to get to sleep I set myself the task of naming every Welsh word I can think of beginning with a particular letter. My favourite is *ll*. Or words beginning with *cyf-*, or ending with *-aeth*. Some words which stubbornly refuse to stick in my head are written out in a new vocab list and subjected to intense and punitive study.

Over the weeks and months I become familiar with the ways in which words shift shape from one part of speech to another, how adjectives and nouns can be recognised by their endings. The musicality of the language begins to assert itself, its elegant folds and rhythmic undulations. It takes a while, but eventually I twig that the only way to achieve any hint of authenticity in Welsh is to speak in a Welsh accent. This may sound logical: the Welsh language after all is where the lilts and cadences of the accent come from. But it's only when you think obsessively about it that these things become truly apparent. The element of the accent which is traditionally described as sing-song comes from a heavy commitment to the penultimate syllable. As you get into the rhythm of it, Welsh words take on the springiness of a trampoline. The rhythm bounces you into the following word. I would be interested in asserting that it's connected on some inchoate level with the dips and rises of the landscape. But that may be a little far-fetched.

'Ti'n gwella yn sicr,' James says at a certain point, one Tuesday evening in the London Welsh Centre. You're certainly getting better. The weekly gain comes at a cost. Three-quarters of an hour into our regular weekly sessions, I can feel a massive blood-sugar low coming on, my brain seizing up, my Welsh articulacy losing its motor function. The bar fills with choristers meeting for a drink before practice. Our table is surrounded, often by Welsh speakers near to whom I sense my tongue turning to stone. The minute hand tumbles ever so slowly south towards half past when James has to go and sing, and I can at last recover from the shattering mental effort required to accelerate towards competence in conversational Welsh.

It takes an awfully long time to walk a male choir of eighty singers into position. I am second on, only a lofty white-bearded second tenor called Howard ahead of me as we process in strict formation out onto the stage of a concert hall in Cardigan. I reach my place on a raised platform in the corner and adopt the Welsh chorister's traditional pose, arms hanging by the side, eyes impassive, head dignified. There is strictly no talking or even whispering. I've seen Pendyrus perform and noted the Zen-like focus.

I'm in the navy-blue jacket. The badge of Pendyrus Male Choir rests on the breast pocket: a golden harp with a sheet of music, a baton and a sprig of corn. I pull it on for the first time in the changing room, also looping the tie round my neck, and feel as never before like the real Welsh thing.

It's strange to see the choir out of their natural habitat, the deep cleft of the Rhondda Fach. On a beautiful late afternoon in Cardigan, a summer breeze whispers in from the bay. The old town is quiet but for a few revellers down on the quayside of the Teifi. At least some things remain the same. The eisteddfod is being held in the town's sports centre. There's a great deal of milling about to do, the day-long programme now running late in the early evening. Pendyrus convenes on its own patch of sports field for a pep talk from Stewart. It's all about lifting our confidence, patting us on the back for collective hard work, and a final word or two on the songs, not only 'Heriwn, Wynebwn y Wawr' but also 'You Make Me Feel So Young', the old 1940s swing hit recorded by, among others, Ella Fitzgerald and Frank Sinatra.

'Remember, gentlemen,' he says, 'as you sing "You Make Me Feel So Young" I want to hear that twinkle. I recommend you think back to a special time with a very special lady.' Manly memories stir in eighty romantic hearts, not all of them ticking so steadily nowadays. 'Some of you,' he adds, 'may have to think back quite a long way.' A bark of laughter fills the open air. By now I really do have the second tenor part locked down. Stewart has kindly recorded

'Heriwn, Wynebwn y Wawr' on tape for me and I have listened without cease on the M4. I have suspended my night-time listing of vocabulary to recite the words. I'm rather fond of them, or those I can understand: they portray a dystopian vision of a grim present in which flames cool in the hearth, mighty oaks wither, darkness descends and the weary body grows ever more frail. It sounds exactly like a depiction of old age, a dire forewarning of death. But one thing can make spirits rise, hearts lift, and allow us to face the future: the power of song. The sentiments expressed are Welsh to the very marrow.

Pendyrus last performed here in 1959. The bright evening light begins to dim. I slip inside the tented awning abutting the sports hall and find a seat next to Stewart.

'Popeth yn iawn, Stewart?' The proceedings from the hall are being piped through a loudspeaker – song after song, between them booming announcements in Welsh from a male master of ceremonies. We talk quietly.

'I'm nervous for the choir really,' he says. 'They've worked so hard and I just hope they give a good account of themselves.' Is he not at all anxious? He looks at me. 'I'll be like that,' he says, holding out a rigid left hand. 'Trouble is I conduct with that.' His right hand is all a-quiver. I am struck anew by the unforced ease of his charisma. After years of choral atrophy, the many men under his baton have been renewed by Stewart.

The male choir category has attracted six choirs from across South Wales. The category is for twenty-five members or more. Ours vastly outnumbers most of them as we are bossed into entrance formation in a corridor area feeding the stage. The choir goes quiet. I catch Mal's eye.

'Nervous, bychan?'

'Tipyn bach,' I say. A little bit. 'You?'

'Nooo,' he says with an admonishing look. 'I'm looking forward to it, I am.' He rubs his hands as the sound of applause ripples in from the sports hall and a long crocodile of choristers in burgundy jackets files past us. The men of Pendyrus put their hands together to clap them off. Fittingly for a sports hall, this is a sporting contest. Eventually Howard gets the nod. I follow his lumbering frame out onto the stage.

Four minutes later Stewart raises his baton, the choir's pianist Gavin swings into the intro, the tenors begin in unison. 'You make me feel so yooooung,' we croon, all snappy and syncopated. 'You make me feel like *spring* has *sprung*.' It's incredible how frothy and frolicsome a choir of eighty well-drilled Welshmen can sound. 'We're just like a couple of tots / Running around the meadow …' The image of the men of Pendyrus skipping brightly through the fields of Ceredigion is not allowed to linger as we bring it right down for the key line: 'And even when I'm old and greeeey / I'm going to feel the way I dooo tooodaaay / 'Cause yoooou make me feeeel sooo yoooung.' Sung entirely without irony. But with considerable twinkle. As Stewart pushes us through the gears, the harmonies get so tricksy that in the surge towards the round-off we're practically clambering on top of one another. 'So yooooooouung!' The final chord is a tight weld of diminished fourths and augmented minor sevenths (or some such).

The audience claps cheerfully. The eighty of us make a point of not smiling. Or I do anyway. As Stewart takes a bow, down in the audience I notice three people making notes. Judges. They are presumably writing things like *ardderchog* and *gwych*, *rhyfeddol* and *siwper* ('excellent' and 'great', 'wonderful' and 'super'). Just you wait, ladies and gentlemen, for the forthcoming explosion of choral gigapower.

Gavin crashes in on the piano and Stewart counts us down to our entry and … Whoosh! 'Miloedd ar filoedd sy'n amau bob dydd

…!!' (Thousands upon thousands who doubt every day …!!) We give it the hairdryer treatment. The sonic force would knock an unsuspecting Englishman off his feet. Then a diminuendo monstroso con legato *mawr iawn*. We can swivel the volume knob at the swish of a stick. I watch Stewart carefully – we all do – as he mouths the words and allows the music to speak through his body. We articulate punctiliously. Such a large choral organism, such a subtle, particular sound. The lyrics paint their dire picture of a palsied present, the heartbeat of the song driven almost to a standstill before the green shoots of a musical revival very quietly suggest themselves: 'Oerni'r canrifoedd fu'n gwasgu yn drwm …' Something about a deep freeze and sleeping heavily for centuries. The pianissimo phrase hints at withheld excitement, at stirrings of passion. Stewart's motions, tightly reined, start to expand. 'Heriwn, wynebwn y wawr,' boom the basses on their own, studiously observing that comma. (Let us challenge, let us face the dawn.) The melody surges towards a climax: 'Gloyw fo'n llygaid a'n gobaith yn fflam.' (Shining eyes, blazing hope!) My voice felt as if it had been mugged the first time I tried this. Up another note for a bar. Now it soars to the heights as if yomping up the flank of a Welsh mountain. And another. Feel that sustain! Understanding of Welsh is probably not necessary for this most pictorial of songs. Down comes the volume again for the urgent, hurried conclusion: 'Mae'r dyfodol yn dechrau.' (The future is beginning.) 'Yn dechrau.' (Is beginning.) 'Yn deeechraaauuu' – socking breath – 'yn aaaawwwrrr!' (Noooooooow!) The roll on that climactic *r* is like a carpet unfurled at pace.

Silence. To much applause, Stewart and Gavin bow. As the choir begins the slow business of removing itself from the stage, I resume my Zen-like focus, in correct choral style. Inside I am exultant, having just participated in an undeniably Welsh ritual.

Back outside, it's a long wait for the result. Two more choirs must sing, including one that others seem worried about called Côr Meibion Taf. They're a small outfit from Cardiff with perhaps thirty members, but they're also singing our song. We wince as we listen through the loudspeaker to what sounds like a crude tele-graphing of the 'Heriwn''s emotionalism. It's the *Pobol y Cwm* version, a soapy oversell. The men of Pendyrus mutter a version of the same thing to one another: we can definitely take this lot. If we don't there'll be an outcry. When Côr Meibion Taf return, being sporting, we politely clap them back in.

Some choristers form an advance party and head to the rugby club over the road. The tension eases as the judges' long delibera-tion extends deep into the evening. It is dark now, though still warm. The Pendyrus committee, including Graham, are conferring in a corner. I am talking to some other second tenors when a rumour ripples out of the awning.

'It's Pendyrus.'

'Pendyrus what?'

'I think we've won. That's what they're saying.'

'We've won?' Owing to the announcement being in Welsh, there is some confusion.

'I don't know but that's what I 'eard.'

I slip into the tent and find Graham with some of the committee.

'Has Pendyrus won?'

'First place,' says Graham, swelling with pride, 'chief male-voice choir competition.'

So it turns out. Côr Meibion Pendyrus has not only won on its first return to competition since 1968, but it will also be taking the overall Choir of Choirs award back to the Rhondda Fach as the best choir in any category. And Stewart Roberts has won the award for best conductor. This is like one of those clean sweeps at the Oscars.

Gratifyingly, we have beaten Côr Meibion Taf and their embarrass-ing rendition of 'Heriwn, Wynebwn y Wawr' into third place. Over the road the rugby club bursts with drinking, singing, beaming tenors. The news has spread. Choral uproar is in full swing. Jakey, nearly half a century with Pendyrus despite his freakishly brown hair, is purring with satisfaction. Colin, whose regular default setting is irrepressible, is a human beacon. Roy, who joined Pen-dyrus even later than me, is beaming. Even the Prof is chirpy. They all greet me as a long-lost friend and are eager to shake my hand.

'How about that then, Jasper?' 'How does it feel to win now, eh?' 'Now you didn't expect that when you joined the choir, did you, bychan?' The implication from all of them is that the big smoke may be rich in many things but it cannot readily supply this sort of sweet experience. Mal informs me that I will remember this moment for the rest of my life. He's right. I will, though not quite for the reason he imagines. It's because, as the night progresses and the beer flows and the songs are dreamily sung, every one of these men from the Valleys thanks me for sharing the taste of triumph and the fruits of hard labour, for becoming one of them. In my case the song turns out to be word perfect. *Mae'r dyfodol yn dechrau.* The future is beginning.

5

Siarad = Speak

' … from henceforth no Person or Persons that use the *Welsh* Speech or Language, shall have or enjoy any manner Office or Fees within this Realm of *England, Wales*, or other the King's Dominion, upon Pain of forfeiting the same Offices or Fees, unless he or they use and exercise the *English* Speech or Language.'

Act of Union (1535)

I'VE BEEN TRYING TO IDENTIFY the most mystical mountain in Wales. Most mystical to me, that is, based on my state of mind at the time of ascent. Of course the English half of me doesn't have much truck with feelings of spiritual uplift. But then we're not listening to him. There's a shortlist of six.

1. Pen y Fan. A Brecon Beacon I first climbed as a schoolboy doing CCF. I didn't like it at all then. I like it a lot now. One afternoon in June I use the mountain to test my Welshness by climbing it rather than sitting in a pub in Brecon to watch a vital England group game in the football World Cup: Wales 1, England 0.
2. Arenig Fawr, at the southern end of Snowdonia. I sprint up one hot cloudless April afternoon. 'Of all the hills which I saw in Wales,' recalled Borrow, 'none made a greater impression

upon me.' It's one of the many peaks in Wales into the side of
which a military plane has crashed in thick cloud. Half of
Wales is visible from the blustery summit.

3. Cadair Idris, up which I once memorably led my spry young
   daughters through spring showers. Its terrors provoked a
   gripping, ghoulish diary entry from the Revd Francis Kilvert,
   the story incorporating a lone English climber falling 440 yards
   to his death and the flesh-stripped corpse being discovered six
   weeks later.

4. Waun Fach, the highest point in the Black Mountains and
   smothered in snow when I glide to the top one romantic sunlit
   day in the very epicentre of February. Curious because from
   the valley it is no more than a rumour; it reveals its pimpled
   summit only from atop a neighbouring mountain.

5. Mynydd Mallaen in the Cambrian Mountains makes it onto
   the list despite – no, actually because of – its utter lack of
   distinguishing features apart from two very ancient standing
   stones, useful for leaning against when guzzling a hard-earned
   picnic. Boggy.

6. Pumlumon, from whose flanks the Severn and the Wye,
   among other rivers, famously spring. 'There is nothing either
   picturesque or fantastic in the form of this mountain,' thought
   the Revd Warner; 'but, rising with dignity above the
   neighbouring elevations, it conveys the idea of massy solidity,
   and substantial majesty.' Not meeting another soul when I
   wander up it, I feel as if I have the desert expanse of Mid
   Wales to myself. I locate the place where the Wye trickles out
   of the mountain and, slightly self-consciously, hunker down on
   all fours to drink from the source of, for me, the Welshest river.

But while all these mountains are mystical to me for personal reasons, I cannot in the end ignore the claims of a mountain which is dwarfed by most of the above. The most mystical place in Wales is in the far north, out on the limb of the Llŷn peninsula, up a mountain called Yr Eifl. I set off alone on a fresh May morning. Clouds scud in off the Irish Sea, one of them gluing fast to the mountain's official peak. But I am heading for the slightly lower peak next door. The going is by no means hard and I summit (to use the mountaineer's verb-noun) after an hour and a half. The view in every direction is breathtaking: Anglesey to the north; Cardigan Bay to the south; Snowdonia rises in the east; while the long arm of the peninsula rolls away to the west, a bumpy carpet of green laid across a wide floor of blue. But the real miracle up here is Tre'r Ceiri – Town of the Forts – a place which hints at habitation reaching back half a millennium before the arrival of the Romans. The drystone circular walls of more than 150 huts dot an oval plateau, some bafflingly intact after 2,500 years. Once upon a time this wind-battered hill fort may have been home to a community of 500. As I do whenever I'm at any of the many miraculous places of Wales, I reflect that if it were in England it would have tourists crawling all over it like head lice. Blessedly, though, as usual it's only me.

One name attaches itself more than others to Tre'r Ceiri. Vortigern, the fifth-century King of Powys in the years after the Romans left, is alleged to have betrayed the Welsh by cutting a deal with the Saxons. 'The stories of Vortigern,' wrote Defoe in another part of Wales, 'are on every old woman's lips.' Legend has it that he retreated into the far north-west, where he gave his Welsh name – Gwrtheyrn – to a place called Nant Gwrtheyrn: Vortigern's Brook.

Nant Gwrtheyrn is not an especially well-known name even in Wales. As far as the Welsh language is concerned, however, it is the crucible. In the end, almost anyone who is serious about learning Welsh as an adult follows the stream to the Nant.

It's James who tells me about it. Our weekly sessions have hauled me along the path towards competence. I'm stuffed to the gills with Welsh words, and able to deploy them for up to an hour at a time without needing to drape myself afterwards on a restorative chaise longue. But perhaps both of us sense that for further development I need to talk Welsh to more than one person, and for longer than an hour a week. Hence the Welsh Language and Heritage Centre in Nant Gwrtheyrn. I go to the website and click on courses. Starting at the bottom and working up, I've got to *Cwrs Canolradd* (Intermediate) before I find anything that sounds remotely at my level. And even that offers guidance on grammar I reckon I've already conquered. The next course up is *Cwrs Uwch* (Higher). Can I really pose as a higher-level student? The potential for altitude sickness seems considerable. I ask James for his thoughts. He sits on the fence, though behind his eyes I can see doubt being silenced with a raised truncheon. I decide to email the Nant. In Welsh.

Are you able to advise me? I would like to go to the Language Centre, but I will not be able to decide between two different courses. I am confident reasonably with the grammar (except the mutations, obviously, like everyone!) but I need lots of to practise with conversation – speaking and hearing. I prefer to challenge myself. What do you think? For example, I have not found difficult to write this letter. I would welcome your judgement. Thank you very much.

Warm wishes,

Jasper Rees

Yes, my Welsh is that good. My written Welsh is. I can write far better than I can speak. A reply returns from someone called Pegi. She advises that my Welsh sounds more than up to *Cwrs Uwch*, on which there is no reason not to enrol. I do as I am told.

'The graph of the number of people speaking Welsh has been steadily decreasing since the middle of the nineteenth century.' I am in the office of the man in whose care the Welsh language ultimately resides. Alun Ffred Jones was appointed Minister for Culture when his predecessor walked into a pub brandishing a lit cigar and his position became untenable. In a way I can't quite put my finger on, it seems a wonderfully Welsh way of losing a job in government. Alun Ffred, as he is widely known, is of course the younger brother of Dafydd Iwan. I've come to ask him how healthy the Welsh language really is. As he's a politician, I'm expecting to be fobbed off with a robust and implausible portrait of ruddy cheeks and rosy glow. But no, at the very top of the Welsh Ministry of Culture, optimism is at best cautious and watchfully hedged about with ifs and buts.

A close reading of John Davies's epic *A History of Wales* tells me what I need to know about the forces which pushed Welsh to the edge of potential extinction. Henry VIII's Act of Union in 1536 sought 'utterly to extirpate all and singular the sinister usages and customs' practised outside England. His daughter threw the language a lifeline with the Welsh Bible, whereafter a kind of stasis endured until the Industrial Revolution duly brought an influx of English-speaking workers to Wales, while the Education Act in 1870 made English the universal language of elementary schooling. The working class grew correspondingly more alive to the economic gains available to those who could speak English. Nonconformity, meanwhile, preferred saving souls to saving the language and began founding English-language chapels. The Labour movement made it a priority to fight for political justice rather than go out to bat for a language identified with the Liberals and the rural vote. And then came the wireless, which piped clipped BBC English into Welsh homes. By the 1960s, with television pinning couch potatoes to sofas up and down Wales, the death of the Welsh language could have been confidently predicted.

Thanks to efforts very much identified with the minister's older brother, a visit to the docks in Cardiff suggests that the forces of history have been defied. The resplendent development is home to the Welsh Millennium Centre and the Senedd, the Welsh Assembly Government. The architectural emblems of contemporary Welsh confidence look like odd spaceships piloted in from distant galaxies. Hollywood imaginations have been at work to give Wales the symbols it needs. The flourishing language is a more earthbound component of the drive towards self-determination.

Alun Ffred Jones is taller and straighter than his brother, and drier, as he starts outlining the parameters of the minister's task with regard to the language – principally, handing over annual subsidies to the Welsh Language Board, which since 1993 has had responsibility for promoting and developing the language through schemes adopted by public bodies, local authorities and the more bilingually inclined private companies. We talk about laws and policies, facts and figures. It's not quite what I came for. I want to know what the Welsh Assembly Government thinks about the language's survival. Is it still on life support? Has it left intensive care? Can it discharge itself from the sick bay altogether? Alun Ffred is like one of those doctors who don't want to be sued for issuing too cheering a diagnosis.

'In the 1960s there was quite a lot of hostility among political parties and perhaps even many people,' says the guardian of the

Welsh language cautiously. 'It's not disappeared, but there is a greater consensus now across the political parties that the Welsh language is a good thing, a bit like biodiversity is a good thing. Officially you won't find any party saying that we're wasting our money on promoting the Welsh language.' Or not in Wales, I forget to add. England is another matter.

The health of the Welsh language is measured, as scientifically as possible, every ten years with the national census. Statistics are available to determine precisely the percentage of Welsh speakers anywhere in Wales. People in featureless offices such as this can look at spreadsheets which tell them exactly how many have Welsh as a first language in any given village. If certain vested interests hold the paper to the light at a certain angle and squint to impart just the right level of distortion, the Welsh language can be seen, for all the Herculean efforts of those with their shoulders to the wheel, to be gradually atrophying. American television is corroding interest in the good work of S4C. Older English in-migrants (as they are carefully known) are refusing to learn the language. Younger Welsh speakers have crossed into England in search of work. And yet one of the problems is that the census doesn't seem to ask the right questions. It is thought that the 20.2 per cent of Welsh residents who said they spoke the language in 2001 did not include another 10 per cent who, for whatever reason, felt their Welsh was not quite good enough to warrant a tick in the appropriate box. The Act of Union casts a long shadow: for many who speak it, Welsh is still not a language which they associate with form-filling officialdom.

'The last census showed for the first time an increase in the absolute numbers,' says the Minister for Culture. 'The growth is in the younger generation between five and fourteen. It shows that the education strategy may be working to a certain extent: creating children who can speak Welsh. The question then is: Do they *speak*

Welsh?' It's a good question. I think of an evening when Mal and I were about to drive over the pass to choir practice. We saw his grandson mucking about in the street in Penrhiwceibr. The boy is part of a generational shift: parents are thrusting their children into primaries which educate through the medium of Welsh, even in predominantly monoglot towns as far east as Wrexham and Newport. The teachers are deemed to be more eager, the teaching more rigorous. But when Mal spoke to him in Welsh he replied in English. 'He says he doesn't speak Welsh at the weekend.' In short, there's a danger that Welsh, having once been brutally expunged from the classroom by the 1870 Education Act and the infamous Welsh Not, may now be confined to it.

'You are able to teach people to speak Welsh,' says the minister, 'but in their everyday lives those young people will probably not use Welsh except in some planned activity. And that is a problem – that you're losing the natural home for the Welsh language. It's not just the fact that it's disappearing from the rural communities.'

I'm starting to feel a bit gloomy. This isn't why I came. I was hoping to be informed by the Plaid Cymru Assembly Member and Welsh Minister for Culture that the future of Welsh has been secured, that English will not finally wipe it off the face of the earth. After all, a survey by the Welsh Language Board in 2002 established that two-thirds of the Welsh population declared the language's future was 'very important' to them. Please can he now give me that assurance? 'That's an impossible question to answer,' he says. 'Minority languages are disappearing at a rate of knots throughout the world. In fact Welsh is probably among the handful of European minority languages which has a fighting chance. But hand on my heart, I couldn't say, "Yes, it will survive."'

I shake the minister's hand, and tell him I'll be off to Nant Gwrtheyrn to do my bit on the barricades.

A few weeks later, on a Sunday evening, I take the scenic route via Welshpool, Dolgellau and Porthmadog, the slate port where my grandmother spent her first ten or so years. The otherness of North Wales for me as a child was a matter of fact. My father had memories of colourless holidays with Welsh great-aunts in Llandudno, but we never went north. As I push on to the Llŷn in darkness, low-lying fog in high-hedged lanes adds to an ambience of peninsular spookiness. Eventually a single looping lane plummets down the side of a mountain.

It being Sunday night, the office is closed. I find a noticeboard where my room number is listed. I'm in Dwyfor (= two seas). One sea roars faintly somewhere off in the darkness. I walk past a long low row of terraced cottages. The place is utterly deserted. I feel as if I've trespassed onto the set of a horror movie. I find Dwyfor, climb a staircase, locate a nice modern room and, irrationally, lock the door.

When the sun rises on the Welsh Language and Heritage Centre, I step out into crisp morning air and a sort of Welsh plaza, a large walled lawn flanked on two sides by the aforesaid cottages. In all directions but one there is a sense of enclosure, rocky slopes heaving upwards. Nant Gwrtheyrn has been scooped out of the side of a mountain as if by giants. Nowhere in the country are peaks in such towering proximity to the sea. To the south-west there's a long view along coastal cliffs as they turn a stern profile to the Irish Sea. I wander down to a swanky new building, all glass gleam and woody shimmer, and enter a huge floorboarded dining room with only a single round table parked in the middle. A woman with short reddish hair and glasses is already eating breakfast.

'Bore da,' I say. Good morning.

'Er, bore da.' She gives me a look.

'Cwrs Uwch?' Same course?

'Ydy.' Yes, she is.

'O ble dych chi'n dod?' The introductory question: Where does she come from?

'Caerdydd. A chi?'

'Llundain.' She raises an eyebrow. There's a pause.

'Do we have to speak in Welsh all the time?'

'Wrth gwrs!' I say. Course we bloody do.

We introduce ourselves. She's called Roisin. I go over to the counter to get myself some breakfast and give us a breather. The door clinks open and into the vast dining room walks a tall, broad-framed man, with cropped hair, looking friendly but wary.

'Bore da,' he says.

'Bore da,' say Roisin and I. He's called David and comes from Conwy. We sit round the table and edge into a conversation as if walking out onto untested ice. There is some nervous laughter, much helpful nodding and considerable stopping preceded by start-ing. As I participate a thought flits into my head. Are they better than me? That would be most unsatisfactory. Or am I as good as them? I try to ignore it. The supremacist philosophies of Mr Darwin have no place here. Wales, lest I forget, was the wellspring of the equals sign, invented by Robert Recorde of Tenby in 1557. Still, there's early evidence that my word larder is an impressive resource. Roisin gives me a startled look as, buttering my toast, I roll out a percussive polysyllable which I then have to translate. Am I actually better than them at Welsh? The door opens again and another woman enters, short with fine fair hair and rimless glasses.

'Bore da. Helen dw i.' We all exchange the relevant information. Helen is from Nottingham. No sooner does she reel off a sentence or two than my fantasies of spending the week at the top of the class are put back in the bottom drawer. In comes Richard, a man with a cheerful round face from Anglesey, then Gerry, a tall thin

woman with ringleted hair from Bangor. Age wise we're all in the
same neighbourhood, mid thirties to mid forties. Apart from John,
who shuffles in last. Wisps of grey hair frame a somehow mischie-
vous face. John must be in his sixties. This is his third time at the
Nant. He comes from somewhere in the Midlands but his Welsh
sounds rooted in very ancient soil. He perorates for a while until a
tall woman in a drapey woollen shawl enters wearing a look of
benign, earnest concern. She announces herself as Pegi. It's the
tutor who told me I'm good enough to be on *Cwrs Uwch*. She gives
an introductory speech about timetables and suchlike, length of
lessons, the dining schedule, the shape of the five days to come. I
understand about half of it.

So far not a word of anything other than Welsh has been spoken.
Or not a sentence. We have started as we mean to continue. There
will be no incursions from over the linguistic border. England and
English could be as far away as Constantinople was to the men of
the Third Crusade. And thus for these five days they must remain.

The original function of Nant Gwrtheyrn grew out of the first
Welsh Language Act in 1967, which acknowledged in law the equal
status of English and Welsh. However, Welsh not often being the
first language of the professional classes, somewhere was needed to
nurture the linguistic skills of those working in public bodies. Since
the centre's inception in 1978, and as that brief widened to include
anyone yearning to learn Welsh or improve what they already knew,
over 25,000 students of the language have visited Nant Gwrtheyrn,
from Cardiff where so many jobs in the media require bilingualism,
from all over Wales and the UK, from countries across the world.
In the summer months the weekly head count can be closer to forty.
But for now, seven of us will be adding ourselves to the tally.

The classroom is a converted Calvinistic Methodist chapel – in a
previous incarnation, from the 1850s to the 1930s, the village of

Porth-y-Nant was home to an isolated and self-contained granite quarry. The chapel, restored like the rest of the village from ruin, is now a tall, light room in which four tables are laid out in a U shape. On the walls are posters about Welsh life, the Welsh language, Welsh celebrities. We take our seats and Pegi begins by asking us to outline our goals for the week. Most of the group need Welsh for professional reasons. Roisin is a town planner (*cynllunydd tref*) in South Wales, David works for the complaints department of Conwy Council (*cwyno* = to complain; *cyngor* = council/advice). Richard is a fireman (*dyn tân*). Helen is about to come and do probation work in Wales. For all of them Welsh is an increasingly vital tool. John, meanwhile, explains that he simply wants to spend a week speaking Welsh, there not being much call for it in the Midlands. Pegi turns to me.

'Beth amdanoch chi, Jasper?' What about you?

'Mae rheswm rhyfedd 'da fi,' I say. I've got a strange reason. 'Dw i eisiau troi fy hunan mewn Cymro go iawn.' I want to turn myself into a real Welshman. The mission statement evinces a perceptible double take from the group. It's a knife-edge moment. It would be awful to be met with suspicion as I was in Welsh Level 1, Module 1. I've got to spend the next five days with these people, and they with me. I look around the room. If I can perceive a distinction, the women have instantly parked me as a classic narrow-focus male from the harmless end of the autistic spectrum, while I'm guessing Richard and David can't quite believe I've volunteered for something so non-specific and unmeasurable.

'Diddorol iawn, Jasper!' says Pegi. Very interesting! She sounds like a reception teacher praising a tot. It's Gerry's turn.

'Dw i'n hoffi just bloody speak as well as you lot.' Gerry has been sent here by her employers at Bangor University. It's clear to her that they've booked her on the wrong week. She drives off at the end of the day. We never see her again.

By five o'clock I'm wishing I could follow her out of Nant Gwrtheyrn. Having advertised my eagerness to build my listening skills, I have my chance all too soon. Pegi presses play on a CD and we listen for a few minutes to a male voice talking about ... the truth is I have no idea what he's talking about. Not even a hint of a clue. Half-familiar sounds now and then materialise like wall lights flitting by in a train tunnel, but there are nothing like enough of them. When it finishes, Pegi looks up and asks us what we made of it. Most of us wear a gormless look. Pegi offers to play it again. I feel like I'm slithering down a snake again, much as I did when starting to teach myself by CD. Eventually we get to see a transcript and I realise why. The whole thing is in dialect, otherwise known as North Welsh.

I've already noticed something of this in the speech of most of the people on the course. Odd words loom in the middle of bog-standard constructions.

I ask Pegi what *efo* means. It's cropping up all over the shop, like some inexplicable rash. She explains that *efo* is North Welsh for 'with'. In the south they say – we say – *gyda*.

'Blydi Gogs.' Roisin emits an imprecation at the next-door table. Bloody northerners. *Gog* is short for *gogledd* (north). The Gogs in the room giggle conspiratorially: they are the masters up at this end of the Welsh compass. Other basic discrepancies are soon making their presence known. I keep hearing the words *o* and *fo* for 'he' and 'him' where I would use *e* and *fe*. And then there are different formulations for ordinary phrases. The Welsh, for example, depersonalise simple expressions like 'I must', 'I prefer' or even 'I hate', as if syntactically distancing themselves from the sentiment. 'There is a necessity with me', 'It is better with me', 'It is nasty with me'. In the south 'with me' is *gyda fi* or *'da fi*. In the north it's *gen i*. And *gen* has different endings, depending on who's doing the preferring or the hating. I've soon discovered that they have alternative words for 'milk', for 'to cry', 'to try', 'to find', for 'out' and 'up'. To my ears Helen even has a different way of saying 'yes'.

These things require a mental recalibration. It's a struggle enough to translate the Welsh you do know into English, but now there's a Welsh you don't know which you have to translate into a Welsh you do know and only thence into English. On the first morning I come across one trim little phrase which encapsulates the fault line running across the middle of the Welsh language. *Dw i'n flin* in the north means 'I'm cross'. In Llanelli, down there on the edge of Carmarthen Bay, it means 'I'm sorry'. It begs a question. What happens when someone from Llanelli accidentally insults someone from Ruthin. 'Dw i'n flin,' says Angry of Ruthin. 'Dw i'n flin,' replies Apologetic of Llanelli. Is it just me, or does Pegi pass on this and other examples of South Walian eccentricity like an Edwardian anthropologist fascinated by the antics of tree-dwellers from Bongo Bongo Land who eat their own hair? But at least I discover a new word. Down south they refer to Gogs. Up here they refer to the people of South Wales as Hwntws: the people from beyond – beyond the mountains.

By the end of the first day, it has dawned on me that at least there's a silver lining to only half understanding what anyone says in the Nant. It gives me a sudden and unexpected sense of belonging. Pegi and the Gogs start to class Roisin and me as Hwntws. I am identified by my allegiance to the Welsh of the south. Therefore, by deduction, at least as far as these people are concerned, I am Welsh.

But the silver lining rims a cloud of exceptional gloominess. Among other things clear by the end of day one is that Helen is basically fluent. John, once you've hacked your way past the habitual coughing and spluttering which ornament his utterances, also has the language creeping through his veins. Both of them, it emerges, grew up in Wales speaking Welsh. Helen, being perhaps three decades younger, has a much fresher memory of these events: she's the only one of us to recognise a Welsh nursery rhyme which Pegi plays. In my head I promote her from pupil to classroom assistant. She wears a look on her face that will become familiar as the week unfurls – patient, serious, non-judgemental – as you demonstrate to her in some disjointed, dysfunctional speech or other the hollowness of your linguistic pretensions. Meanwhile, Richard the Anglesey fireman and David the Conwy complaints officer are both inclined to hurl themselves into sentences without the least anxiety about grammar. They're like boys diving into creeks whose depths they have not taken care to fathom. I'd give a lot for a piece of their confidence. The impression I have is that they understand everything that's being said, perhaps because their exposure to Welsh has been longer and is more regular. They hear it every day in work. I've been on the go, in effect, for just over a year, and I continue to be hampered by my English deafness to foreign sounds. As I tire towards the end of the afternoon, Pegi's radio-crackle Gog increasingly fails to penetrate. I sense one of my almighty Welsh-induced blood-sugar lows coming on, possibly even some kind of diabetic shutdown. That first evening at supper I buy a bottle of Merlot to share. As there are six of us, that's one glass each. No one else seems impressed by my notion of making a start on a second bottle.

The others have their low moments too. Roisin's face wears a long look if the course strays into literature. When poetry hour comes round on day two – we look at a longish poem overflowing with verbal goodies about the founding of Nant Gwrtheyrn – Richard's bright and open face grows hangdog and glum. He prefers to talk.

And talk we do, from the moment we sit down to breakfast till we part after supper. In the morning coffee break, the lunch break, the tea break, we talk as we refuel. The standard of the Welsh is variable but it seems not to matter. We are in this together. What do we talk about? Standard stuff: Welsh life, the Welsh universe, anything Welsh that pops into our heads. There is a running joke or two. Richard and David claim that from the terrace outside the dining room they have spotted Ireland (*Iwerddon*). It's theoretically possible, but I'm having none of it. We extract excellent mileage out of this piffling gag. (Guess you had to be there.) As Roisin and I are heading down to the pebbly beach after lunch on day two, I make my own sighting on the terrace. There are two women, one tiny, the other tall with a big bird's nest of white hair. It's definitely Jan Morris. When we get back from the beach no one believes that I've spotted an actual Welsh celebrity.

Another source of amusement is in the dogged refusal of us all to slip into English, however great the ensuing indignity. Vocabulary being limited, this involves a certain amount of perfectly innocent pilfering. Welsh is often accused by the more ignorant English of purloining half its word larder. After all, Taffy was a Welshman, Taffy was a thief. British English is of course an entirely self-generated language with no roots at all in Indo-European, Sanskrit, Latin, Greek, Old German and their later descendants, etc. It's true that some words have slipped across into Welsh via the portal of English. *Tacsi* is one that causes widespread hilarity. Never mind that 'taxi' hails from Germany. *Sgio* is the Welsh word for 'ski', which English and several other languages half-inched from Old Norse. When S4C was introduced. the Welsh had their own television *sianel* and could also see Welsh-language films in *y sinema* (source of both words: French). And so on and so forth. In fact the Welsh have made inventive use of modern technology to generate their own vocabulary. You use your *cyfrifiadur* (computer) for *ebost* (email) and *trydar* (Twitter). You enter a *gwefan* (website) via *y hafan* (its homepage, lit. haven). You heat up food in *y popty ping* (microwave). When the general subject of borrowing from English comes up in class, I get the chance to tell my first ever joke in Welsh, passed on to me as a true story. An Englishman behind the bar at the London Welsh rugby club is serving a Welshman up in town from Wales. 'The thing about Welsh is it's just English, isn't it?' the barman says. 'They take a load of English words and add an *o*, don't they? Eh? That's all Welsh is.' 'Fair play,' says the Welshman. 'I can't argue with that. Now can I have a pint of lager please, Fatso.'

And as I say, we too occasionally succumb to a version of Fatso syndrome. Verbs are usually the first port of call in such circumstances. You can't think of the word for whatever locomotive action it may be. If Pegi's not listening, or anyone else from the Nant's Welsh-language police – the women who work in the kitchen or the office – then you might in a dire necessity and on a strictly extemporising basis use a word which occupies a no-man's-land between English and Welsh and nonsense: *jumpio*, for example, or *rejectio*; *splashio* and of course *snoggio*. (This last comes up because over supper one night it emerges that Helen as a teenager in Clwyd enjoyed an intimate moment with one of the Welsh celebrities depicted on the wall in the classroom.) And other such cod-Latin gobbledegook. We apologise to one another and to higher Welsh powers as we do it. But the key thing is that we do not utter a single sentence of English. That is the one unbreakable rule. To lapse into English would feel like treading on the cracks in the pavement. No good could possibly come of it.

Sometimes, when Richard or Roisin or Dave is reaching for the right Welsh word, it happens that I'll know the one they're after. That in turn becomes my defining identity in the group. My red vocab book is filling at a hell of a lick. Words with no conceivable use in everyday speech are noted down, just in case. Richard looks at me in mock alarm when I know the word for 'culture' (*diwylliant*) or 'international' (*rhwngwladol*), 'authority' (*awdurdod*), 'punctual' (*prydlon*) or 'emergency' (*argyfwng*).

'Ti wedi llyncu geiriadur,' says Helen in the mid-morning break on the third day. Through the window the sea twinkles pleasantly as we guzzle hot drinks and biscuits.

'Sori, Helen?' I've done something to a dictionary, but what? She takes a sip of her coffee and theatrically gulps. The others, who hadn't a clue what she meant either, emit a burst of collusive laughter. So they think I've swallowed a dictionary.

It helps that I have been reading stories in Welsh. I started where many a Welsh learner embarks on an appreciation of Welsh literary language. I chanced upon the book ten years previously when poring over Teilo's attic library as he prepared to enter monastic life and divest himself of earthly possessions. His world-class collection of Byroniana, including a near complete set of first editions, was bound for the University of Delaware. Rummaging through the remainder, my eye was caught by a rich variety of books in other languages. Assuming I might one day want to brush up on them, I selected *Madame Bovary*, *La Sacra Bibbia* and for some reason, presumably sentimental as I had no plan at that point to learn it, a slim volume in Welsh. One day I open it and begin.

> Un tro roedd yna bedair cwningen fach, a'u henwau oedd – Pwtan, Cwta Wen, Fflopsi, a Mopsi.

In Welsh *The Tale of Peter Rabbit* turns out to conceal a terrifying array of booby traps, tripwires, potholes and landmines, principally in and around the verbs, which drive the story forward in a past tense that no one has previously mentioned to me. The story has been rendered in scrupulously correct pre-war Welsh. Teilo tells me he was always teased by his grandmother for speaking formal rather than oral Welsh. Now I can see why. He was speaking the New Testament Welsh of Beatrix Potter. I dump *Hanes Pwtan y Gwningen* with the fluffy-tailed protagonist still in mortal peril among the cabbages and move on to a book with a more contemporary urban edge. The familiar spine leaps out at me one day in a bookshop.

> Broliai Mr a Mrs Dursley, rhif pedwar Privet Drive, eu bod nhw'n deulu cwbl normal, diolch yn fawr iawn ichi.

Shrewd move. *Harri Potter a Maen yr Athronydd*, it turns out, is an absolute goldmine, in which I learn such useful words as *mellten* (thunderbolt) and *craith* (scar), *porffor* and *piwis* (purple, petulant), *neidr* and *Myglars* (snake and Muggles). Not forgetting *Wyddost-Ti-Pwy* (You-Know-Who). I lap it all up as fast and feverishly as ability allows. Which isn't very fast.

'Where've you got to in the Welsh *Harry Potter*?' a daughter will ask, her interest in my Welsh quest suddenly perking up.

'I'm halfway down page four.' Irritatingly, the translation has been done in Gog. Very nice for the young Rowlingians of Gwynedd and Merionnydd, etc., where the proportion of Welsh speakers is much higher, but there are actually more Welsh speakers in the south. A *Harri Potter* for us Hwntws would have been appreciated. That said, after two days at the Nant, where I have made it my bedtime reading, it becomes increasingly easy to tolerate if not fully endorse the boy wizard's use of northern dialect. By the time the *Cwrs Uwch* draws to a close, I am more than bearing down on chapter two.

I may have swallowed my *Modern Welsh Dictionary*. John seems to have ingested the whole of Bishop William Morgan's Bible. His vocabulary – he knows the Welsh words for 'gooseberry' and 'rood-screen', 'limekiln' and 'hoe' – harks back to an evanescent world in which the Welsh were closer to the soil, to their bardic heritage, to God. He acquires a nickname: The Oracle. John's Welshness is so gnarled and primordial I wonder whether he's not part-fashioned out of coniferous tree root.

The presence of fellow students in possession of a Welsh child-hood ticks all the boxes of my inferiority complex. Richard may be the only one of us who has lived in Wales all his life. But of those who haven't, David and Roisin are in-migrants and Helen and John out-migrants. I've never migrated in either direction. There are moments in class when I can feel myself succumbing to the self-pity of the outcast. I am jolted out of one such moment when Pegi presses play on a CD and I recognise the strains of a tune which my grandmother at almost ninety used to coax out of arthritic fingers on the piano.

'"Gwenith Gwyn",' I say, humming along to the lilting strains.

'Da iawn, Jasper,' says Pegi. My chest swells. Not that I've any idea of the words or their meaning. So we translate them together. 'Bugeilio'r Gwenith Gwyn' – the title means 'watching the white wheat' – tells of the thwarted love of farm labourer Wil Hopcyn for Ann Thomas, a well-to-do farmer's daughter who is forced by her mother to marry a man of equal status. Wil leaves home, only to dream that Ann's new husband has died. He returns to discover that it is Ann who is dying of a broken heart. It's all quite choking, especially when we are encouraged to sing it together. I allow the Welsh tide to wash over me.

George Borrow is the only notable author of a travel book about Wales who took the trouble to learn the language. Wherever he went, predominantly in North Wales and always on foot, he performed a sort of informal census, measuring levels of Welsh and English among the people he encountered. The further north and west he went, the more Welsh he found. 'Dim Saesneg,' passers-by and tradesmen, maids and farmhands would say when he asked them a question. No English. The further south and east, the less Welsh he heard until just beyond Newport the language petered out altogether.

Borrow was a gifted amateur philologist who had learned Welsh as a young man in Norfolk, to which he added a knowledge of Latin, Greek, Sanskrit, Gaelic, Romany and several more mainstream languages. When *Wild Wales* was published in 1862, eight years after the travels it describes, reviewers noted his eagerness to parade his linguistic skills. He faithfully recorded all conversations in which it was discovered with amazement that he could speak the language. 'I never heard before of an Englishman speaking Welsh,' said a man in Wrexham. 'Is the gentleman Welsh?' wondered another man near Llangollen; 'he seems to speak Welsh very well.' 'It will be a thing to talk of for the rest of my life,' said a carpenter on the road to Bangor. One hostile Welshman, Borrow noted on the road to Llanfair in Anglesey, was 'confused at hearing an Englishman speak Welsh, a language which the Welsh in general imagine no Englishman can speak, the tongue of an Englishman as they say being not long enough to pronounce Welsh'. On the way to Llanrhaeadr another woman 'had no idea it was possible for any Englishman to speak Welsh half so well'. None knew quite what to make of him. In the north they mistook him for a South Walian. In the south they assumed he was North Walian. He sometimes pretended that he could barely speak Welsh, before gradually revealing the full extent of his fluency. 'I have a little broken Cumraeg, at the service of this good company,' he said on sitting down to a beer in

Anglesey. 'Your Welsh is different from ours,' he was soon being told by an old man, 'and of course better, being the Welsh of the grammar.' And no wonder. 'How were you able to master its difficulties?' asked a doctor in Snowdonia. 'Chiefly by going through Owen Pugh's version of *Paradise Lost* twice,' Borrow replied, 'with the original by my side.'

He seems to have been racked with insecurity. Time and again, as he sought out conversations with those he met in Wales, his instinct was always to best his interlocutor. He travelled with the humility of a pilgrim paying homage to his bardic heroes – Goronwy Owen, Twm o'r Nant, Dafydd ap Gwilym – but also the zeal of a preacher spreading his own certain knowledge. Nothing delighted him more than to engage lowly shepherds and innkeepers and indoctrinate them with his enthusiasm for their culture, often in absurdly long screeds. He wandered across Wales lecturing Welshmen about their own history, the derivation of their own place names, sometimes reciting his own poetic translations. His intentions can be read honourably as a project to re-inseminate Wales with its own oral history. But for all his evident love of language and landscape, how does one respond to a man who was so careful to record every compliment paid to him? After one pleasant encounter with a slate miner and a mountain ranger one Sunday on his way down to Beddgelert, he couldn't resist reporting what he overheard.

'What a nice gentleman!' said the young man, when I was a few yards distant.

'I never saw a nicer gentleman,' said the old ranger.

Wild Wales is at its best when Borrow is tearing through the mountains, neither pace nor zeal dimmed by an August sun or an

autumn drenching, ingesting experiences of every stripe as they
come at him. One of the finest passages finds him waking up one
morning in Machynlleth, where memories linger of the freedom-
fighting Owain Glyndŵr, and setting off against all advice across
the naked hostile hills of Mid Wales. Pumlumon is a passing landmark, the spectacular waterfalls of the Devil's Bridge his eventual
destination. On a twenty-mile walk of epic drama, he meets a
typical cross-section of Welsh society: a modest old man who
believes the Church of England 'is the best religion to get to heaven
by', then two women who refuse to speak to an Englishman, four
shoeless red-haired children, a sullen man with a donkey who 'had
the appearance of a rather dangerous vagabond' and a half-naked
deaf mute working at a lead mine.

When he arrived at the inn in Ponterwyd, having traversed the
barren hills, Borrow was greeted by a pompous innkeeper who
affected not only to know 'the ancient British language perfectly'
but also to be a poet. As usual Borrow took pleasure in triumphantly besting him. In due course, having butted into the kitchen
because the parlour fire was belching smoke, he explained to the
host the reason for his visit: the stunning waterfalls in the river
Mynach at the Devil's Bridge a couple of miles to the south. The
host greeted the news indignantly. 'We have a bridge here too quite
as good as the Devil's Bridge; and as for scenery, I'll back the scenery
about this house against anything of the kind in the neighbourhood of the Devil's Bridge. Yet everybody goes to the Devil's Bridge
and nobody comes here.'

A century and a half later I sit in the same room of the same inn,
now upgraded to a hotel, and read out this testy lament to the
current owner. 'It's still a bit like that, to be honest.' She's a short
woman from East Sussex. They bought the place a few years earlier,
her husband being a quarter Welsh. Propping up the bar is a thin

retiree, all fag ash and burst capillaries, with a blotchy Black
Country accent. There is a powerful sense that we are far from the
beaten track. Outside, much as Borrow described it, the Rheidol
still clatters noisily through a chasm at the end of the garden, as if
in a roaring hurry to escape the region. The mountains of the Pumlumon range patrolling the horizon are quite as desolate and abandoned as they ever were. It feels like the ghostliest corner of Wales.
Borrow was more than happy to move on to the Devil's Bridge. But
in a sense Borrow has never left. The inn has had its revenge on
him: of the many places he stayed in Wales, this was a long way
from his favourite, but nowadays it's known as the George Borrow
Hotel. He would have been appalled.

On Wednesday morning it's all change. If my comprehension is
correct, Pegi has a domestic issue to attend to, though I wonder if
she hasn't just seen the way the wind is blowing: after two days
assessing the abilities of the class, she has perhaps determined that
two-thirds of us are not as clever as we claimed to be on our application form. For the rest of the week *Cwrs Uwch* transforms imper-
ceptibly into *Cwrs Canolradd* – from Higher to Intermediate – as we
are placed in the hands of Eleri. Eleri has huge blue eyes and dresses
with the discreet formality of a strict grammarian. On the down-
side, she is another northerner whose Llŷn accent mostly consists
of sea breeze and the crackle of pebbles in surf. But she enunciates
with marvellous over-emphatic clarity. At first my heart slightly
sinks at the realisation that we are being brought down a notch or
two. It feels like a firm slap to one's Welsh chops to be spoken to so
slowly. But a firm slap is what, if one is being honest, one craves.

On Wednesday afternoon we go on an outing to Caernarfon.
From the minibus I see in daylight for the first time the perilous
route carved into the side of the deep valley of Nant Gwrtheyrn,

gouged out of the side of Yr Eifl. It might as well be Kashmir, the road teetering on the very ledge of a precipice. From this perch it's easy to see why the Nant, one of the ancient places of Wales, has many legends attached to it as limpets to rocks. As we sway about in our minibus, Eleri tells the story of Rhys and Meinir, two local cousins who were betrothed to wed in the church at Clynnog Fawr. On the morning of the wedding, Meinir sought out a hiding place from which, according to custom, Rhys would come and fetch her to the altar. He looked high and low but failed to find her. As the weeks passed he would climb each day to a cliff top and, next to an oak tree where they used to meet, howl her name. Years slid by. One night he sheltered from a storm under the oak tree when lightning split it open to reveal the skeletal remains of Meinir still encased in her wedding dress. When she couldn't escape from her hiding place, it became her tomb.

The cafe at the Nant is called Caffi Meinir. We stop at Clynnog Fawr, one of the way stations on the pilgrims' route to Bardsey Island (three trips to Bardsey were worth one to Rome), and inspect the church where the wedding would have been. I wonder if the story's moral has some kind of modern application. Could Meinir be taken for a symbol of the Welsh language, her death a dire warning of irretrievable loss?

Closer to Caernarfon Richard points through the window up to a house in a field.

'Dyna'r ty Bryn Terfel,' he says. That's Bryn's house. It seems a modest property for a man who towers over the musical landscape of Wales. I think of his recommendation to me: 'If you showed any enthusiasm towards the language you would be welcome here with open arms.' Never has a truer word been spoken. I hope it counts as enthusiasm that I've not allowed English to pass my lips since Sunday afternoon.

Nor is any spoken in Caernarfon. The idea is to practise our Welsh in shops. The shops are presumably long used to tongue-tied adult learners from the Nant swarming the premises. We head for an outlet which sells books and music opposite the statue of David Lloyd George in the shadow of the castle. The cheerful face of Dafydd Iwan stares out from the racks of CDs. I tell the others I've got a signed copy of *Goreuon* at home. They are gratifyingly impressed that I move in the high echelons of Cymru Cymraeg. We split off and wander about the place like teenagers on a school outing, hands slumped in pockets against the cold under skies continuing clear. I find another more heavyweight bookshop and decide to make an impulse purchase. The moment has come to plunge headlong into the vasty deeps of Welsh literature. I've had it with *Pwtan y Gwningen* and *Harri Potter*. It's time to move through the gears. After a bit of browsing in the Welsh section I spot just the thing. The English part of me baulks at coughing up somewhat over the odds for a single book, but almost immediately it proves a worthwhile investment as I walk back through the darkening alleys of Caernarfon, the shops closing all around, while brandished under my arm in the traditional scholarly posture the name on the handsome hardback jacket is clearly visible for any impressionable passer-by to read and take in and admire: Dafydd ap Gwilym, the great medieval Welsh poet. Back in the minibus I open to the first poem and read what is, in effect, music.

Hawddamor, glwysgor glasgoed …

The less euphonious English version opposite has this down as 'Greetings, splendid greenwood choir'. I feel like George Borrow bar the small discrepancy that I recognise only half the words. But there's time yet.

The next morning Richard reports back from Anglesey, where he has had to return home for the night. He has a son who attends a Welsh-language primary school. For the first time ever, he says, the previous evening they had a conversation in Welsh. We practically burst into whoops and cheers. It feels as if a small but important victory has been won on behalf of all of us.

The morning is devoted to marrying Welsh verbs to Welsh prepositions. As with all languages, the little words in Welsh have their behavioural quirks which, like small boys picking their noses, one would like to erase but can't. *Gwrando ar y radio*. In Welsh they listen *on* the radio. *Chwarae dros y tîm* = to play over the team. *Maddau i rhywun* = to forgive to someone, which seems somehow more forgiving. Eleri wants to make us correct but also colloquial. Thus we spend the afternoon in the company of Welsh idioms. *Llyncu mul*: lit. swallow a mule = sulk. *Gwneud ei gorau glas*: lit. do his blue best = do his very best. *Tipyn o dderyn*: lit. a bit of a bird = a bit of a lad. *Mynd dros ben llestri*: lit. go over the top of the dishes = go too far. This is all done through games and competitions. During the breaks – morning, lunch, tea – as we continue to yak and crack jokes ('Dyna Iwerddon!'), the feeling dawns that I have somehow known my classmates for aeons longer than four days. Such has been the intensity of the learning experience. I think of the Welsh camaraderie described by Charlie and Wayne whom I met half a mile underground in the Vale of Neath. We have bonded at our own kind of coalface.

In the evening we are sent up on our own to dine in the village pub in Llithfaen at the top of the hill. Our linguistic task after eating is to watch a weekly broadcast of a Welsh drama on the big screen. A big right-angled bar juts out under a low ceiling. There are a few cloth-capped hill farmers round one table by the fire. We sit at another next to the window and order a bottle of wine. Helen and I somehow get into a discussion about hill farming, both of us obviously being experts in the field. Somehow it sharpens into an argument about the Welsh word for 'ram'. I insist that it's *hwrdd*. She wrongly thinks it's *maharan*. As I've swallowed a dictionary I stick to my ground when, halfway down my first glass and thus duly emboldened, I decide to consult our neighbours. Being hill farmers, they can probably settle this one. I get up.

'Esgusodwch fi.' The three hill farmers look up from their pints of *cwrw da*. 'Dyn ni'n dadlau yma am gair Cymraeg.' We're arguing here about a Welsh word. It should be *am air*, but we'll let that pass; I am brimming with new-found Welsh confidence. The three of them hold their heads expectantly, exuding a general atmosphere of wizened tolerance and fertile sideburns. 'Beth yw'r Cymraeg am ram?' What's the Welsh for ram? One of them – he's extremely old and has thick glasses – pipes up affirmatively.

'Maharan!'

'Diolch yn fawr iawn!' says Helen – thank you very much indeed – to whom the three of them now direct flirtatious nods and conspiratorial winks, which she disgracefully does nothing to discourage.

'Dim hwrdd?' I ask disconsolately. Not my word then?

'Hwrdd?' one of them expostulates. 'Hwrdd? Hwrdd yw gair hwntw.' *Hwrdd* is a southerner's word. They chuckle among themselves, Helen complicit. 'O ble dach chi'n dod?' Where do I come from? (*Dach* not *dych*, as per Gog usage.) I could give them the strict, literal truth, but my week at the Nant, plus the full glass now emptied into my system, induces a sudden fit of poetic licence.

'Dw i'n dod o'r de.' I come from the south. 'Yn wreiddiol.' Originally. I am starting to believe it myself. And why not? Borrow, after all, was often taken for a southerner in the north.

The group have been persuaded to move on to a second bottle. The six of us talk as the dishes come and go of how we'll use our improved Welsh in times to come. Helen is persuaded to divulge more titbits about her *snoggio* with the Welsh celeb. My near encounter with Jan Morris is picked over for hidden significance. The Oracle shares a few more words from Bishop William Morgan's Bible. Richard tells grim tales of fatal conflagrations across North Wales. We speculate about the kind of complaints David will be fending off in Welsh. Roisin wonders whether her Welsh hasn't gone backwards in the Nant. She is firmly advised that this is not the case.

We've now spent four days in total Welsh immersion. There is only one day left. As the others talk I am suddenly blindsided by an out-of-body flash. Tomorrow in class we will be tasked with writing and reading out a story about ourselves. I will craft something riddled with errors about a child's Christmas at Mount Hill, my grandfather with the carving knife, my grandmother busy in the kitchen, a great-uncle shouting 'Shut the door!' and an uncle talking without cease. And then after a short afternoon session in which Eleri will cover our stories with corrections in red ink, we will get into our cars and drive back to our anglophone lives and perhaps never see one another again (although firm assurances will have been made to the contrary, *ebost* swapped, etc.). And for a few days I will go into mourning the way actors do at the end of a play's run. But that is tomorrow. Today, now, half a dozen of us are in the back room of a pub on the side of a mountain on a remote peninsula in North Wales. Somewhere up there in the dark the round stone huts of Tre'r Ceiri have endured since long, long before the birth of Christ. None of us really needs Welsh. None of us even really needs a past or a heritage or a place we can say we come from. We can all live happily ever after in the eternal present of the cyber-sphere in which even English will soon be reduced to the utilitarian codings of vowel-free txt spk before eventually Mandarin chokes the planet. So why not let the old ways go? The march of progress, surely, will kill off the Welsh language anyway, as it has all but killed off Welsh coracling and Welsh congregations and Welsh miners.

But reason not the need. Why else are we gathered here this evening round this table? We have stumped up our money and time, volunteered a diminishing stock of middle-aged brain cells to staff the barricades and in our small grammatically challenged way helped stem the predatory forces of English, which has the might of history behind it. We have gone out to bat for this older purer language to which we all feel an ever-deepening allegiance. As do thousands of others. It's an epiphany: a moment when suddenly everything is utterly clear. None of them notices the embarrassing detail of my eyes filling as I formulate my conclusion.

Were we to meet in the future, I say, I couldn't imagine speaking English with any of them. It could be better expressed by a more melodious Welsh speaker, but they know what I mean and we all drink to it. In fact I could no more speak English with these people than Mandarin. Perhaps we'd learn much more about one another in English. Vast hinterlands would presumably open up. We could maybe joke about more than the whereabouts of Ireland. But a contract would be broken and something vital lost. Welsh – at least here and now – is our first language.

6

Chwarae = Play

'They've taken our coal, our water, our steel. They buy our homes
and live in them for a fortnight every year. What have they given
us? Absolutely nothing. We've been exploited, raped, controlled and
punished by the English – and that's who you are playing this
afternoon.'

Phil Bennett, Cardiff Arms Park (1977)

THE SUCCESS OR OTHERWISE of a London Welshman's visit to
the Millennium Stadium is subject to various variables. Time of
kick-off. Identity of match companion(s). Quality of opposition.
Weather. State of the rail network. Team selection. Current level
of knowledge of words of the anthem. Side of bed key players got
out of. Capacity of bladder. Luck/lack of same. Availability of
Shane. Anxiety about getting a seat on the train back.

The journey begins at Paddington. With each stop the train
decelerates along platforms lined with red-shirted clusters of the
Diaspora. Carriages fill. We slip under the Severn and emerge into
the land of our fathers, the hills rising out of the north-facing
window. By Newport there is standing room only as the corridors
are cramped with gentlemen of all ages, sizes and states of inebria-
tion. Celts have a bipolar relationship with optimism. At this

preliminary hour, hope still abounds. Fatalism is for later. Rivers of red are starting to surge towards the great steel-girdered cathedral that rises like a city within a city on the Taf. Through the gate, tickets ripped, up several staircases onto a long floor where there is Welsh beer to be bought. Stairwells open out towards the sky or, on rainy days, the roof. The amplified sound of a brass band is playing, a choir singing. Someone in a luminous jacket points you upwards and it's now a steep clamber to your row and thence a sideways shuffle past Welsh knees to your seat, where you and whoever you're with, who is also Welsh, turn and sit and take in the sight spread before you of, by general consensus, the finest rugby stadium on earth.

A hundred jacketed seniors with silken voices shuffle from one corner of the pitch to the next, dodging punts from the visiting squad who are now out on the grass doing drills. They lead the crowd in Welsh songs to which you do not know the words. Apart from 'Guide Me O Thou Great Redeemer'. You feel an uncomfortable twinge of self-reproach that you cannot sing along to 'Sosban Fach' like your grandfather.

As the 75,000 red seats fill, the players trot back into the tunnel, shoulders rolling, pectoral overdevelopment rippling under stretchable neo-fabric. Rugby players used to look like human beings. It's your perpetual worry that the Welsh team will somehow be less pneumatic than the visitors. Meanwhile up in the stands the disciples granny-step towards their seats. Between songs from the choir, a disembodied voice makes deafening announcements in English and Welsh, the two languages merging in an acoustic muffle. The teams are announced, stern glowers from symmetrical screens mounted high above the posts, young faces ever so slightly aged before their time by thunderous hits to the body. For the favourites: cheers; for the visitors' best player: boos.

And during all of this, the anxious thought runs through my head. Do I really belong here? Can I claim with my Harrovian hinterland to be an organic component of this seething whole? I look around me and see Welsher faces than mine, hear Welsher voices. Gaggles of plump, peroxided luvlies, their dimpled faces cased in daffodil wimples. Hordes of hard men with bullet heads and tattooed necks. We Welsh. Can I actually say that? Dare I use the first person plural in this holiest of shrines to which the face of the nation turns as the clock ticks down to kick-off? Strategically placed fire-jets ejaculate spurts of hot flame towards the roof with growing urgency, the tunnel belches pink-orange smoke and the team suddenly spew like red dragon's breath onto the grass as the stadium emits a primordial roar of deathless allegiance. I find that I am bellowing too, without having to will the noise out of myself. It's there in my lungs.

'Come on, boys!!'

I have no idea why, but this always comes out in a Welsh accent. The stadium stands and sings the anthem, the choir serried behind the teams and conducted by a small man on a box. Imagine harnessing the energy of the sound. You could power the Glamorgan grid. I don't know the words. I sing the important bits – 'Gwlaad! Gwlaaaad!' – and make a stab at the rest. One time I write them down and self-consciously sing with my eyes lowered, though at that point my Welsh pronunciation is barely up to snuff. And then the teams scatter to either end of the pitch, the choir and band march off towards a corner and the disembodied voice on the stadium Tannoy delivers a final address, which thunders over the gathering noise.

'Ymlaen, Cymru! Come on, Wales!'

We need no encouragement. 'WALES! WALES! WALES! WALES!'

Yes. I belong. When the fifteen men of Wales take to the field, I am Welsh.

I have a friend in Wales called Leighton, or Leight, or, when he's texting, L8, who I am convinced was propping for Llanelli when, on the very famous day in Welsh rugby, they beat the All Blacks in 1972. Leighton is edging towards sixty nowadays, so is the right age. And he's certainly the right size, a solid slab of Welsh beef. I'm sure someone told me he was playing, and now no amount of sweet-faced denial from Leighton will convince me otherwise. If he wasn't on the pitch in person, he was there in spirit. Or someone very like him, wise in the old Welsh ways of legalised GBH and licensed assault. That was how they played rugby back then. Over a generous glass of something red, Leighton is fond of sharing his memories of thuggery and skulduggery, of thumpings and stampings, gougings and gashings. His big soft eyes will open wide at the memory. This was in days of yore when referees turned a blind eye. Back in the 1970s I don't suppose Leighton got his hands on the ball very often. That wasn't a prop's job. They were mainly employed in the privatised application of natural justice. Retaliation was preferably administered in a pre-emptive capacity with these words: 'Welcome to Stradey.' Stradey Park is the home of Llanelli RFC.

These stories chill me to the marrow. Why? Because it has dawned on me that, in order to turn myself into a Welshman, I need to think about getting a game in Wales.

'No problem, cariad.' Leighton is affection personified (*cariad* = beloved, darling, dear). 'We can sort you out with a game for Clwb Rygbi Cymry Caerdydd.' Leighton's son Hywel, he explains, is the club captain. I smile brightly in his kitchen and glug some more red. In my head, I'm already booking myself into casualty. I am forty-five. I have not played rugby for twenty-eight years. And when I did play, it scared the bejesus out of me.

I don't know why I grew up fearful of physical contact. A testosterone deficiency? Infant spindliness? I cut a puny figure on wintry afternoons under H-shaped posts. A deep trauma happened when I was first stuck in a rugby shirt. I still remember the day in the depths of January 1976 when the ball changed shape. My known world ever so slightly tilted and I learned something new about myself: that I had a lily liver. I didn't even fancy tackling the opposition at football, which put only feet and ankles at risk. Suddenly they were telling you to throw your *face* at someone's flying studs. In the trenches they shot my kind in the back.

At the school I went to there was an index of fearlessness. The rugby master, Mr Youle, who also taught maths, was a terrifying ogre with wild grizzled curly hair planted atop a giant frame like tufts of grass on a lofty crag. He lived for rugby – or rugger as they called it in that corner of West Sussex. What he really lived for was tackling. He harboured deep suspicions of anyone who liked football, because football involved kicking. You didn't kick in rugby. You tackled. To encourage a tackle-based culture of kamikaze valour, he would mount a large display board up in the corridor. The names of every rugby player in the school were listed there. If that afternoon someone pulled off a heroic tackle he'd put a capital T next to their name. A more perfunctory effort, but still identifiable as a tackle, would merit a small t. Most boys accumulated a respectable set of Ts and ts. Even those who preferred to steer clear of a scrap would generate enough ts to spare their blushes. But I just couldn't seem to hurl myself into the danger zone. It looked like it would hurt. Even maim. As I was a new boy my name was bottom of the list. I used to look at the board in break, wondering if anyone would notice the blank squares next to Rees 1. The humiliation was such that one week, having dredged up the courage to wrestle a midget to the floor, I reminded Mr Youle that I'd done a tackle. He had the board in front of him at the time and was busy distributing upper-case commendations. With a disdainful squiggle he deposited a small lonely *t* next to my name.

There was something Mr Youle found particularly baffling. He could make no connection between the long-haired skeleton who refused to tackle and the evidence enshrined in my surname that I must on some level have something to do with Wales. On Sundays he would invite the older boys down to his cottage in the grounds to watch the highlights of the Five Nations. As an honorary Welshman I was asked along and more or less told to support the fifteen men in red. So I did.

It was on those Sunday afternoons in 1977 and 1978 that I was introduced to names that still echo around the hills and valleys of Wales and far beyond: Gareth Edwards, Phil Bennett, J. P. R. Williams, J. J. Williams, Gerald Davies, Mervyn Davies, the Pontypool front row. The great men had mostly retired by the time I saw Wales play for the first time. It was an away game at Twickenham in 1980. I went with my older brother and, reaching our seats ten minutes late, we were met by a stadium in eruption as the flanker Ringer was pointed towards the tunnel by a referee. Wales scored two tries, including one by Elgan Rees. To boost my sense of Welsh belonging I would for several years after spread the story among my fellow Harrovians that Elgan Rees was my uncle. In a boarding school full of credulous hoorays, the claim was hard to disprove. He wasn't the greatest wing to play for Wales. He wasn't even the only Rees to play on the wing in that era. There was a Clive Rees too, but as he resembled a short, mad-haired professor who zigzagged about the pitch as if frantically hunting for his mislaid specs, I stuck with Elgan.

But Elgan was not my brother's uncle. My older brother supported England, who hoofed over three penalties that afternoon at Twickenham. Result: England 9, Wales 8. Two national histories summarised in scoreline: plodding victory for pragmatism and force, bitter defeat for adventure and romance.

It was the romance of Welsh rugby which seduced me. I was educated by Mr Youle to believe that Wales played the proper way. They created shapes of glistening beauty, never better demonstrated than in the Greatest Try Ever Scored, when the Barbarians playing the All Blacks in 1973 crafted an attack of astonishing dynamism and flair which, started by Bennett and completed by Edwards, involved seven players: one Englishman, six Welshmen. Of course Wales engaged in the rough stuff too. To gain possession of the ball in rugby you have to go about the necessary business of physically subordinating the opposition. But the best teams are remembered for what they do with that possession, and no team in rugby history is better remembered than Wales in the 1970s.

Even before the birth of Project Wales, I start to travel to the Millennium for every home game, hoping for history to repeat itself: for Wales to stick it up the English, to bring home the Grand Slam, to terminate a losing streak against New Zealand which stretches back to the year of the coronation. Hope walks shoulder to shoulder with realism. These things would be nice, but they are never expected. Not any more. However often you go, the All Blacks will always maraud and destroy. I am there when Wales beat Australia, and when Wales win a Slam. Those are very good days. Very good indeed. But I am also there one dreary afternoon when Wales are playing like muppets against Scotland. As ever I have half an eye on the return journey. The queues outside Cardiff Central can be punitively long, even without the cold and the rain. It's always a good idea to beat the rush. And if things are looking gloomy, why not nip off a little bit early? Half-time analysis with match companion goes as follows:

'This is shit. Wales are playing like muppets. How many points do they need to be losing by for us to escape five minutes before the end?'

'Ten or more.'

'Agreed.'

Wales continue to play in the aforesaid manner. They have never looked less like winning. A Scottish player is injured and after a long delay is stretchered off. The clock ticks down, though we can't actually see it from our seats. The crowd grows tetchy. Time is clearly ebbing away. Wales, ten points down, have a line-out five metres from the try line. It's now or never. The Welsh line-out is as skittish and unreliable as an ill-trained thoroughbred. I'll bet my house on Wales losing the line-out.

House saved. Line-out lost. In unison, 75,000 fatalists groan.

'That's it,' I say. 'Let's go.' We get up, shuffle out of our row and walk with heads held high out of the stadium. No one follows. Out in the street it is eerily quiet. But we've made the right choice. On the grounds that we're well ahead of the rush, we slip into a Welsh Rugby Union souvenir outlet where the match is being played out on a screen behind the counter. The first thing we see is the clock. Still eight minutes to go. How could we have got that so wrong? Must have been that injury. Then a Scot is sinbinned. Then Wales score a glorious try. Five points behind. Conversion. Three points behind. Three minutes to go. Wales break, a Scot trips our fullback and is sent off. Scotland down to thirteen men with forty-three seconds left. Wales take the penalty. No points behind. Good comeback, well done, boys, a bit shaming to have missed it, but a draw after all is not a win. We start for the station. We've gone fifty yards when a pub on the other side of the road all but explodes with noise. The game, inexplicably, is not over. We dash up and are just in time to peer in a window and glimpse through crowds of red shirts a screen on which Shane is touching the ball down under the posts. The pub goes berserk. The air above us detonates. Since we left the Millennium Stadium, the muppets have scored seventeen points. It's the most pulsating finish to a rugby match in living memory. And Wales won. And I missed it. If I'd taken a Welshness test on that day, there could have been only one verdict.

Fail.

Late July. Mount Hill. Early 1970s. The sun beating down on lush green fields flanked by oaks in heavy bloom. Pylons march across distant hills. My grandfather in a garden chair out on the spongy lawn. It's the annual sports day. I am seven or eight. Bert's two junior partners from the surgery have brought their brood. We liked the pair of brothers, one thin, one tubby. The three sisters – we had no experience of girls – slightly unnerved us. We weren't familiar, for example, with gender etiquette in relation to competitive sports. Should we give them a sound thrashing with egg and spoon or keep it courteous?

I went all out for victory. And these were games at which I could win. The race was the blue-riband event. The course consisted of an anticlockwise circuit of the Mount Hill property. You were gone and out of sight for what felt like for ever but was probably less than a minute. And all the time Bert sat there with his stopwatch, keeping an eye on things. One year I was victorious a lot. At the ceremonial prize-giving I'd already had my hand shaken and my palm greased with a 50p bit, when Bert announced the high jump prize. I'd won this one fair and square, so to spare my grandfather the bother of reading out my name I broke from the circle of adult spectators and junior competitors without waiting for the announcement, strolling up with a proud, entitled air to collect my next winnings. I was met with a glare which shrivelled the soul.

'I haven't said your name,' said my grandfather with chilly calm. My legs petrified. Confused by shame and terror, the blood had no idea whether to rush to my face or vacate it. I also got a public dressing down from my father, backed up by my mother, because this rebuke would have been meant for them too, the ones responsible for raising such a presumptuous, arrogant little English monster. And then the winner was announced. A girl. Wales, to repeat, was the wellspring of the equals sign. Bert, the former High Sheriff of Carmarthenshire, parcelled out the winnings fairly, and that was that.

In those summer visits the perimeter of our Welsh world would expand with outings to the Tywi estuary, with the castle above Llansteffan on one side and the train chugging along the shore on the other. There are snaps of my father and uncle playing on the same patch of sand in the 1930s, Bert with dark hair sitting immaculately on a blanket. But there came a time when our parents would want to be in and out of Mount Hill as rapidly as they could manage and there was no time to go anywhere. Then the perimeter would not expand but contract as all hours not spent sleeping or eating were passed in the old kitchen down a little flight of stairs off the hall. A large table dominated the red-tiled room. For years it had lain camouflaged under sewing and knitting things. But one day when I was ten the shiny wooden top was removed in three pieces and beneath it was an expanse of green baize. My older brother was the first one to be inducted. On the next visit it was my turn. Finally we were all three of us playing snooker on a round-the-clock vigil. The colours of the balls were odd: the pink was orange, the green khaki, the yellow off-white. For several years we'd tip out of the car at Mount Hill at perhaps four o'clock, see our way through the minimum formalities, then one of us would ask another of us if we fancied a game of snooker. By five past four we were racking up the balls and cueing off. We stopped playing five minutes before leaving two days later. Thanks to the many hours of Welsh practice, I carried off the snooker championship two years running at my boarding school. They are the only sporting trophies I ever won.

One Saturday lunchtime Leighton takes me to a bowling club in north Cardiff where Clwb Rygbi Cymry Caerdydd meet whenever Wales are playing home. I'm to be introduced to Hywel, his son and the club captain. But the person I really have to schmooze is the club chairman, introduced to me as Rhys the Voice. He's shorter, fairer, with an air of irony settled permanently on his brow. I guess that he plays scrum half – part correctly because he's an actor and he can't afford to turn up on the set of the Welsh-language soap *Pobol y Cwm* with his face rearranged. So nowadays he runs the club from the touchline. He came by his name because whenever Wales are playing at home at the Millennium, the disembodied voice making the announcements over the Tannoy in Welsh and English belongs to none other than Rhys the Voice. I feel as if I'm in the presence of minor Welsh royalty. ('Ryce, the appellation of the great clan …' said Borrow; 'of old the regal race of South Wales.') We sit down with a beer and I tell him in Welsh that I'm turning myself into a Welshman and need to play a game of rugby in Wales.

'Dim problem,' he says. 'Ti'n gallu chwarae dros y vets.' I can turn out for the codgers XV.

'Gwych!' I say. Great! I'm lying.

'Pa safle?' What position do I fancy? Good question. Ideally touch judge, but I fear I need a more immersive role on the other side of the white line.

My optimal efficiency as a rugby player was as a wing at the age of nearly fourteen, when I was taller and faster than the boys around me. Then they started to thicken and solidify in ugly hormonal spurts. I still remember the sickening thud on the side of my head when once I was scragged in possession and smothered by a grunting heap of post-pubertal maulers. I switched to fly half and at the faintest hint of trouble would punt the ball away in an elegant spiralling arc towards the far side of the pitch for a wing to chase. Countermanding the wrathful diktat of Mr Youle, I swore by the kicking game. So handy for avoiding contact. Bugger passing. Sod tackling. Safety first. Keep out of harm's way.

Rhys the Voice is waiting for answer. I've got to play somewhere. Where's the safest place on the pitch? Think. I'm not fast any more, of course. Nowadays I run through treacle. I am halfway to ninety. But fly half – outside half, to use the correct Welsh terminology – is far too close to the action.

'Asgellwr?' Wing? I'm going back home.

The game of rugby famously took its name from an English public school where, one afternoon in 1823, it is alleged that during a game of football a certain William Webb-Ellis caught a football (which was legal back then) and decided to run with it (which still isn't). In England, the whiff of privilege and entitlement has clung to rugby union ever since. 'Drop a bomb on the west car park at Twickenham before the Varsity match,' the journalist Hunter Davies once memorably advised upon first experiencing an English rugby fixture, 'and you'd wipe out Fascism in Britain for the next ten years.'

The game migrated across the border when the Anglican college in Lampeter adopted the rules in 1850. Rugby fanned out into places where there was no middle class or further education, and took root above all in the industrial communities where choral singing was the only other organised activity. When in 1881 an official Welsh team first took on England – at 'Mr Richardson's Field' in Blackheath – it was drubbed by opponents who had been playing internationals for a decade. Within a month the Welsh Rugby Football Union was formed. It would require six further attempts for Wales finally to defeat the neighbour. That was in 1890. Rugby rapidly became a defining facet of Welsh identity. In the same decade as the *Encyclopaedia Britannica*'s entry for Wales said '*see* England', the newly adopted national sport offered the Welsh a symbol around which a country without its own institutions could gather. It was so much the better that the team prospered on the pitch.

Wales dominated the Edwardian era. In 1905 they beat the already formidable All Blacks, then the Springboks in 1906 and Australia in 1908. That year they became the first side to defeat every other home nation and so win the Grand Slam; they did it again in 1909 and, with France newly part of the Five Nations tournament, once more in 1911. After the war, the harsh years of the Depression left its imprint on the national side. Welsh hearts fluttered anew for a period in the early 1950s, including in 1953 the most recent victory against the All Blacks. But it would be another twenty years before the second golden age would return. It lasted for the duration of the 1970s – which yielded three Grand Slams – and came to an abrupt end at Twickenham in 1980 when a fourteen-man Wales was defeated by a single point.

That, at least, is the opinion of the man sitting opposite me.

'We just lost something. We lost our physicality. That's the way it is. Welsh rugby didn't recover for a long, long time.'

Elgan Rees has silver hair nowadays. The eyes and cheekbones are still sharp, the body trim. At fifty-seven I imagine he can still execute a proficient sidestep.

'I could if it came to a situation where I had to.' He laughs. Elgan is a sales rep for a company which manufactures protective clothing – has been for over thirty years – and spends much of his time on the M4, which is why we have met in the motorway service station just to the west of Cardiff. If he'd played in any other era he'd be a more integral part of the Welsh collective memory. But injury would curtail an international career which had taken longer than normal to get going. With Gerald Davies and J. J. Williams parked on either wing for much of the decade, there was simply no way into the team.

'I think I've got the record number of caps for Wales B,' he says. Elgan had the very rare honour of being selected to tour with the British Lions in 1977 two years before he represented Wales. He recalls the welcome he received in the Welsh squad. This was back in the amateur days when no one did warm-ups or stretches, Sunday-morning training was at low tide on the beach at Aberavon and players paid for their own boots. 'I remember Gareth Edwards said to me, "What size boots are you?" I said, "Size nine, Gareth," and the week after I had a brand-new pair of Adidas boots. I just could not believe it. It was like Christmas. And having them given to me by Gareth Edwards? Oh my gosh.'

Elgan made his Wales debut at twenty-five, away to Scotland. 'I had one of the worst first halves ever. I dropped a few high balls. They could see there was a weak link there. My head was really down at half-time. I remember I had a word from J. P. R. Williams: "Keep your head up and don't worry about it." And fair dos, J.P.R. chipped ahead for me to score in the second half.' He scored on his debut at Cardiff Arms Park too. By the following year when Wales went to Paris for the first game of the Five Nations, he was a fixed member of a side which was tipped to win yet another Grand Slam. He scored, Wales won easily, but the game cast a long shadow.

'We were accused of over-rigorous play. And after that game there was a build-up during the week in the press of the Welsh being too physical. And I think it set the tone for the Twickenham game. I've never been in a game where the atmosphere was so intimidating. British Lions that you had toured with just blanked you. After ten minutes Paul Ringer brushed past John Horton and he was sent off. For nothing! And from then on in there were skirmishes going on all over the field, physical battles going on everywhere. We were criticised by our own union after that game. A lot of English players were at fault as well and we were blamed for it.'

Wales would not win another Grand Slam for twenty-five years. It didn't help that the great generation retired. Nor that Thatcherite policies caused the two main sources of Welsh rugby talent – the mines and the grammar schools – to dry up. But that game, says Elgan, was a watershed.

I tell Elgan that it was the first international I ever attended and I vividly recall that sense of menace. But I've got something else to tell him too. We've been talking for an hour about his memories of the golden age. Elgan is a delightful man, modest and apparently thrilled to recall with a stranger those now distant years when he strutted, jinked and sprinted upon the world stage. I'm suddenly nervous.

'Elgan, I need to come clean about something,' I say. 'When you broke into the Welsh team I used to identify with any player called Rees.' I'm easing him in.

'And Clive Rees as well obviously,' he reminds me. 'He was called Billy Whizz.'

'You were a lot cooler than Clive. And I have to say it went a bit further than that.' Deep breath. 'The thing is, Elgan, when I was at school, in order to enhance my Welshness I used to claim that you were my uncle.' I take care not to mention which school it was.

Having no idea how a former Wales international will greet this bizarre form of hero worship, I am relieved when his face creases up and a peal of laughter echoes around our bit of the motorway service station.

'Well, if you can get away with it, Jasper, get away with it, I say!' He even thanks me. I rather feel that thanks are due to him. But anyway, now that's out of the way I have a question. At the age of forty-five, I tell him, I've booked myself in to play for Clwb Rygbi Cymry Caerdydd. Does Elgan have any advice? He doesn't hang about.

'Don't play!' he says. 'Don't take the risk. It is a physical game at the end of the day and your body is not quite used to taking the dumps and actually having to do tackles and being tackled as well. It's difficult to go on the field and just do it. I wouldn't go there, to be honest.'

Oh. I tell Elgan that's not exactly the advice I was looking for. Does it make a difference that I've been asked to play on the wing?

'On the wing you've got a chance,' he says. 'As a winger I would try to run away from trouble.' He's laughing again. 'I tried to avoid tackling as much as I could.' This is an excellent development. Beyond the coincidence of our Welsh surname, my rugby uncle, who scored six tries in thirteen internationals for Wales and twice toured with the British Lions, and I have something in common after all. If Elgan Rees can run away from trouble, then so can I.

An *ebost* arrives from Rhys the Voice offering a choice of two Sunday games, a week apart. I'm busy elsewhere in Wales on the first, so plump for the second. Rhys the Voice hopes I'm fit and healthy. I get into training. Running round the park. Running round the river circuit. Press-ups. Sit-ups. Sit-ups. Press-ups. The usual malarkey, utterly hellish. My knees in particular set up a protest. I am a victim of cartilage complaint and joint malfunction. But I must face my Welsh destiny. Then two days before the game a text arrives.

'Dim gem! Wedi canslo!'

The game's off. I can cancel my appointment in casualty.

To soften the blow, Rhys the Voice issues an invitation to watch him work at the Millennium. Thus a few Saturdays hence I turn up at Gate 4 in Cardiff and am handed a laminated pass with my face on it. I am inordinately proud to be an officially badged insider. Rhys the Voice leads me through the tunnel from which in a couple of hours the simulated dragon's breath will be snorting and the XV men of Wales emerging.

I have taken the precaution of wearing my Welsh rugby shirt. Sadly, the appropriate attire does not qualify me to trespass onto the actual pitch, nor even the grass this side of the touchline. The turf really is that hallowed. I stand and look up at 75,000 empty seats, all of them to be filled within two hours. Voices of stadium workers echo around the vast hollows. Rhys the Voice is in conversation with someone from the outside broadcast team. A message has come down from very high up in the Welsh Rugby Union that he's not allowed to be so pro-Wales in his pre-match announcements. Apparently it's not very hospitable. So 'Ymlaen, Cymru! Come on, Wales!' will have to go. His patriotism has been gagged.

We wander along the side of the pitch down to another tunnel in the corner. From down the slope comes the magnificent noise of a choir and band in rehearsal. We walk towards the sound of 'Sosban Fach', past a glinting semicircle of red-jacketed brassbandsmen (and women, and boys and girls). A well-fed conductor is tucked tight into his livery, face puce under a steepling bearskin hat. Rhys the Voice and I plant ourselves next to a box on which a small conductor stands, the same man I've often seen from the

stands. In front of him is a vast choir – two choirs, in fact – consisting in the front row of young blowdried men in black suits and
shirts with white ties, and behind them white-haired gents in thick
zip-up anoraks. You can tell which choir are the nancies coached in
from London.

They pump out a rousing national anthem. Surrounded by hard
walls and ceiling, the sound pings cleanly around the space like a
bullet around a room. I stand and sing, a few more words having
gone in, but I still start Redwoodising somewhere in the third line.
No one's looking at me. When it's over and the choir wanders off,
Rhys the Voice introduces me to the conductor, who rejoices in the
name of Haydn James. There are a lot of Haydns and Handels in
the Valleys, he explains, a legacy of the oratorios first performed in
the nineteenth century.

The stadium is now no longer quite empty. Rhys the Voice takes
his place behind a bank of equipment next to a dapper silver-haired
man in pinstripes called Iestyn who shares the announcing duties.
Their schedule is full of highly specific timings. Announcement of
this at such-and-such a minute, choir to sing so-and-so precisely
here. Teams to warm up at this point. We are right by the tunnel. I
sit next to him as these predictions come precisely to pass. Rhys the
Voice holds a microphone to his mouth, speaks into it and lo, his
words boom out of vast speakers mounted high above us. It's as if
the stadium is responding to his disembodied instructions. The
choir walks on. The squads jog out past our left shoulders to do
their drills. Rhys the Voice appears supremely relaxed as he
addresses an audience of 75,000 in English and Welsh. The choir
is now in front of us, the brass band led by its spherical conductor
off to the right. The barrels planted around the touchlines start to
spit vertical flames the heat of which lightly toasts my eyeballs. To
my left the tunnel froths with bilious smoke, though close up the

effect is curiously less dramatic than up in the gods. And here as if
at the command of Rhys the Voice come the contemporary deities
of Wales into a stadium detonating in welcome. Iestyn announces
the anthems. Haydn James, mounted on a box, raises his baton. We
stand to sing and I give it currently my best shot as just out there
on the grass the XV men of Wales put their arms round one another's shoulders. Their inflated torsos bulged and rolling like bald
Welsh hillscapes, they look up towards a middle-distant heaven and
draw on the moral sustenance offered by a whole stadium singing
'Gwlaad! Gwlaaad!' Country! Country! The choir marches off with
the band to their corner tunnel. The teams line up. As usual I
expect to hear the bilingual exhortation for the boys from the
Tannoy. But the source of those stirring words is obedient to the
command from high up in the Welsh Rugby Union. There is no
'Ymlaen, Cymru! Come on, Wales!' I am sitting next to Rhys the
Voiceless.

On 20 September 1977, fifty years after they married in the Capel
Yr Annibynwyr in Lammas Street, my grandparents celebrated
their golden wedding. All Carmarthen made its way up to Mount
Hill for the party. My main memory of the gathering is of a short,
middle-aged guest collaring my father during drinks before lunch.
    'Dr Rees,' he said, 'I got a terrible problem with my back.' There
was a lot of this for Dr Rees whenever he returned home. In those
days particular respect was reserved for doctors who plied their
trade up in London. This stuff was discussed in the car on the way
back home. 'Dr Rees, I got a terrible problem with my back' became
a catchphrase – English shorthand for classic Welsh hypochondria.
How we roared.
    But then not long after, and without the slightest complaint,
Bert lost his sight. Near total blindness didn't keep him from the

golf course. His friends parked him in front of the ball and he would stoically make his way round as if his disability simply didn't exist. A Christmas or two later Dorothy, now nearly eighty, kept slipping away to the bathroom and staggering back a few minutes later as if nothing was wrong. Being glued to the snooker table, we didn't notice much, but within days her gallstones had been removed in London and a woman who had spent a lifetime cooking in the luxuriant Welsh way was put on a penitential dairy-free diet. Again, there was no self-pity.

We went to Wales for one last Christmas, driving to a local carvery to guzzle all we could eat. It wasn't the same. I wonder whether having to spend the following Christmas with us in England wasn't the end of Bert. By April, at the age of eighty-four and preceded by all of his eight siblings, he had died.

I took the train from Oxford to Carmarthen for the funeral. The small diesel chugger from Swansea rounded the corner into the Tywi estuary, yards from where Bert and Dorothy had taken their small boys to the beach before the war. This was my first journey into Wales under my own steam. I was dimly conscious that, from now on, I'd be seeing it through my own eyes.

St David's was an Anglican barn thrown up at high speed in the 1830s, its spire hurtling importantly to the heavens, in order to give the Church of England a more visible presence in Carmarthen as people defected in droves to Nonconformity. We went to the front row, five Reeses each put through five anglicising years at Harrow School. Behind us it felt as if the whole town was there, arrayed in black. His Grace the Archbishop of Wales read the lesson. I remember feebly attempting the one hymn that was in Welsh, the language Bert didn't speak with his wife and sons. Light peered dimly through an impressive stained-glass window behind the altar, donated by my grandparents in 1962: Christ in majesty surrounded by images of music and dancing. It must have cost a fortune. But then Bertram Rees had done very well for himself until a crash at Lloyds took much of it away. A cortège of black cars prowled through Carmarthenshire countryside in the rain towards the crematorium in Narberth.

The next day Dorothy decided to sell Mount Hill. The contents were duly auctioned off but for the most treasured items of furniture, and she moved into a bungalow with a small garden and a view of the Tywi Valley. She then disbursed many of her financial assets as gifts, and in order to prevent the recipients from having to pay tax on them she determined to survive for the next seven years. So at eighty-three she took up an exercise regime which involved walking around a small circuit in her garden for a mile and a half every day. She kept a check on the distances with a pedometer. If it was raining, she'd do the even smaller circuit inside. She continued walking in circles for five years until, nearing ninety, she started falling over and was persuaded into a home. But she more than met her target of surviving those seven years. Steady tapping breaks the stone.

DOUF! A rock-hard shoulder thwacks head on into my right thigh. I can feel myself toppling backwards and brace for impact with the earth. OUGH! My coccyx crashes into the turf. I tense and my tautened neck whiplashes on landing. CRICK. That hurt. A lot.

Not that I haven't been warned.

'Bydd e anodd heno.' It's a text from Rhys the Voice. It'll be hard tonight. 'Physical iawn am awr.' An hour's worth of jerks. 'Llawer o contact.' The interpolation of English words in these dire predictions suggests that Welsh doesn't have the vocab to encompass the sheer ghastliness of what's in store. Needless to say, my feet turn to ice. But I am in the area and Clwb Rygbi Cymry Caerdydd are meeting for their regular Tuesday evening training at the university grounds in Llanrhymney. I drive through Cardiff as if to an execution. My own.

There's no sign of Rhys the Voice as young Welshmen reeking of ointment clatter in studs across the floor and out into the floodlit night. Time ticks by. I study the noticeboard intensely, twice. I don't think I've felt this out of place since ...

'Sh'mae, Jasper! Ti'n barod am y sesiwm?' Enter Rhys the Voice, club chairman, full of the usual complement of beans. I'm not particularly ready, no, but I do seem to be changing into the appropriate gear, although how appropriate it is to wear a Welsh rugby shirt in this company is a moot point.

We jog out onto the pitch. A wooden H towers overhead as we gather, perhaps forty of us, in a circle and listen to a head coach address us in Welsh then English. I don't know the average age of the veterans, but no one else here seems to be in their forties. It emerges that Clwb Rygbi Cymry Caerdydd is under a cloud after the first team the previous Saturday snatched feckless defeat from the jaws of victory. We are to be punished with a gruelling workout, even innocent parties such as myself. We fan along the try line and start jogging up towards the twenty-two. Then back. Then up again. Then back faster. Then to the halfway. And so on. Jogging, sprinting, walking, breathing, stretching – this could go on all night and I'd pass with flying colours.

Our next drill involves finding a partner and scrumming down opposite him. I select Rhys the Voice. We lock shoulders and in turn try to use our upper-body strength to twist the other out of the horizontal. Upper-body strength and me are not often found in the same sentence, but Rhys the Voice is half a head shorter than me, and besides, I'm determined not to look like some floppy-sleeved nancy from over the Severn. So I put a lot into it and come up unbelittled if ever so slightly twingey in the neck area. A side effect, I tell myself. Ignore. Go with this feeling of macho empowerment.

We gather in the middle. Two blokes in their twenties are pulled out of the group and one is asked to tackle the other, who is stationary. He piles in, grabs his quarry round the thighs, lifts him off his feet and dumps him upside down. Traditionally known as the spear tackle. The perpetrator is roundly chastised for dangerous play. If someone does that to me I'll be more than twingey in the neck area, I think, as a co-coach demonstrates how to tackle safely: shoulder to the thigh, head on the hip.

We are instructed to form groups of six and mark out a square of five metres by five. On the whistle, one player in the square has to put in as many tackles as possible in thirty seconds while the rest provide a moving target. I start jogging about while a rhinoceros in shorts charges around, crashing into moving objects. Thump. Down goes one of the five. Up. Sprint. Thump. Another one. I try to veer out of his eyeline. Thump. Another one down. But sooner or later he's going to catch my eye. Up. And I am conspicuously wearing red. Sprint. So far he's got three of the others. It's my turn any min– THUMP.

My instinct is to stay on the deck and gently recover. However, it wouldn't do to lie about looking wounded so I roll onto my front, push myself very slowly onto all fours, gingerly stand and re-enter the square. The others are still being biffed by the rhino. When the whistle blows it's now the turn of a compact, bow-legged unit who gets me twice; after him a tearaway whippet whose tackles make up for in snap what they lack in heft.

On the grounds that I'd look like a wimp to put off my turn till last, I volunteer to go next. I've not tackled anyone for the best part of three decades. Even Elgan Rees avoided tackling where possible.

The whistle goes. I look around the square and size up the options. Five young Welshmen are circling. A cheetah must feel something like this upon sighting a pack of wildebeest. A cheetah approaching retirement, with arthritic knees. The whippet is closest, so I have at him with maximum force, shoulder on the thigh, head on hip, and wait for him to crash to the floor. He is conveniently light, so only a bit of extra shove finds him toppling, and me with him. THONK. Hitting the hard earth is slightly less painful when someone under you is cushioning the blow. I lever myself up and look for more prey. Another player is passing so I thwack into him. Down he goes. Up I get. This is actually quite bracing. I can feel my testosterone levels surging. I don't know why I didn't do more of this at school. The rhino is in the corner of the square. Time to take him down. A three-yard sprint and BIFF! My arms barely reach around his tree-trunk legs. He barely budges. Tumble, dammit, you lump. He's immovable. I dig my studs in, drive with all my middle-aged might and begrudgingly he sinks like a slow-mo sack of spuds. I get up and keep going. Hit. Down. Up. Sprint. I've already done more tackles than in my first term at prep school. Hit. Down. Up. Sprint. Surely Mr Youle, now deceased, would look upon me more favourably. The tackle board would record five, six, seven new *t*s, some of them *T*s. Hit. Down. When the whistle blows I'm on the floor, panting heavily.

'Faint?' calls out the co-coach. How many tackles? 'Rhywun yn well na deg?' Anyone better than ten? *Wyth* for me. Eight.

When the rota begins again we are tasked with improving on our previous score. I ratchet up the intensity and hurl myself at a queue of bodies. Hit. The lungs are starting to feel it. Down. And the right shoulder. Up. But I keep going. Sprint. The rhino consents to keel over first time. Hit. Just as I'm wondering if the whistle will ever go, it does and I've scored ten. I am starting to feel like quite the meathead. If it moves I'll fly at it so I will. Bring it on! Testosterone now at danger levels. Bring it all on!

We jog up towards the tryline and form into more queues of six. This time, taking it in turns, we have to run from the touchline to the five-metre line, crouch, then sprint and crunch hard into a tall yellow rectangular crash pad held up by a volunteer. After the first crash you retreat three metres and, at the call, crash into the pad again. I await my turn. It seems perfectly doable. After all, a crash pad can't hurt you, can it? I reach the front. And sprint to the line. Crouch. Sprint. SMASH! The crash pad, and the volunteer, take the impact of a monstrous hit. Or as monstrous as I can manage. I shuffle back and await the call. Go! SMASH!

'Da iawn,' says the crash-pad holder. This goes on for ten minutes. In all I manage a dozen or so crashes. If only I'd been this aggressive at rugby as a schoolboy, I think, as the head coach asks for two teams of six to line up against each other. One has the ball and, passing it up and down the line, has to try and break through the other team's defences. Suddenly the pretence is over. A dozen young Welsh men are clattering into one another for real. *Llawer o* contact. One of them is the giant Hywel. Physical *iawn*. I suddenly decide that my body might object if after twenty-eight years of no impact it is suddenly asked to take on this extra burden. I've done enough for now. I can congratulate myself. Project Wales has taken a vast step forward. I shower, wash, dry, dress and get into the car feeling thoroughly pleased. This is it, I think. I am one of the boys. Finally.

The next morning there is not a single muscle about my person that hasn't succumbed to paralysis. It is virtually impossible to get out of bed. Or sit. Or stand. Or walk. I move like a lobotomised Frankenstein's monster. My joints have locked. It's as if I've been caught in rockfall. The worst of it is not the arms and shoulders, back, coccyx, rump (which *really* aches), thighs, knees or ankles.

The real problem is in a more vital part of the body. My neck. Something feels badly wrenched in there. I suddenly realise why rugby players have necks the width of barrels, to go with all their other pumped-up musculature. It's chainmail.

My phone beeps. A text from Rhys the Voice.

He names a date for the codgers' match two days before my forty-sixth birthday. Only a couple of weekends hence. The vets play very infrequently. All things being equal, this is likely to be my main chance.

The next morning I can't move either. I wonder whether my body, which is after all my temple, is trying to tell me something. And even if it isn't, I know someone who is: an email arrives from my parents.

'We think your intention to play rugger is not only foolhardy but downright stupid. Please reconsider.' Without waiting to be asked, Dr Rees has ventured an opinion. Trust him to say 'rugger'. I can't move on the third day either. By the fifth I am in negotiation with myself. If I play only half the match, I halve the risk. If I trot on with twenty minutes to go, so much the better. Even with ten minutes I can at least say I've played rugby in Wales. But in the small dark hours fears start to assail me of getting ransacked in a seething maul and having my unarmoured leg snapped like a dead twig or being spear-tackled by a psychopathic wing who doesn't like the sound of my English accent. My visualisations are all about survival, not glory. But I must do it. Against medical advice. And against that of Elgan Rees. Who played for Wales. 'Don't take the risk,' he said.

With five days to go, snowstorms are massing on the east coast of England and Scotland. The unseasonal weather races west and smothers all Wales. I text Rhys the Voice, ostensibly to ask for directions to tomorrow's game, in reality to seek confirmation that, while I was always willing, I won't actually have to put my body on the line after all. A reply comes back by return.

'Dim gem! Eira!' (*Eira* = snow.) Another cancellation. Is it just my body which doesn't think it's a good idea to play? Is a guardian angel trying to prevent my participation? If I really pushed it, if I really hustled, I could presumably get myself onto another team sheet. But I feel as if I've dodged a bullet with my name on it. There is no point in pretending. I cannot duck the unWelsh truth about myself: Dr Rees, I got a terrible problem with my backbone.

7

Cystadlu = Compete

'Restoring the Welsh language in Wales is nothing less
than a revolution. It is only through revolutionary means
that we can succeed.'

Saunders Lewis (1962)

WHEN MY GRANDMOTHER could eventually no longer drive, she
gave me her car. It was beige. And somewhat of the old school,
being a Simca saloon with plush red upholstery, a handbrake in the
dash and a petrol cap behind the rear number plate. It felt like an
Eastern European taxi.

No car in the history of motoring can have had two more con-
trasting owners. She was a slightly flappy driver, if memory serves,
but ever so careful. I remember racing away from Carmarthen on a
golden Sunday evening behind the wheel of my new motor at the
age of twenty, feeling enriched by new possibilities.

While staying with friends in the Black Mountains, I had to
collect a latecomer from Newport station. Two of us set out on an
icy night. My passenger and I decided to kill time in conventional
OCD style by compiling sports lists. We fixed on first-class Welsh
rugby clubs. A mile into our journey we had already listed Llanelli,
Cardiff, Swansea, Neath, Bridgend, Aberavon, Pontypool,

Pontypridd, Maesteg and South Wales Police when one of us – I forget which – proudly introduced the untoppable, championship-clinching decider.

'Ebbw Vale.'

At which point, because I had not really been concentrating on the road, I veered round a left bend a little too vigorously, skidded on sheet ice, slammed through a thickish hedge and came to rest, *Italian Job* style, in precarious mid-air. I was forced to ring up my grandmother and explain what I had done to her car. She was all too forgiving.

So I associate Ebbw Vale with my inner halfwit. It's not a good association to take into Welsh Learner of the Year, being held this year in Ebbw Vale. Or Glyn Ebwy, as we say in Welsh. This is my moment. I'm competing as a Welshman against other Welshmen and Welshwomen.

It's not quite pissing down. Rain dribbles dismissively onto the windscreen, as if holding back the monsoon for later. I've come down from the northern end of the valley, along the ridge fringing the top of the old coalfield. I drive past formerly prosperous towns which once powered the British Empire, each at the head of its own valley: Aberdare, Merthyr Tydfil, Tredegar – they turn a hardened face to spitting skies. Coniferous forestation smothers the slopes hereabouts. Where it doesn't, the hills are scorched bald, purple heather scattered like alopecia.

I hear about Learner of the Year when nosing about the BBC Cymru website. Four people had got through to the previous final. There were pictures of them, all wearing smiles. You could click and find a paragraph in quotation marks, with a helpful translation underneath. They were all resident in Wales, I noted. And had learned Welsh for the usual reasons: needed it for work, or lived with a Welsh speaker. Somewhere inside me, envy fluttered its mean little wings. I bet they didn't write those blurbs themselves. A fiver says they had help, that the syntax police swooped and sprayed it with Cymrifying anti-toxins. I wish one of those pictures were of me, grinning false-modestly in contemporary casuals, semaphoring to the world how marvellous I am at Welsh. Well, it could be, couldn't it? I could enter, couldn't I? I could do that. It's just a question of application.

The application form can be found on the National Eisteddfod website. Needless to say, this corner of cyberspace is in Welsh. Rather official Welsh, cluttered with pedantic grammatical formalities and long abstract nouns ending in *-aeth*. *Cystadleuaeth* = competition. *Gwybodaeth* = information. To be honest it's all kind of a bit Gree ... Ooh look, you can click on that tab there and get the whole site in English. The devil on my shoulder urges me to click. No, says my Project Wales voice, that would be *very wrong*. Cliiiiick, whispers the first voice sulphurously. Reader, I click. Instantly, the entire site of the National Eisteddfod, the site which celebrates Wales and Welshness and the Welsh language, transmogrifies into the language of world domination. It's a jolly easy read. There's bags of digestible info about categories of competition, rules and regs of entry, deadlines, addresses. I am hoovering it up, like moreish polyunsaturates that corrode your stomach wall. After three web pages I start to feel uneasy, then queasy, then actually soiled. This is the language which once set out to smother Welsh into actual extinction. I must return to Welsh at once. If I don't, how can I claim to be learning? Click. We are back among pedantries and abstractions.

'Wyt ti wedi dysgu Cymraeg?' it asks in large jaunty italicised white letters on a hot-flush pink background. The tense is ambiguous. It could mean 'Have you learned Welsh?' or 'Have you been learning Welsh?' They don't draw a distinction, so I'm not sure of the answer. Yes, I have been learning Welsh. No, I have not learned Welsh. Not yet.

'Beth am gystadlu?' Soft mutation: how about gompeting? This competition, it explains, is open to anyone over eighteen who has been learning Welsh. The preliminary round happens in the spring, and something something chance to chat and something with a team of judges. I don't understand it all. Five will be chosen to compete in the final during the National Eisteddfod week. There's £300 in it for the winner, and £100 for the finalists, not to mention a year's subscription to *Golwg* magazine.

I fill out the form, and set down to compose a supporting document of 300 words. I quite like writing in Welsh. You get as long as you want, a dictionary, the Internet, a chance to scope your work for errors. And you don't have to answer someone firing mutations at you with a self-loading rifle. So I tell the story – of the two trips a year to Carmarthen, of my grandparents' abandonment of Welsh as the marital language, how the language has reseeded itself in my uncle and now, maybe, in me. The supporting document is probably chockful of cock-ups – erratic conjugations and rogue consonants, omitted mutations and misattributed plurals. But it is sincere and enthusiastic; and it's undeniably in Welsh. I post it, and email the Eisteddfod office in Wrexham asking for acknowledgement of receipt. 'Disgwyr o'r Blwyddyn', I type carefully into the subject field. A few days later a reply lands in my inbox, confirming receipt. The subject field has been subtly edited to 'Dysgwr y Flwyddyn'. Clear subtext. 'Get it right, plonker. It's not "Lerners from the Year". Don't expect to get far if you can't spell. Or master the basic tenets of the genitive case in Welsh. Muppet.'

I've been practising Welsh all week. A session with James, a lot of BBC Radio Cymru on the website. I've been mainlining vocab too, like I used to at school before an exam. It doesn't feel enough.

I am visited by an urgent need to warm up my Welsh before I go in. I text Rhys the Voice: competing in Dysgwr y Flwyddyn, *beth am ymarfer*? How about some practice? While I wait for a reply I get out the little red book and go through more vocab. Thanks partly to *Harri Potter*, partly to Nant Gwrtheyrn, I have ingested some random and frequently arcane vocabulary. I know the Welsh for 'to ramble on', 'to dart' or 'flit', for 'a bit of a lad' and 'climate change'. I know the word for 'noble' and 'science fiction'. Will I ever use any of it? My phone buzzes. It's Rhys the Voice: 'Can't,' he texts in Welsh. 'Working at the stadiwm. Pob lwc! [good luck!]'

I scroll down my list of contacts. Leighton? Might be humiliating if I can't understand him over the phone. I try Catrin, the only Welsh speaker I know in London. She texts back in Welsh that she's busy at the mo but some time next week?

'Too late! I'm competing in forty-five minutes.'

'Fyc!' she replies, then adds that her Welsh at the moment is *yn grap* (= crap – mutated). I ring, and we have a nice chat. Its function, we both tacitly understand, is to stiffen my collapsible vertebrae. Cat compliments my accent, and tells me how well I've done to get so far so fast. I lap it up. At this juncture I need to believe.

'Pob lwc!' she says. It's showtime.

The competition is taking place in a school. There's a quiz in progress, questions in Welsh with piecemeal English translations. The front two rows are occupied by happy-looking types. Other Welsh learners and their families, presumably. I seem to be the only person who hasn't dragged along an entire carful of children. It would have been nice to bring a daughter or two. I've tried to get them interested in Project Wales. Right from the off I drummed their quarter-Welshness into them with missionary persistence. 'You're supporting the team in red,' I'd advise two small girls fresh out of nappies whenever the Six Nations was on. One of them was even given a Welsh middle name to put in her passport: Mair, Welsh for Mary. They've been driven over the border often – once upon a time to visit their great-grandmother, latterly their monastic uncle Teilo, but also to take the air in Carmarthenshire, Pembrokeshire. They've been up Cadair Idris. Unfortunately, they've enjoyed a bit too much sun in other parts. They associate Wales with walking, walking with effort, effort with reluctance, and reluctance with saying no to stuff. Principally, inducements to visit Wales.

Plus they've got their own oral exams to sit, more important ones like A levels and the International Baccalaureate. So I'm on my own.

I feel as if I've trespassed into some sort of pre-established environment. These people all look naturalised, as if they've lived here for ever, even though they can only have got here this morning. It's like when you turn up on holiday somewhere, but for some enforced reason a day later than everyone else, who by the time you arrive have already scoped the parameters of this new world, colonised it with routine. This, they say, is how we do things here. We *know*. We have long experience. Longer than you anyway.

A woman with a clipboard approaches busily. She ticks off my half-Welsh name on a long list. I'm at the bottom, the last one unaccounted for. 'Da iawn.' Ten minutes before my interview, she explains, I'll be taken upstairs. I should settle in, get a *paned* (cuppa), enjoy the *cwis* (quiz). Obediently, I edge towards the edge of the raked seating and park myself in a red-plastic bucket seat.

A woman in the row behind asks me in Welsh if I'm here to compete – *cystadlu*.

'Ydw,' I say. Yes I am. This is another quirk of Welsh: they don't say yes in Welsh if they can help it, or no. Yes I am, they say, or no you don't. Yes we would. No they will not have. The tense is immaterial: if the question contains a verb, so should the answer. Are you competing? Yes I am. Are you nervous? Yes I am. (One is cacking oneself, to be specific.) Don't worry, she advises. They're very nice.

They are the two judges. In Welsh they call them *beirniaid* – *barn* being the word for judgement or opinion. But I can't help thinking of them as examiners. Sorry, but a situation in which you go into a room for ten minutes to answer questions in a language you have by no means fully conquered and then discover at the end whether you've passed or not is, for my money, an exam. The last time I sat an oral exam was twenty-eight years ago. If memory serves, they've never not been problematic.

No, insists the woman, it's just a gentle chat. I ask her where she's from. *O ble dych chi'n dod?* was one of the first sentences I ever learned in Welsh. She's from Bridgend, she says, and points to her name on the list of competitors we've all been given. To kill time I peruse it studiously. There are twenty-nine of us this year, apparently the largest entry ever. Among adult learners, Welsh is on the up. I peruse the long column of names. They are all very Welsh-looking: lots of Ieuans and Angharads and Hywels, sundry Joneses and Llewellyns and ap-Morgans.

At the bottom it says, 'Jasper Rees, Llundain'. The familiar relief: at least my surname doesn't look out of place.

I assume I'm the loner here, the one who has travelled furthest. After their names it says where they're from – in Welsh naturally: Aberteifi, Caergybi, Llantrisant, Y Gelli, Pen-y-Bont, Yr Ariannin. Oh. That'll be Argentina. He must be one of the Patagonian diaspora. Welsh speakers are tuppence a dozen down there, I tell myself, thanks to the nineteenth-century migration to a remote pocket of South America. Rhys the Voice once went on a rugby tour there and, while failing to find anyone who spoke English, couldn't move for Welsh speakers. I look around the room for a vaguely Hispanic-looking learner. More intriguingly, there's even one from Gwlad Belg – Belgium.

To kill more time I look down the order of play:

9.30–1.00: Preliminary tests. Everyone will have a ten-minute conversation with two judges and at the end of the morning they will choose a shortlist to go on to the semi-final round in the afternoon.

1.00–1.30: Lunch (*cinio* – one of those Latin-root words that helpfully link Welsh to the etymological mainland).

1.30–4.45: The shortlist of competitors to have a second interview of fifteen minutes each with three judges.

4.45: We release the names of the five who will go through to the final round in Glyn Ebwy – Ebbw Vale – on 4 August.

And then there's some stuff about 4 August, competing at the National Eisteddfod and announcing the winner and giving him or her the prize, interviews with the press, etc. But we are getting ahead of ourselves. The question is this: am I Welsh enough to get past lunchtime?

'Jasper?' The clipboard woman taps me on the shoulder. Would I like to follow her? Not particularly, but I get up anyway and trudge in her wake. It's not just me. There's a tall bloke called Dai. We are herded into a small office and asked to wait. Dai, who's from somewhere off the M4, says he took up Welsh for work: something to do with youth groups if my internal translator is functioning correctly. He seems alarmingly fluent. I ask him how long he's been learning, and it's well north of three years. Great.

Two extremely jolly ladies keep popping in and out, beaming reps of the National Eisteddfod. I ask them how many contestants they had last year. Half as many, it turns out: only fifteen. Among adult learners, on this circumstantial evidence, Welsh is twice as popular as it was a year ago. A comparable take-up pattern of constant annual multiplication will bring about total bilingualism in sixteen years. I've just done the maths. No wonder the reps are so jolly.

We chat about this and that – why we are learning, where we come from. London raises an eyebrow or two. There aren't many opportunities to speak Welsh there, I make a point of saying, just in case either of them is involved in the judging process. There's no point, it occurs to me, in not letting them know that some of us are operating under a handicap. The evidence is stacking up that Dysgwr y Flwyddyn is not a level playing field. It's not some gentle sub-GCSE paddle in the shallow end for dilettantes and newbies. People who've been at it for literally aeons can enter – who have to use Welsh at work every day and/or who are married to a fluent Welsh speaker. I've been learning for fifteen months. Count them. *Un deg pump*. It is now dawning on me, in this airless anteroom, that I am about to commit an act of hubristic folly. Long tall Dai sits opposite me trotting out lovely looping Welsh sentences without a care. He's like one of those natural sportsmen you sometimes get elegantly thrashed by at, for example, golf. The energy is minimal, the efficiency maximal, the result a flawless mechanism built for economy and ease. Dai's sentences land on the green, near the pin, as planned, as required, and this they do every time. His mind is able to translate thought into word.

I tee off my sentences honourably intending to fetch up some-where over there, having travelled in a smooth arc that bisects the air. I address the thought in my head, eye on the ball, check the tense, right arm locked, think about the object, keep my head straight, plan for mutations, feet firmly planted, watch out for that relative clause ahead, ease in and whoops you've used the wrong verb there and that's a declining preposition you've just omitted to deploy correctly and wrong plural, you jerk, *wrong plural*, call yourself a Welshman?!?

My Welsh lives off the fairway. I spend a lot of my time scratching around in the tufted undergrowth.

'O ble dych chi'n dod?' The question comes from an angular man in his thirties with long swept-back hair and a slight bulge to his green eyes.

'Llundain,' I say. My answer is toploaded with heavy implication. At the foot of the rainbow in the east, mate. That's where I come from. The dim and distant mouth of the M4. I am the outsider here.

'A chi?' And you? Might as well ask him. He has a thick accent I can't quite place. He's obviously another contestant with the built-in advantage of living and breathing the language in his daily round. Anglesey maybe? Somewhere impenetrable in Mid Wales?

'Gwlad Belg,' he says. Ah. So this would be the Belgian contestant. Now he mentions it he does have a Flemish tinge to him. He looks like he's walked woodenly off a canvas by Memling or Van Eyck. It's difficult to suppress a faint annoyance. Why the bloody hell would a Belgian learn Welsh? Back to Ghent with you, Lowlander. I'm all set to ask when one of the ladies pokes her head around the door and summons him to his interview. All eyes and elbows, he grabs a bulky black briefcase and exits with a friendly wave.

Maybe I should pipe down about London.

There's another bloke in the room from Dorset, short, wiry and ginger. My accent bitch-slaps his salty yokel burr. Yes! Ha! This is one contestant I'll wipe the floor with. Easy. Competition brings out one's loveliness ever so. Come on! Let's do this now! I must pump myself up. None of this bile foams out of my actual mouth.

I'm all modest charm and beaming politeness. We're all in this together – that's the public position. But these ugly Darwinian feelings run free in the pastures of my mind. I want every other contestant to seize up in front of the *beirniaid*. If we were confined to a desert island I would want them all to be struck mute, even if it counterproductively depleted the number of Welsh speakers. Just so long as I could go through to the next round.

It's just me and Dai now. Dai says something. I must keep up this confidence. So I nod cleverly. I am your equal, I think. He looks at me expectantly for an answer. Can't he tell I'm nodding in agreement? Oh sod it, I'm going to have to admit I didn't understand. So much for Darwin. I'm way down the evolutionary chain of command. He repeats the question. It's the basic one about my Welsh roots.

'Wel,' I say, bartering for time. I've noticed I've been saying this a lot. 'Wel.' I'm not quite sure where it came from. It seems to have sprouted in my speech like a weed between paving stones. There's no lexical reason for it to be there. It's not even Welsh. It's 'well' but without the double *l*. Probably its function is to suggest intelligence.

'Wel,' I say. 'Mae fy nhad yn dod o Gaerfyrddin.' A perfect sentence, please note. Not a mutation out of place. I learned it off by heart about a year ago and have been trotting it out ever since. My father comes from Carmarthen. Not that you'd know it to meet him, I don't add. I'm all set to expand on the fascinating theme of deracination when Dai is summoned to the examiners.

It's only me now, and the two ladies who have quit flitting in and out and sat down. They have a satisfied air about them of having almost completed their morning's work. Twenty-nine contestants. Imagine how it will be next year. Who knows what geographical oddities it will produce? Lest we forget, Welsh has travelled. There must have been a Welshman on one of those voyages of exploration that discovered a flightless seabird that lives in large waddling flocks on the rim of the southern seas. Why else would penguin – *pen gwyn* – mean white head?

Talking of the southern hemisphere, this reminds me. It's a long way to come for a ten-minute interview, I suggest. One of the jolly ladies asks me what I mean. Patagonia is hardly next door to Ebbw Vale, I volunteer.

'Mae e'n cystadlu ar y ffon,' one of them explains. I nod. It's all being done telephonically. There's a pause. In which one of them thrusts a leaflet in my direction.

'Beth am ddod i gwrs Cymraeg?' This time my heart really does actively sink like a stone. She's suggesting I come on a Welsh language course. Is my Welsh that bad? But I'm here competing in Dysgwr y Flwyddyn, I want to say. I've done quite enough learning, thank you very much. I've completed the second-highest course available at the National Language School in Nant Gwrtheyrn. How dare she undermine me? How dare she cut me off at the knees? It's so unfair.

I take the leaflet and pretend to study it. The ladies talk among themselves. I decide to commune with myself. To enter the zone. I used to be good at exams, I remind myself. Passed a bunch of them with flying colours. If not oral ones. I'm a writer, I think. Can't we just write the exam? *Scribo ergo sum*, as someone once nearly said. Or in Welsh: *Dw i'n ysgrifennu, felly* (*felly* = so = therefore) … And then what? Marvellous. I don't know how to translate 'I am' into Welsh. *Dw i*? Sounds a bit incomplete. *Dw i'n bod*? But that means 'I am being'. I am writing therefore I am being. Ridiculous. I would so like this language to unveil just a few more of its secrets, preferably in the next few minutes.

'Jasper?'

It's time. Enough. I get up and follow her out of the anteroom. And into a classroom.

The two *beirniaid* are waiting. There's a man and a woman. The

man comes welcomingly round the table to shake my hand. I introduce myself, although needless to say I don't catch any names. I
never do anyway, even in English, but on this occasion one's mind
is fixed on nether things. The shallowness of one's breathing, for
example, plus maybe a hint of neurosis in lower localities. They are
both in their fifties, both dressed in smart Saturday casuals. As
usual I am wearing my red Welsh rugby shirt, just in case it feels
like bringing me some luck.

'Braf cwrdd â chi,' I say. They have lovely Welsh faces, open with
an undertow of melancholy. It is indeed nice to meet them. They
smile in welcome, but without any suggestion that this is a laughing matter. We've got a language to support here.

I compose myself. They compose themselves. I notice I have
crossed my legs clubbably. We are all of us composed. Without
waiting for permission my body seems to have decided that this
will be a cosy fireside chat. I'm projecting an image with which my
bowels, for example, are not in sympathy. Placidly I look at them
as they go through the business of putting on reading glasses,
looking at papers, removing reading glasses. The male *beirniad*
furrows his brow and speaks.

Tell us why you decided to learn Welsh, he asks me. I am able to
translate fluently. A good sign. Everything should flow from here. I
take a breath and …

'Wel.' My first word of Welsh in my Learner of the Year interview
is English. In a driving test this would be marked against you. But
once is surely permissible. I reapply my foot to the accelerator pedal.

'Mae fy nhad yn dod o Gaerfyrddin.'

They raise their judging eyebrows in a show of interest. I have
embarked on the familiar narrative. But now what? Very occasionally my staggering arrogance is revealed to me with the utmost clarity.
My reports at school always parroted the word. Clever, they said, but

arrogant. Report after report, term after term. Thinks a lot of himself. It's a function of your arrogance that of course you don't believe them – they really don't know what they're talking about – and then suddenly thirty years later you realise that they knew all too well. Ever since I decided to enter this competition many months ago, I knew that this would be the first question. What else do you ask the adult learner of a minority language? The slight bummer – no, the miserable truth – is that I never quite got round to composing the answer. I could have filled the next minute or two with a beautifully crafted peroration, full of charming tangents and persuasive digressions. The chance was there to scatter complex polysyllabic words about the place, like throw cushions. I have after all swallowed a dictionary. 'Ti wedi llyncu geiriadur,' they said back at the Nant. *Llyncu* is a lovely word for swallowing: you can hear the gulp in it. There are an awful lot of words in my little red book: consumed hook, line and sinker, learned and laboriously relearned. But somehow I've never quite got round to arranging them into the speech needed right here, right now. And now it's too late. Here's one I didn't prepare earlier. I am having to rely instead on something I've always relied on: my belief, embedded and enhanced over many years of professionally winging it, that I'm sufficiently bright that all will be fine. That theory has occasionally held water.

Not in Welsh.

My opening statement isn't entire hogwash. But I speak Welsh at a slow ramble – the correct grammar won't gush forth any quicker – and as I listen to myself I can still hear the tentative toddler taking its first steps, bumping directionlessly into things. Out the relevant facts stammer, the building blocks of my story, but the whole speech is full of false starts, hesitations, culs-de-sac. I mention, for example, that I have two brothers, and then find that I have nothing extra to add. The bit about celebrating as we crossed the Severn Bridge would have gone down a treat, but I suddenly realise that I never learned the word for 'to cheer'. On the hoof I have to make do with *mwynhau*, to enjoy. I tail off with something about wanting to rediscover – *ailddarganfod*, though I've no idea if such a word exists – my roots.

The *beirniaid* nod inscrutably. They're thinking either there's no such word or he's swallowed a dictionary. Next question: does anyone in my family speak Welsh? Ah, I know this one.

'Mae fy ewythr yn siarad Cymraeg.' My uncle is always helpful here, a great icebreaker. Though I never quite know how to pronounce *ewythr*. He's a monk, I explain. Not a lot of families can boast one of those. You can't get a lot more Welsh than a Welsh-speaking Cistercian monk for an uncle. He lives on Ynys Bŷr, I expand. I hope they notice that my mastery of Welsh place-names is confident. It's off the coast near Dinbych-y-Pysgod. They nod. They don't need me to tell them that Caldey's next to Tenby. His Welsh is rather formal, I explain. *Ffurfiol*.

I remember to tell them that my grandparents spoke Welsh, albeit not to each other. Albeit I don't use the Welsh for albeit. It's good to reflect on these things, I think, as I launch on a discursive socio-historical tour of the forces which governed such choices between the wars (*rhwng y rhyfeloedd* = between the wars). English was simply the language of the house – the parents, the children, the widowed grandmother who lived under her son-in-law's roof for a quarter of a century, the, er, servants. Damn, I wish I didn't know the Welsh for servant. But I do. Everyone sees the word *gwasanaethau* on the M4. Services. Servant is *gwas*. I might get marked down for having elitist forebears.

Across the table and through their bifocals the *beirniaid* consult my supporting document, photocopied in duplicate. The sight is unnerving. I suddenly can't remember what I wrote. Was it all

complete crap? The possibility distracts. How much grammar did I
cock up? It's not natural submitting your conversation to examiners,
I think, however lovely their melancholy Welsh faces. The consensus
around the table is that we're all adults. The accepted pretence is that
this is a chat among equals. I am second to none in adopting an air of
breezy social confidence. But we all know the truth.

I suddenly remember what I wanted to say about my brothers. I
want to say that one of them is a chip off the old block. Although
how do you actually say that? Important to divest oneself of this
anglicised lexicon, this Saxon persiflage.

'Mae fy mhrawd' – excellent use of nasal mutation, though one
says so oneself – 'yn bod Sais go iawn.' He's a real Englishman. For
example, I add, he supports England – *cefnogi Lloegr*.

'A chi?' They want to know who I support.

'Does dim dwywaith,' I say – there is no doubt. My first collo-
quialism. Tick. 'Dw i'n mynd i'r Stadiwm Mileniwm trwy'r amser.'
I'm always at the Millennium, me. Oh yes, practically live there, *dw
i*. It's important to impress these *beirniaid* that there's a broad span
to my Welshness. It's not all aspirate mutations and periphrastic
verbs. I have met my rugby uncle Elgan Rees, I want to say, but it
seems improper to boast. Plus they're probably his personal friends.
Everyone in Wales knows everyone else.

'A ble dych chi'n dysgu Cymraeg?' This from the female *beirniad*,
who, without wishing to stereotype anyone, may not wish to dwell
on rugby. She wants to know where I learn my Welsh.

'Wel …' This tick is losing its charm. 'Dw i ddim yn siwr.' I'm
not sure. I can't believe I've just said that. Where on earth did that
come from? I know *exactly* where I started learning Welsh. I wonder
if I'm trying to sound enigmatic. For some reason. Not a good idea
in Welsh; there are no two ways. What I mean, I tell them, is that
I did learn for a term at City Lit, but then I stopped.

'Pam?' Why? Suspicion in their voices.

Because I was getting ahead of the rest of the class, I explain. Turns out I am boasting after all. I was learning on compact disc – *cryno ddisg* – and hoovering up a lot of vocabulary and so decided to have private lessons. They weren't really lessons, I add, more like conversations. The *beirniaid*'s faces are illegible. Behind the masks I feel certain they're thinking, who is this joker? But it's been very hard learning in London (*anodd iawn iawn*), I make sure to stress again. London has its Welsh speakers, but there's not much chance to practise. And even when I come to Wales, I say, you can never be sure that the person in the shop or the pub you address in Welsh will understand you.

This is shameless fishing for sympathy. It seems the utterest folly to imagine the *beirniaid* won't see clean through it. But there's just a chance they won't.

They want to know where I meet for conversation.

'Y Canolfan Llundain Cymraeg,' I say confidently, wondering if they know it, 'yn Gray's Inn Road.'

'Y Canolfan Cymry Llundain.' The male *beirniad* corrects me. They do know it. Then I suddenly remember Nant Gwrtheyrn. Amazing what you forget to say in these situations, until you remember them. I mention my week in the national language school, and now they smile. It turns out that the female *beirniad* knows the teachers there. Everyone really does know everyone.

'Fwynhewch chi'r profiad?' Did I enjoy my experience at the Nant? Oh yes, I tell them, I loved it. From Sunday night to Friday afternoon, not a sentence of English was spoken by any of us. It really was quite the Welshest of weeks. Maybe we didn't sound that intelligent, but we didn't sound very English either. Plus it didn't rain, I add. Much. And I spotted Jan Morris. I'm collecting famous Welsh people, I tell them.

Who else have I met?

'Wel …' That's definitely the last one. 'Bryn Terfel.' The *beirniaid* rearrange their eyebrows approvingly. 'Dafydd Iwan,' I add. This is definitely scoring me points. 'The Culture Minister. He's Dafydd Iwan's brother.' They know who Alun Ffred is. It suddenly occurs to me they're all men. And mostly related. Apart from Jan Morris, that is. The Clwb Rygbi Cymry Caerdydd are also all men. 'Plus I've joined the Pendyrus Choir,' I say. That's another eighty men right there. Why are all my Welsh acquaintances men? Furthermore my grandfather was one of eight brothers and one sister. My father has one brother, who lives in an all-male monastery. I have two brothers. Not a lot of women down the pit either. Apart from two teachers and two pupils at the Nant, it would appear that my grandmother is the only Welsh woman I have ever properly known. Perhaps finding my inner Welshman is no more than finding my inner man. An effete member of the urban metrosexual intelligentsia is getting in touch with his masculine side, the suppressed daredevil within who yomps up hills and down mineshafts and rugby-tackles men built like rhinos and brazenly sits oral exams despite inadequate preparation.

'Faint o bobl oedd ar y cwrs?'

'Chwech myfyriwr,' I answer. There were six of us on the course. I never know how to pronounce the second half of *myfyriwr* (student), so I find it's best just to commit heavily to the front bit and let the back end look after itself. We were four Gogs and two Hwntws. Nor am I sure if these slangy geographical specifications are offensive or not. On the final night – *Nos Iau* (in Welsh they like to specify if it's day or night) – we went out to dinner, I say. In a very good pub. And as we were sitting there, I continue, talking and eating and drinking with these people, I suddenly had a … I had a …

Oh shit.

I can't remember the word. I know the word and don't. I can feel it somewhere in the ether, sense its vague outline. But it refuses to come. Don't panic.

You had a …? This from the male *beirniad*.

'Beth oedd e?' I say. What was it? I stare into space. Silence. I know it's from Greek.

'Dw i wedi anghofio'r gair hyd yn oed yn Saesneg.' I've even forgotten the word in English. You pillock. Why does it refuse to materialise? Embarrassment. I can feel a slight moistness in the undercarriage.

'Mae'r gair wedi diflannu,' I say. The word has disappeared.

'Teimlad?' suggests the female *beirniad*.

Yes, I agree. A feeling. It's not the word, but it'll have to do. *Teimlad*. A feeling that we were all here together, doing our bit to help the Welsh language. To help it continue.

And that's the reason why I'm learning Welsh. I want to do what it says in the last line of the national anthem. *O bydded i'r hen iaith barhau*. It seems a remarkably hubristic statement. How dare I believe that my sclerotic Welsh stutterings, learned in London, could possibly underpin an entire language? But the *beirniaid* are all smiles. They really are.

'Wel,' says the male *beirniad*. Suddenly everything is OK. 'Diolch yn fawr a phob lwc.' Thank you very much and good luck. They get up. I get up. We shuffle round the table and shake hands. I thank them in return, and leave the classroom. It's over. I have competed.

Cinio. I go downstairs. I'm suddenly famished. And parched. Competition is draining. In a big classroom quiches, salad, cheese, ham have been spread. I load my paper plate and wander back into the main room. The blonde woman from Bridgend is still in the same seat. She asks how it went. The truth is I have no idea. It happened. 'Dw i ddim yn siwr.' I scoff my salady bits. A man in his

twenties comes over – another competitor from somewhere along
the M4 corridor – and yaks camply in Welsh. How infinitely malle-
able is this great language, I reflect as I excuse myself and go next
door to retrieve a reviving pile of Welsh cakes. Oral examinations
do that to you. I must have been pumping adrenalin back there,
and am now depleted. Dai, the suspiciously fluent one, slips into
the seat next to me. 'Sh'mae, Dai,' say I. We are all in this together,
Welsh people talking in Welsh about competing in Welsh. We
wouldn't dream of saying a word in English. Are we not Welsh?
How Welsh are *we*? I feel this with sudden intensity.

There is movement. Two people, a man and a woman I've not
seen before, stroll up to the front, looking official. We all know what
this means. The man is very tall, with a moustache. I notice my
pulse embark on its predictable acceleration – the foolish gambol-
ling heart which should know better. He pulls himself up to his full
height at the lectern. Is it really necessary to feel nervous? How
tiresome. This is the hour of judgement. Who is going home? Who
is staying? How Welsh in fact are you? As Welsh as the person
sitting next to you?

The tall man with the moustache opens his mouth to speak. We
already know the speech. The standard has been exceptionally
high, he is saying. Higher than ever. I am worried by his compassionate tone. The judges have been very impressed. This is going to
be a bloodbath. And we have had more competitors this year than
ever before. Half of whom are about to be culled. We have had
competitors from Patagonia and even Belgium. Not to mention
London, I think, which he doesn't in fact mention. The judges
have found it incredibly difficult to make a decision. Yeah, yeah.
Get to the meat, lanky.

These are the names of the twelve competitors who are going on
to the semi-final. Is it my imagination or is there an entirely

synthetic and deeply irritating pause for dramatic effect? I find
myself randomly cursing Simon Cowell. The grammar of his talent
shows has bled across the border and into the doings of the National
Eisteddfod. And then he starts reading out names. They are of
course all Welsh names. Eifion this, Sioned that, Gruffudd the
other. The names – twelve of them – ring out like a tolling bell. Do
I hear a Dai? Chances are I do. I half listen, almost disembodied by
the knowledge, the *certainty*, that I'm not on the list. I'm not going
to *mynd ymlaen* (lit. to go forward, to go onward). Arwel this, Catrin
that. The word *ymlaen* pings around inside my cranium like a baga-
telle ball. Forwards, onwards, upwards. Out they come, name upon
Welsh name. I should have prepared that opening peroration. *Mae
fy nhad yn dod o Gaerfyrddin.* This is not my moment. I never truly
did get my hopes up. My ticker is already slowing down. It knows
something. I should never have tried speaking Greek. What a tit.
That was the moment I failed.

The names stop. Mine as predicted not among them. Flunk.
The bar not cleared. I look around me. There is a general sense of
rabbits blinking in headlights. Of atomic aftershock. I look to my
right. The face of the blonde woman from Bridgend has mysteriously elongated.

'Dych chi'n mynd ymlaen?'

'Nac ydw.'

'A chi?'

'Na.'

'Beth am chi?' I ask the man in his twenties.

'Na.'

They are much better speakers than me, and they've not got over
the first hurdle either. The Bournemouth Welshman – I can see
him shaking his head ruefully – isn't going anywhere either, other
than Bournemouth. I turn to Dai on my left.

'Dych chi'n mynd ymlaen?'

He smiles modestly. His body language says it all: don't hate me, I must have been lucky, etc.

'Ydw,' he says. Yes I am.

'Gwych!' I say. Great. 'Llongyfarchiadau.' Congratulations. I really mean it. 'A phob lwc.' Note correct deployment of aspirate mutation. These things are going in.

'Diolch,' says Dai. He's all shy smiles. And total fluency. I hope he gets through to the final. Come the revolution, we'll be needing Welsh speakers like him.

Wel, my work here is done. I say the odd goodbye, the odd *braf cwrdd â chi*, then walk out of the room, down the corridor, out of the school building, over to my car half-blocking a fire exit, get in, gun the engine and slip out of the Ysgol Gynradd Glyncoed, up onto the road leading through unlovely Ebbw Vale and off down the valley. It's still spitting. And I am seething, *boiling* with self-hatred. Thin driplets slither across the windscreen. My misplaced self-belief really is a curse. If you're going to rain, please rain properly. My casual faith in the persuasive powers of charm is truly contemptible. Let's have a proper Welsh deluge. How could I sit there pretending I was somehow above all the business of competition? A plague on my English swagger. This mindset must be *scrapped*. The road follows the Ebbw along the valley floor. This is one of the things Project Wales is teaching me: to think of myself as part of a community that is wider, larger, deeper than one cocksure individual. The car snakes and weaves between conifered walls. *Teimlad* = a feeling. The sun is putting up a struggle. Specks flick across the glass, now irradiated by light. Who wants it more? The rain, the sun? Ebbw Vale = halfwit. Who wants to learn more? I think as I drive carefully down towards the sea plain. The Englishman or the Welshman? It's a competition, and there can be only one winner.

8

Tyfu = Grow

Welsh sheep numbers by category
June 2009

Breeding ewes	3,996,000
Other sheep, over one year	204,000
Lambs under one year	4,038,000
Total sheep and lambs	8,238,000

Little Book of Meat Facts:
Compendium of Welsh Meat and Livestock Industry Statistics 2010 (2010)

'TI EISIAU TYNNU?'

The mother, a swollen bulk of wool, lies on her side, noiselessly straining. One leg is in the air, exposing a rosy undercarriage. She is primed for parturition. Her vulva gapes elastically, like a neat circular tear in a stretch of bright-pink Lycra. Through the opening peeps a foreign object, grey and glistening. Do I want to pull what exactly?

Dewi reaches out a hand and carefully pulls the stretchy membranes of flesh apart. I continue to stare. One has been present at only two previous births, and both times it was a human that popped out. That, I do believe, is a pair of feet. If you look closely you can see they are cloven.

He's a big unit, is Dewi – he plays loose-head for Dolgellau. The sense of heft is offset by a shy smile and soft enquiring eyes.

'Pam lai?' I say. Why not? I've been on site for an hour. I sort of assumed there'd be some kind of preliminary initiation. Maybe yard-sweeping or bale-lugging or just general rope-learning before the deep end beckoned. But no. Dewi tells me to grab and tug.

It's hard to get a purchase on a lamb's foot copiously slimed in amniotic slick. Between the little knobble of hoof and the tiny ankle there's a handhold of sorts, but it's a smeary grip. I'm reminded of pulling on a wishbone dripping with chicken lubricants. My hand slithers clear off the foot. I'm reluctant to impart too much pressure. I don't want to snap this thing's leg before it's even been born.

'Mae'n llithro,' I say. It's slipping. (Am rather proud of knowing this word. Picked it up in *Harri Potter*.) This lamb appears to be stuck, possibly for good. Dewi indicates that I can afford to pull a little harder, so I do. The owner of these legs won't thank me for this assertion but, begrudgingly, something budges. I yank again. No, there's a bottleneck in there. Dewi leans in again and slips a hand inside the rim of the vulva, pulls it clear to reveal another form poking indistinctly into the light. As I suspected. There's too much lamb trying to get out all at once. It's some sort of snout. Dewi slides a few fingers in and pulls a head clear of the cervical tunnel.

That's it, I'm out of here. I'm not pulling on a head. Dewi clamps a firm fist around the legs and pulls properly. A small form slides gloopily forth, soaked in sludge, till it is entirely free. And after the birth, the afterbirth, a little sacklet of bright-red gristle, follows it onto the floor of the concrete yard.

'Rhaid siecio'r ceg,' says Dewi. You have to check the mouth. *Siecio*, pronounced 'checkio': one of those verbs that has wandered across the border and snaked its way along the alleyways of Wales as far as this isolated valley. Dewi shoves an unceremonious finger into the creature's mouth and rummages around at the back of the throat to clear any blockage. A new-born lamb is now free to take its first breath.

It's hard not to feel a bit biblical as this scene unfolds, but I master the urge as I crouch over the fresh life lying in a pool of spilt fluid, rippled in blood. Its tiny head nudges up off the hard floor. Dewi has stood and now the mother follows suit, struggling to her feet to prod an inquisitive nose at the newly delivered package. She sniffs, then speculatively licks. Dewi touches my elbow. It's time to step back, he indicates, so mother and lamb can bond. Otherwise she might reject the fruit of her womb. He uses the word *gwrthod*: to refuse. We edge backwards to the corner of the enclosure.

After ten seconds or so, Dewi says something in Welsh that I don't quite catch. There's another one coming within ten or fifteen minutes, he repeats. Another lamb showed up on the scan. Can I stay and watch and if she needs help, *tynnwch* – pull. If there's a problem, he says, come and get him in the shed. And he ambles off in the direction of a big ugly barn with corrugated walls.

It's just me and the ewe and the lamb now. If ever there were a Welsh test and a half, this is it. I watch with adamantine intent. She licks and nuzzles and generally cossets her first-born, which bleats feebly. Its legs buckle after all that time folded tightly into the uterus. I hoist myself onto a low wall and look around. Straight ahead is a mountain. The only way ahead is up. It feels as if I've come to the very epicentre of Wales.

At the top of Cwm Cywarch is a hill farm where I am to spend a working Welsh week. Blaencywarch – *blaen* meaning head – is only a slight misnomer. From the farmhouse, the valley in fact turns sharp right up into a vast amphitheatrical *cwm* of near perfect symmetry, a glaciated spoon-scoop. Somewhere out of its flanks is where the Cywarch spurts forth. It tra-la-las along the valley floor, turns left at the farmhouse, then tumbles down the cleft between the high walls until two or so miles downstream it flows into the river Dyfi, which itself eventually fans out into the famous estuary before debouching into Cardigan Bay at Aberdyfi. That feels like a long way off from here.

A balmy hint of sun warms the hilly air. The odd puff of cloud drifts lazily across, casting mobile shadows on the surrounding ramparts of this astonishing place. It's been a good nine minutes now. No sign of urgency from the expectant ewe. I wish she'd hurry up. A faint roar overhead growing louder. Flitting across the blue heavens is a dark silhouette which disappears at warp speed over the brow of the hill just as the roar swells to an ear-splitting climax. NATO is on manoeuvres. My ewe doesn't bat an eyelid. Sixteen minutes. Dewi reappears from round the corner of the barn and saunters towards me.

'Does dim cig oen eto,' I call. There's no lamb yet. His eyebrows wander upwards in surprise as he wrestles her to the floor and thrusts a forearm into her cervix. He delves around and then stops.

'Mae e wedi marw,' he says. It's dead. He yanks out a thin sliver of lifeless flesh, mauve with decomposition. Great. My first role as a Welsh farmer is to be a harbinger of death. I ask Dewi when it would have died. He thinks a few days ago. And what, I ask, would have happened if he hadn't pulled it out?

'Basai'r mam wedi marw hefyd.' The mother would have died too. Lucky she was in the yard then, near a helping hand. Except it wasn't luck. Of the hundreds of ewes dotting the fields that slope up and away from the farmyard, this was one of the few brought in specifically for close observation. There's only one person here who doesn't know what he's doing.

'You?' people say. 'Working on a sheep farm?' I admit it: the weeklong rural element of Project Wales is the biggest category error, bigger even than mining or rugby. I've been indoors all my working life. But no one turns himself into a Welshman without disappearing into the hills and experiencing the Welshest thing of all.

I read about Dewi's father in the *Western Mail*. 'Hedd Pugh takes home another prize as the Welsh Rural Community Champion,' announced the headline. The Royal Welsh, the annual agricultural show, was on at the time, in its regular week in July on its regular patch in the eastern midlands of Wales, near Builth Wells, timed as ever to coincide with an Old Testament deluge. 'Hedd and his family,' ran the report, 'farm 1,600 acres rising from 500ft to 2,900ft in a stunning location at Blaencywarch, Dinas Mawddwy, with 1,200 sheep and a small herd of suckler cows, but he still finds time to play an active role in 24 local and regional organisations.' He sounded like the kind of Welsh hill farmer who might be just about broadminded enough to welcome an urban dweller from the *mwg mawr* (= big smoke). I decided to write – in English (in case he didn't speak Welsh). I mentioned my language studies (in case he did).

A few weeks later my mobile throbbed in my pocket.

'Could I speak to Mr Rees?'

I couldn't quite place the accent.

'My name is Hedd Pugh. So you'd like to work on a Welsh hill farm?' He thought the lambing season would be the best time for it.

'I was wondering if there'd be an opportunity to practise my Welsh now and then.'

'On the farm,' he replied, 'we speak nothing but Welsh.'

The dead lamb has been consigned to a plastic sack and dumped by the roadside for later collection when a stout blue Ford 4x4 pick-up rolls up the lane. Hedd gets out and strides over in wellingtons. He is of medium height, with thick walls of unsheared greying hair, bright beady eyes and a stout beer gut.

'Croeso i Flaencywarch,' he says. I shake his hand. 'Ti wedi tynnu oen yn barod?' he says – have I already pulled out a lamb? – in a tone of voice of someone who wishes me to think he's impressed, though we both know it is a polite pretence. We lean on the gate and look at the ewe in the pen. Her surviving lamb has struggled to its feet and is nosing blindly around her undercarriage.

'Mae'n chwilio am laeth,' says Hedd helpfully. It's looking for milk. My ears prick up. *Llaeth* is very much the test word for telling where you are in Wales. In North Wales they say *llefrith*. Linguistically therefore I must be in the south. To confirm my theory I suddenly think of a clever question to ask Hedd.

'Hwrdd neu maharan?' Which word for 'ram' do they use round these parts?

'Hwrdd,' says Hedd. As I suspected. I am definitely among Hwntws. My people. We watch the lamb take its first glugs of mother's milk. The peace is broken by the roar of a fat, squat quad bike materialising along the lane. Off it steps a darker bantam-weight version of both Hedd and Dewi. I'm introduced to Owain, Hedd's second son, who is twenty. (The youngest, Carwyn, is off training as a builder's apprentice in Machynlleth.) We get talking about foxes, possibly because Owain is wearing an Anglo-Saxon T-shirt which says 'FUCK THE BAN'. At first I don't know what nameless peril they are talking about – for 'fox' Hedd uses the Gog word *llwynog* whereas the one I know is *cadno*. Perhaps it makes sense to use an alien word for an enemy predator, I reflect. But as father and two sons talk I start to hear other sorts of Gogisms I first came across in Nant Gwrtheyrn – the different constructions and syntactical quirks which are the lingua franca up north. It seems I am standing on some sort of linguistic fault line. We're just north of the Dyfi river, which Gerald of Wales described as the border between north and south. But there is a much more natural border straight ahead: the mountain wall. It's easy to imagine how vocabulary from the north struggled to filter down into Cwm Cywarch. Until NATO started flying over, not much will have made it past that forbidding barrier.

'Merionithshire, or Merionydshire, lies west from Montgomeryshire,' recorded Daniel Defoe as he made his way into North Wales:

> The principal river is the Tovy, which rises among the unpassable mountains, which range along the centre of this part of Wales, and which we call unpassable, for that even the people themselves called them so; we looked at them indeed with astonishment, for their rugged tops, and the immense height of them … There is but few large towns in all this part, nor is it very populous; indeed much of it is scarce habitable, but 'tis said, there are more sheep in it, than in all the rest of Wales.

Defoe's tour of Wales was a catalogue of the country's bounty. Chepstow 'furnishes great quantities of corn for exportation'. Brecknock-Mere, he reported, is said to be 'two thirds water, and one third fish'. From the mountains of Radnorshire 'they send yearly, great herds of black cattle to England'. He approved of the 'very good, fertile, and rich soil' of the southern Welsh plain which helped supply Bristol 'with butter in very great quantities'. The cattle-rich fields of Carmarthenshire impressed him, and Tenby was admired as 'a great fishery for herring in its season'. The flourishing port at Milford Haven, a corner of Wales 'so very pleasant, and fertile, and … so well cultivated, that 'tis called by distinction,

Little England, beyond Wales'. He made note of Montgomery-shire's stocky but highly prized horses. And then Defoe ran out of compliments to pay Wales.

A *Tour Through the Whole Island of Great Britain* pre-dated the emergence of the genteel eighteenth-century traveller. Roads had scarcely improved since Gerald of Wales passed along them, and no one went to Wales without some present business to lure them. Published as a series of thirteen letters, the *Tour* saw the light of day in the mid 1720s towards the end of Defoe's life, by which time he had enjoyed an eventful career in commerce including bankruptcy and prison, worked as a government spy, composed a great deal of seditious journalism and invented the English novel.

The Penguin Classic edition runs to 679 pages including Defoe's own prefaces and appendices. Of those, his dispatch from Wales merited fourteen, part of a letter titled 'The West and Wales'. The problem, simply, was the terrain. Defoe approved of Wales where its landscape aped England or, even better, its land supplied England. 'Mountains of antiquity ... are not the subject of my enquiry,' he sniffed soon after entering the Principality, but he found them hard to ignore. He and his travelling companion had barely entered the Black Mountains when 'we began to repent our curiosity, as not having met with any thing worth the trouble; and a country looking so full of horror, that we thought to have given over the enterprise, and have left Wales out of our circuit'. Travelling through Brecknockshire, he reported that the English 'jestingly called it Breakneckshire'. The joke was lost on the creator of *Moll Flanders*. "Tis mountainous to an extremity,' he complained, and you can hear in him the voice of all travellers who repent of their intrepid decision to seek out adventure. And this was before he traversed the south of the country, reached Pembro-keshire and turned north towards Mid Wales.

Pumlumon soon loomed out of the mist. He declared it probably
the highest point in Wales. For twenty miles around it, all he could
see was more mountains 'so that for almost a whole week's travel,
we seemed to be conversing with the upper regions'. Being 'so tired
with rocks and mountains' they headed inland, came into Montgomeryshire and fell with relief on the Severn Valley – 'the only
beauty of this country' – before turning back towards the west and
the coast. 'Here among innumerable summits, and rising peaks of
nameless hills, we saw the famous Kader-Idricks.' And so the
mountains of Wales towered higher and higher over Defoe until he
came to 'Caernarvonshire, where Snoden Hill is a monstrous
height, and according to its name, had snow on the top in the
beginning of June'. In the town of Caernarfon he approved of the
castle built by Edward I 'to curb and reduce the wild people of the
mountains'. But Wales had curbed and reduced Defoe. From his
hotel in Chester he concluded that 'even Hannibal himself would
have found it impossible to have marched his army over Snowden,
or over the rocks of Merioneth and Montgomery shires'. And with
that, he turned his face to England and the east with the relief of
Robinson Crusoe being rescued from his desert island.

Anyone who clambers about their family tree will eventually come
upon a forebear who worked on the land. They may be only a generation back, or maybe several. My great-grandparents Thomas
and Eliza Rees were married in their twenties – she was four years
his senior – in 1887 and in the same year took on a farm called
Bwlch in the village of Meidrim in Carmarthenshire. It may have
been to mark this occasion that one day they travelled into
Carmarthen to have their portrait taken by a photographer. They
pose in their smart Sunday best, a splendid bowler and cane for
him, a white hat frothing with plumes for her. Thomas sits and

looks formally off to the right. Eliza stands, her left elbow leaning on a carved table, dark eyes fixed on the lens.

The following year their first son was born. After Bill came three more boys: Davy in 1890, Jim in 1892 and Harry in 1894. Edith, their only girl, was born in 1895. A gap of four years followed and then came four more boys: Percy in 1899, Bertram in 1901, Howell in 1903 and Robert in 1905. Soon after Bert's birth they moved to a farm called Corn Gafr – Goat Horn. Eight boys may have made for a lot of helping hands on a livestock farm, but Corn Gafr could not support them all. In 1911, Bill took passage for Australia and planted a citrus farm in New South Wales. The other older brothers volunteered when war was declared, and Bert had to withdraw from the local grammar school to work on the farm. Around this time, presumably through inexperience, he lost two fingers in a chaff-cutter. In 1915 he lost his mother.

The 1901 census records that they had three servants. In 1911 there was only a niece. The mother of nine may have succumbed at least in part to exhaustion when she died in her early fifties. Her youngest son, who would grow up to be my great-uncle Bob, was only ten. When in 1918 the older boys returned from the front and it presumably became apparent that they would not be coming back to the farm, Corn Gafr was advertised for sale. Six years later Thomas followed his wife to the grave.

The first four boys went into farming. Edith married a farmer. Percy was the first of the family to abandon the land as a way of life. He went up to London to train at St Bartholomew's Hospital as a doctor and in due course became an eminent psychiatrist. Bert and Howell trained at Guy's Hospital as dentists. Bob also went to Bart's and became an obstetrician. In each case their training was paid for by loans from their older brothers. Apart from Bert, they all practised in England.

After Bill's emigration to New South Wales, the nine siblings would not gather together again in one place for over forty years, when Bill returned with his wife for a visit in 1952. His absence did not prevent the oldest brother from being carefully added to a group photo featuring all nine, spruced and sprigged in morning dress, on the occasion of Bert's wedding in Carmarthen in 1927. In 1952 there were two family reunions, one in England, the other in Wales. At Edith's home near Winchester the nine siblings stood for a photograph with the nine spouses sitting in front of them. They also attended a service in Meidrim. They will have gathered at the foot of their parents' grave and remembered a hard but idyllic childhood on a farm over the hill before cars and telephones and internal plumbing. Perhaps they returned to Corn Gafr too, but I suspect not: the women look far too smart for stepping daintily through Welsh mud.

Six decades later, I ask for directions to Corn Gafr. An old woman who lives opposite the New Inn tells me to drive a mile or so up the hill then bear right up another hill. Wind blows high-speed clouds across Carmarthenshire. I turn west and suddenly through the window I see a low conical mountain prevailing over the landscape. It can only be Preseli, perhaps ten miles distant. What a view to grow up with. I drive on till I reach a modern con-creted farmyard.

'Keep going down that track,' says a farmer in his fifties. 'There's not much there now, mind.'

A book called *Historic Carmarthenshire Homes and Their Families* records for how long there once was. A lease was granted 'in the manor of Korn Gavor' to Thomas Griffith Ap Howell by the owner Thomas John Phillipps, gent., of Llanfihangel Abercywyn in 1587, the year before the Armada. In 1672 one resident was High Sheriff of the county, more than three centuries before my grandfather.

Corn Gafr, when I get there after half a mile, feels a long way from anywhere. I edge around a small herd of Welsh Blacks sprawled across the grass in anticipation of rain. The farmyard is surrounded on three sides by ruins. Holes gape where windows used to be, roofless rooms bid welcome to the heavens, and time has bitten chunks out of walls.

It's not immediately clear which of the half-dozen buildings they would have lived in. Some of the boys certainly slept in a barn above the cattle. I walk back towards the mouth of the track and notice that the nearest ruin has a small sturdy porch. This must once have been the family's front door. Francis Jones, the author of *Historic Carmarthenshire Homes*, visited in 1980 and found the house 'empty and deteriorating'. 'The interior is roomy,' he writes, 'there is panelling in the small entrance hall and some much older panelling on the left-hand side of the staircase. From the upper floor, a short flight of stairs leads to a commodious attic.' Panelling and stairs have both gone. Even the livestock, found grazing in the barns on previous visits by Reeses, have left them to crumble.

They always kept an extra place at the table, I've been told, for unexpected guests, who would have heard nothing but Welsh, even if the language was marginalised at school. Among themselves they continued to speak it deep into old age. The rain is coming now. I try to summon the ghosts of eight boys and a girl, raised on this farm among cattle and sheep, hens and geese, dogs and cats. It was here that Bert made his first extraction. It was here that Eliza must have died, probably in the same bed in which she gave birth nine times. In the early 1970s someone decided that it wouldn't do to live in this lonely impractical spot down by the river at the bottom of the hill, that a classic Welsh bungalow overlooking the sweep of Preseli and Pembrokeshire – Little England Beyond Wales – made a great deal more sense. So Corn Gafr was eventually abandoned by all, if not forgotten. Percy built a home in Surrey and called it Corn Gafr. In New South Wales one of Bill's children called their dog kennel Meidrim.

From the porch I look at the Welsh Blacks. One or two of them look back at this interloper in a red rugby shirt. A notion nudges me in the ribs that the Reeses of Corn Gafr have somehow left these sentinels here in the yard to keep watch over the old place as another westerly breeze whistles along the valley and rain taps steadily on the old stones.

Hedd and I wander down the lane. A sheepdog tags along beside us. The sun is still caressing the walls and floor of the valley. We talk about this and that until we meet a tiny stooped figure wearing a bright-blue over-pinny and a thick woollen hat. She must be in the tail end of her eighties. Hedd introduces her as Beti.

'Mae'n braf iawn cwrdd â chi,' I say in my politest Welsh.

'How are you?' she croaks. At least I assume that's what she says: her English is so accented as to be impenetrable. Not that I can understand more than a word or two of her Welsh, as she and Hedd slip into a conversation about sheep. They've probably never spoken about anything else. She has a bucket of feed she is scattering over a fence to a tiny flock in a field at the mouth of her lane.

'Wel,' says Hedd. 'Rhaid dal ati.' Must keep going. I smile at Beti as we walk down the lane and Hedd explains that she has lived in Cwm Cywarch all her life, having never married. Since her brother died she's been alone. There's another farmer in the valley who's even older, he says, and still going at over ninety.

I ask him at what age he learned English. In primary school in Dinas Mawddwy, he explains. 'I was about nine year old when I remember an English-speaking family moved to the village and we just couldn't understand them.' Did he find it hard? 'Very hard.

After we went on to the Dolgellau school we were having English lessons.' Nowadays Hedd is president of the agricultural college in Dolgellau and is active in the National Farmers' Union so he mixes with English speakers a lot. He doesn't consider himself fluent. 'There's a lot of people a lot more fluent than I am. Day to day we never speak English. If I was at home on the farm every day I could go for weeks without speaking in English at all.'

Up along the edge of the field a distant dog flies round the rim of a flock. The goal, says Hedd, is to move them on to a greener pasture. It's a wondrous thing to behold, I reflect contently, this age-old harmony, this trust nurtured across centuries between shepherd and sheepdog. Sheep have been cajoled and corralled in this way since time immemorial, I think. This is truly the Welsh way.

So much for my romanticism. Dewi and the quad bike fly over a brow in the field, bumping and throttling, scaring rogue elements of the flock into formation. It's mightily effective. They're through an open gate in a jiffy. The Welsh way, it seems, is essentially a partnership between man, dog and Kawasaki.

'It's easier for the hills,' explains Hedd. 'We've got a lot of land to get around.' As if to prove it, later in the day we head up in the other direction, past the farmhouse and into the higher, hillier fields towards the valley's cul-de-sac. My task is to be another mobile fence post discouraging the sheep from breaking formation. Hedd does the same. Owain is careering about on the quad bike while Dewi has switched to a bright-orange scrambling bike which whines and whirs across the open slope. The two dogs do their bit too.

Across the day and into the next, a pattern begins to develop. Flock A needs moving from field B to field C to join flock D. Flock E needs its daily ration of vitamin-enriched sheep feed in Field F.

Ewe G and her lambs H and I need shifting from barn K to paddock J. Pasture L containing flock M needs its newly born lambs counted. Fields N, O and P need to be checked for orphans and dead, but I misunderstand the instructions in Welsh and also check fields Q and R. Flock S needs to be returned from the yard to field T. Sheep U belongs to neighbour V and needs catching but it's a cussed bugger and escapes from sheep truck W, leaps over drystone wall X into field Y, where the person tasked with bringing it down is farmhand Z. Me. Owain and I corner sheep U in a field and when it attempts to sidestep through a gap I dive headlong across the grass, grab it by the fleece and wrestle it to the floor. Resistance is futile. I lie there smothered in a kicking sack of wool. Owain has a top tied around his waist which he places over the head of the sheep.

'Iawn sefyll nawr,' he says. It's OK to get up. I let go and stand. The sheep's head is obscured by the material. She won't move, Owain explains. They're so stupid that if you cover their heads they just lie there.

Meanwhile, the barn brings out one's maternal side. Past the huge corrugated flap which constitutes the barn door is a maze of pens and runs constructed of iron gates and wooden wickets. This is where I meet Hedd's wife Sian, who seems to be in charge here. Sian is a teacher's assistant in Dolgellau, but the school holiday coincides with lambing so she spends her Easters in the shed trying to persuade orphaned lambs to take on sustenance. I can't quite decide who the boys look like. And then I realise that it's an uncanny combination of both. Hedd and Sian are one of those couples who must have instinctively gravitated to each other at least partly because, with strong cheekbones and beady eyes and pleasant open faces, they look wonderfully alike.

Radio Cymru blares out of a wireless on a ledge. The floor is carpeted with straw and an occasional topsoil of hay. In one large enclosure a bunch of ewes are waiting to drop. In another there's a collection of motherless lambs. They've either been rejected by ewes, or the ewes have died out in the field. The five under my feet come in various sizes. The littlest are ineffably sweet, quivering in corners on pipecleaner limbs. There's a thuggish-looking class bully type that, if it had only two legs, would be in borstal before the summer's out. As it's got four, it will be on someone's plate instead.

I tell myself not to forget this. The Pughs certainly don't. First thing one morning Dewi and Owain are in the yard sifting ewes brought down from the hills. They grab each under the forelegs, kick away the hind legs and upend it so that the undercarriage is exposed. They feel the belly and squeeze the teats and if there's a milky excretion it is consigned to one pen. If there's none it goes to another. These are the barren ones whose pregnancies, at least this year, have failed. A dozen or so have been rounded up to be moved up the road into a field.

'That's about £400,' says Hedd, pointing as unaccusingly as he can manage at the ewes responsible for the lost revenue.

No wonder, back in the barn, the orphaned lambs are carefully nurtured through their loss. They fight over a pair of rubber teats sticking through a fence and attached to an upturned flagon of high-protein milk substitute. The thug gets it all unless you drag it out the way. Which I do, assertively, for the whole week. The tiny one needs a bit of guidance. I grab it by the neck and force its mouth onto the teat. After a few seconds it loses concentration and after further force-feeding you have to conclude that actually maybe it's just full. Other lambs, either rejected or orphaned, are thrust upon new mothers. It's the sheep-farming version of an adoption agency. The only way to get the mother to accept her new charge is to pin her in the corner of her pen with an iron crook so she can't turn and shove the interloper away. I do quite a lot of iron crook work across the week. Eventually, says Sian, the ewe will accept the lamb once it smells of her own milk.

Regularly at midmorning, I follow Hedd across the yard and into the old two-storey farmhouse. Boots are left outside, hands washed in a cluttered anteroom. The kitchen is snug, with a square table. A tin of biscuits is proffered with a pot of tea. There's the local paper to read – in Welsh – and S4C is on in the corner. On the wall is the clock Hedd won as Welsh Rural Community Champion (there was also a cheque for £500). At lunchtime Sian serves up hearty pies and stews followed by filling puddings. I look at Owain's whippet frame and wonder how long it can last. Maybe he eats less as an agriculture student in Aberystwyth.

The Pughs acquired the farm from an uncle and aunt of Sian's in 1985; her father was born here. A photo album shows the work that went into renovating the place. Hedd previously had worked on his father's farm, three miles away at the bottom of the valley. The farm cost £100,000 for a thousand acres. 'It sounds a big farm,' he says as we get into the 4x4 and head off down Cwm Cywarch, 'but it's mostly mountain.' A sheep per acre is the accepted norm on a hill farm, he explains. Five years later they expanded the flock and the farm by renting 600 further acres. By then the boys had started coming. At three or four they were already helping and in due course it became clear the older two wanted to go into sheep farming too. 'Once you have boys you're thinking if they want to farm you've got to find land for them.'

The 4 × 4 noses along the lane. We pass Beti on her corner and wave. The sun seems insistent on hanging around. I've barely seen a cloud since arriving. Round a pair of bends we come to a small chapel, long since closed, where they used to take the boys to Sunday school. Google's Street Search cameras filmed this far and no further up the valley. 'We're in no-man's-land,' says Hedd. He doesn't have to add that that's how he likes it. We reach the main road and drive south-east for twenty miles. The landscape grows notably tamer, the hills more reasonable. Eventually Hedd pulls in at a caravan park, heads up the hill into a network of four or five fields and proceeds to drive very slowly around the perimeter. Sheep look up at us inquisitively, trotting out of the way where necessary. This, Hedd explains, is one of his farms, acquired four years previously.

'There was no land going for sale by us so you've got to expand and buy wherever you can find it.' He barely gets out of the car. This is purely a tour of inspection. With the rising cost of petrol, coming here every day must be ruinously expensive. 'That's why we brought the sheep from this farm home to the shed for lambing.' Every time he shifts a sheep from one farm to another he has to fill in a form. We spend no more than half an hour at this farm before, the inspection completed, we head back the way we came. I ask Hedd if in his time farming has changed.

'I think we've had the best times for farming, especially the hills,' he says. 'I used to produce, produce, produce, and then the emphasis changed to conservation. Going back about twenty years ago. It works well with us. We've done double fencing, looking after hedges, planting trees. You've got to make sure that you don't put too many sheep on the mountain so that the heather comes back. There's a new scheme coming out now. The new scheme is going to be on water quality and carbon footprint. At the moment I can't see getting into the new scheme. It's voluntary. If I can't get into it I'll be losing 40 per cent of my income. And without that I haven't got a chance of surviving. What we get from selling the lambs is not enough to survive on.' He and Sian restrict their holidays to a couple of days at the Royal Welsh each year. But then you'd have to travel a very long way to find anywhere more peaceful than

Blaencywarch. Does the beauty ever pall? I ask him. 'You get used
to it,' he says with a smile.

   A few miles from Dinas Mawddwy Hedd pulls off onto a narrow
road and follows a tight valley for a few miles until at a tiny village
called Abercegir he parks at a pretty whitewashed farmhouse. This
is yet more land owned by the Pughs, acquired twelve years back.
We load a couple of sacks of sheep feed on a quad bike and head up
the one-in-three slope. After a climb of 300 metres or so a column
of sheep is chasing along behind the quad bike. To a chorus of
bleating I get off and distribute the feed along a line of about five
metres. The trick is to make sure the lambs get some too. Back on
the quad bike we climb higher and higher until the slope starts to
level out and we are near a ridge. Hedd directs me to go up and
have a look. I do as I'm told and all of a sudden am overwhelmed
by a panoramic view of bristling peaks. I unfurl a map in my head
and start ticking off the mountains. To the south is the bare mound
of Pumlumon, to the north-west the triangular crag of Cadair
Idris, to the north the bristling ridge of the Arans, which sit just
above the Pughs' farm. In the distance a NATO fighter takes its
regular route over Cwm Cywarch, sound trailing behind it like a
dog after sheep. It's up here that I have my answer to the question
I've been meaning to ask Hedd. Why is it that sheep are so embedded in the national consciousness of Wales? The pretentious
urbanite in me is hoping for a riveting answer which I can scope for
embedded meaning. But while the ancestral heart of a bard beats
somewhere inside every Welshman, hill farmers are above all practical people. Hedd sits on the quad bike and surveys the magnificent array of mountains rising in every direction.

   'You've got so many hills and on the hills you can't do nothing
else,' he says. 'Only put sheep on it.'

One summer's day I am summoned to a lunch party in Ascot, hosted by one of the grandsons of Corn Gafr. There are seventy of us spanning three generations, descendants of five of the nine siblings from Meidrim. (Two of the brothers did not have children, one line has died out, and the Australian diaspora couldn't make it.) Bert's line, I'm proud to say, is the only one that produces a full house: two sons, three grandsons (plus other halves), six great-grandchildren.

We are given name tags, and a noticeboard with a family tree explains who everyone else is. The photographs of the nine and their wives from 1952 sit alongside the portrait taken in Carmarthen of Thomas and Eliza Rees in their Sunday best towards the end of the nineteenth century. I look around and see the faces of Corn Gafr iterated across the generations, strong resemblances among the sons and daughters of the nine, genetically diluted until the great-grandchildren reveal little or no visible trace of their Welsh ancestry. Nor in the next generation down will many still bear the name. Of Thomas and Eliza's fifty-two great-great-grandchildren, four male Reeses seems a poor return. Thus does nature, which gave them eight sons, correct itself.

This is a revival of a tradition. When the Rees siblings were still alive they used to meet every couple of years for large family gatherings at hotels in southern England. I remember large crowds of people to whom I knew I was related but in whom, as a child, I had no interest. We kept ourselves to ourselves, or talked to our grandmother and those Reeses we knew. The same rules of disengagement now apply to the large brood of begrudging children hauled here along motorways from all over England. Various boys play cricket in the baking heat. Three smartly dressed young girls sit in a corner looking horribly bored, as do their parents. But most of us make an effort to work our way round the room. My part of the conversation is always the same.

'Yes, we're descended from Bert and Dorothy. I've got two brothers and here are my two daughters. Girls, come and meet your
second/third cousins once/twice removed.' In all this, Teilo is a
phenomenon. The only person who has this family tree photocopied in his head, he could not be more in his element, making con-
nections, tying up loops, telling people things they didn't know
about their own grandparents.

The gathering is an abiding testament to the nineteenth-century
Welsh belief in education, and the social mobility it catalysed in the
twentieth century. There is much quiet wealth. The Reeses have
carried on being farmers and doctors. And then among the quirkier
callings we also have not only a monk but also a pilot, a bus driver,
a violinist. And a writer. The majority of the assembled will have
benefited from private schooling, or still do, or will. One little girl
is freshly sprung from the womb. We eat and drink as we sit and
mingle, and eventually my father takes it upon himself to stand and
thank our hosts for their great generosity in reviving this tradition.
I telepathically urge him to mention the remarkable fact that we are
all the descendants of a small farm in the middle of Carmarthenshire. Or at the very least to give Wales a name check. The telepathy
doesn't work. And maybe that is appropriate. Wales for most of
these people is a ghostly memory, its DNA thinned out till it's all
but imperceptible.

After lunch it's time for a group photograph. On such an occasion I cannot let the opportunity pass to slip off to my car and
change into the appropriate dress. As the party ambles across the
lawn towards the large tree under which a long row of chairs have
been laid out for the elders, I come back in the other direction
newly attired. Several people catch sight of me.

'What the bloody hell are you wearing that for?' barks someone.

'What in God's name do you call that garment?' parrots another.

Forgive them, I think, for they know not what they say. England has marinated their brains in old assumptions. Amid the chorus of snipes and catcalls is an approving smile or two.

'Excellent choice, Jasper.'

'Daad! Typical.' As seventy descendants of Corn Gafr in Meidrim smile for the camera on this boiling English summer afternoon, I quietly hope my daughters standing just in front of me are proud that I for one am wearing the red shirt of Wales.

On my last day in the Pughs' kitchen at Blaencywarch, Owain produces his passport. Out of curiosity I ask if I can glance through it and on the first page I notice that it has Welsh writing in it. I've not seen Welsh in a British passport before. It so happens that my passport is about to expire. Where better to renew it than in Wales? Perhaps I can get my mitts on one of those Welsh-language ones. How Welsh would that be?

The post office in Machynlleth is at the back of Spar, only yards from the seat of parliament where Owain Glyndŵr was crowned Prince of Wales. It's after him that all Owains are implicitly named. Not to mention all Owens and Owenses – the surnames of my grandmother's parents. There's a queue. When they get to the counter everyone seems to speak Welsh. And the post-office mistress speaks Welsh back. I've taken the precaution of looking up a word or two and step forward confidently.

'Oes ffurflen am gael pasport yn Gymraeg?' (*Ffurflen* = form.)

'You can *apply* for a passport in Welsh.' Irritatingly she's decided I need to be addressed in English. She rummages on a shelf behind her and returns brandishing two envelopes. 'Here is the Welsh-language form. But the language is quite technical so it might be an idea to have the English one as well.' She slips them both through the narrow slot on the counter.

'Diolch,' I harrumph. But at least I have in my hand a Welsh-language passport form. No one can take that away from me.

A mile or so beyond Dinas Mawddwy Hedd pulls in at a house. We enter a low-ceilinged room full of large sofas and chairs and a kitchen table on which afternoon tea has been laid out by a small friendly woman in her eighties Hedd introduces me to as his mother Margaret. On the piano is a snap of Hedd and Sian on their wedding day in the 1980s. Hedd, looking uncomfortable in a suit with a fatly knotted tie, is rather thinner, but the same glint shines in his pebbly eyes. After tea we go out and help Margaret shift some of her flock into a trailer and thence up into a field at the near end of Cwm Cywarch. We do four trips in all, a dozen or so ewes plus their lambs quad-biked in from the field to an enclosed yard, gates positioned so that the sheep can be corralled into a tight space and pushed into the trailer, then taken up to the field to have their fleeces spray-painted with a green dot by me, shoulder or rump according to gender, then released. My movements become mechanical. I am aware of a pleasant sensation of feeling natural-ised. The city is a fading memory. I am living and working in Welsh. In one week I have returned to the land without a backward glance. It helps of course that the weather has been unremittingly benign.

It's past my regular time for knocking off when we get back to Blaencywarch. Normally I'd slope off, but I slip into the barn to see how the lambs I've been helping to feed all week are doing while Hedd potters about. The smallest one has learned to take milk from the bottle. The ewe has accepted the lamb foisted upon it. My work here is done, I think. Radio Cymru still blares tinnily from the wire-less. Suddenly I hear my name.

'Jasper, ti eisiau tynnu?' Do I want to pull? Hedd is over among the pregnant ewes. One of them is prone on her side. He's kneeling next to her.

'Pam lai?' Why not? I clamber over the metal fencing and into the enclosure. I've not seen another birth since the morning I arrived. Hundreds of lambs have appeared in ones and twos in the fields, but always when I've been looking the other way. I crouch down. Hedd tugs aside the vaginal membrane and two cloven feet materialise. This time I know to grip firmly and pull properly. I pull one, then the other slithery leg until they come clear, and soon enough a tiny snout has nudged out into the air. I take both legs. At first nothing happens. You really do have to haul hard on these things. I pull again and feel movement. A small head pops out and with one more determined heave the entire body of the lamb slips clear, followed by the dark shiny glob of the afterbirth.

Hedd pushes a finger into its mouth to check for amniotic blockage. The lamb lifts its head and emits the merest wobble of sound, a tiny bleat. The ewe looks round. We stand and retreat so that the mother can bond with her newborn. Hedd looks at me and smiles.

'Da iawn,' says the Welsh Rural Community Champion. 'Ti wedi tynnu cig oen o'r diwedd.' I've finally pulled a lamb out. I smile back.

9

Eistedd = Sit

'When I see the enthusiasm which these Eisteddfodds [*sic*] awaken in your whole people … I am filled with admiration.'

Matthew Arnold (1866)

AT FIRST SIGHT it looks like any other countryside festival. Armies of attendants in Day-Glo livery wave you through muddy fields to park precisely where they tell you. Happy humanity in cagoules and fleeces brandishing costly tickets flows on foot towards clicking turnstiles. People of like mind congregate under open skies to cheer and drink and commune.

But here, in a small town in the British Isles in the twenty-first century, you pass through a portal and something is definitely different. As I wander along tented avenues among families, couples, teenagers and busy-looking officials, the scene could not be more English. Beers and beverages are sold along with sandwiches and salads from outlets in a manner recognisable the length and breadth of these isles. Plastic awnings flap in the wind. Gun-metal skies glower overhead. There's a classic August chill on. They've managed to get every detail right. It's uncanny. This could be anywhere in England. But there's one thing that's different. Everyone – *every-one* – seems to be speaking Welsh.

This is the annual celebration of Welshness, of *Cymreictod*, known as the National Eisteddfod. There are local *eisteddfodau* galore across Wales, held in village halls, theatres, churches, chapels and sundry other makeshift performance spaces. There's an *eisteddfod* for the young known, somewhat sinisterly, as the *Urdd*, or Order. But this is the big one. Every summer, in the first week of August, Cymru Cymraeg attracts thousands of visitors to its festival of nationhood. The venue alternates each year between north and south. This year it's in Ebbw Vale. I hand over my ticket to a smiling attendant and wander into what in effect, with only one or two small discrepancies, is indistinguishable from the Quidditch World Cup.

Every conceivable representative of Welsh life has an outlet. The political parties are all here, from Plaid Cymru to the Tories. So are the farming and teaching unions, the universities from Lampeter up to Bangor, museums and tourist trusts. You can have your fill of Welsh publishers and printers, manufacturers and designers, harpists, jewellers, cottage rental companies, single-issue agitators of various hues. I buy a hoody blazoned with the legend 'Cymdeithas yr Iaith cymraeg': the Welsh Language Society.

And then there is the parked pantechnicon of S4C, who are broadcasting round the clock from a gated paddock. Presenters with bright faces and cheerful hair sit on garden furnishings under television arc-lamps. The focus of their attention is a huge pink pavilion, a jaunty big top which dominates the Maesfield. Inside here, Welsh musicians, actors, singers and choirs compete across a range of categories defined not only by art form but also age, gender, number. The Welsh Learner of the Year is presented with his or her prize on the stage of the pavilion (in this case her: my mate Dai got to the final but did not win). The competitions are numerous enough to fill the week from Monday morning through to Saturday afternoon.

It's Friday today. I am here on reconnaissance as I follow a stream of people flowing into the auditorium. I take my place and turn to be greeted by one of the great Welsh sights. Onstage is a seated array of Druids and bards in various shades of eye-catching hoods and robes: forthright blue, searing turquoise, ultimate white. This must be the Gorsedd, the bardic circle. To their right and left are big screens. Television cameras are in fixed positions, lights hanging from rigs. The National Eisteddfod has journeyed a long way from the earliest gathering at Cardigan Castle in 1176.

The lights dip. An organ softens the atmosphere with gentle mood music. From the back of the auditorium various figures process wearing robes of burgundy or British racing green, variously bearing cushions, trumpets and, in one case, a huge monumental sword. Soon enough a man in a white robe and a small round hat enters holding a book, whom I recognise as the Archdruid of Wales.

The Archdruid's bardic name is Jim Parc Nest, after the farm near Newcastle Emlyn where he was born. He also trades as T. James Jones. He is the Welsh equivalent of the Poet Laureate, but with one key difference: the Archdruid is at the hub of a long poetic tradition which is still central to the contemporary culture.

I first met Jim and his wife Manon Rhys, the eminent Welsh-language novelist, through my friends Leighton Jones (aka Leight or L8) and his wife Rhian. Rhian and Manon were at school together in Prestatyn. 'We'll get you round and introduce you to the bards,' said Leighton. Since then, Jim and I have corresponded by email. I have taken him as my guest to an international at the Millennium. But this is the first time I've seen him operating in an archdruidical capacity.

When the group reaches the stage, the Archdruid takes his place on a throne as the trumpets blow a fanfare to all corners. We are open for business. The Archdruid comes forward to say some words, which, not being adept at understanding amplified Welsh, I allow to wash over me very much like the mood music of the organ, now taken up by two onstage harps. A dainty Arcadian tune brings green-clad children haloed in flowers to their feet to perform a pixyish sort of dance.

Let us gloss over the fact that the stage is not filled with real Druids of the type who were once slaughtered by the Romans on Anglesey. There is no pagan connotation at work here. Nor does it pay to seek deep-rooted antecedents for the elaborate theatrical construct being enacted in front of us. But while they are not exactly ancient, nor are the procedures of the Gorsedd exactly modern: they have been in existence for slightly less time than the United States of America. This is the climax of the week of ceremonial devised in the 1790s by an enthusiastic celebrant of Welsh bardic traditions who called himself Iolo Morganwg. Indeed he was so enthusiastic that he invented some fresh traditions, and it is thanks to these that the National Eisteddfod's penchant for ritual is sometimes derided by outsiders as ever so slightly bogus.

What is indisputably antique is the Welsh veneration of poetry as a public and democratic art form. In the courts of the princes the leading bard's stature was enshrined for all to see in the splendid chair reserved for him. The first bardic competitions flourished in medieval times, but the skills associated with Welsh poetry were allowed to slide into abeyance after defeat by the Normans, and more dramatically after Henry VIII's Act of Union. The Eisteddfod in its current form took shape as a political response to a public inquiry into the state of Welsh education. This wrong-headed Anglocentric document, drawn up in 1846, attributed the perceived indolence and ignorance of the Welsh to the twin influences of Nonconformist Sunday school and the Welsh language. The report ignited an upsurge of fervour which manifested itself above all in Cymru Cymraeg's determination to celebrate its musical and literary traditions at an annual gathering. The first official National Eisteddfod was held in Denbigh in 1860. On the National Eisteddfod's website, the records of prizes handed out to poets go back to 1880.

The two principal prizes consist of the Crown, awarded for a sequence of poems not exceeding 200 lines, and the Chair, awarded for the best poem written in a strict metre known as *cynghanedd*. And this is where the traditions of the National Eisteddfod are not remotely bogus. The rules governing metre and rhyme in Welsh poetry are fiendishly exacting and uphold literary values which were established back in the golden age of the bard in the Middle Ages. Reverence for those skilled in Welsh poetry is undiminished. It's difficult to imagine the scene which now unfolds in the pavilion happening in any other culture. The Archdruid gives a short speech, the climax of which is the naming of the winner of the Chair. When Welsh bards compose they use bardic pseudonyms. Thus everyone turns to look around the auditorium to see if they can see someone called Yr Wylan, the tradition being that he (and much more rarely she) identify himself (or herself) by standing up. A few rows back from me a stocky red-haired man in early middle age sheepishly rises to his feet. No sooner has a swivelling spotlight fixed on him than a quartet from the Gorsedd approaches to clothe him in a purple robe with gold braiding and lead him through the audience to the stage. Everyone claps furiously as 'Men of Harlech' loops out of the organ. Yr Wylan is duly installed in the tall-backed Chair, commissioned for the occasion, while the ceremonial sword is held over his head by a member of the Gorsedd who is none other than former front row forward of Wales as the Archdruid says some more words. There is more applause, more harp music, and before long the Gorsedd is processing out of the auditorium, the Archdruid and the newly chaired Yr Wylan in the vanguard preceded by a cameraman walking carefully backwards to capture every hallowed tread.

As I watch the proceedings unfold, it occurs to me that the time has come for Project Wales to turn poetical. In order to approach ever closer to the citadel of Welshness, I must publish my own bardic contribution. However bad.

Dorothy's project for survival was a great success. She lived until the age of ninety-six, lucidly almost to the last. For six years she trekked around her bungalow overlooking Carmarthen and the Tywi Valley, surrounded by old bits of wooden Welsh furniture which looked hulkish and neutered in this small characterless space. As her own world continued to shrink – she lost her sense of smell – and the piano, knitting, painting, cooking, flower-pressing and other accomplishments receded beyond her reach, she kept a busy mind ticking over by learning large swathes of the atlas by heart: the states of America, the countries and capitals of Europe and Africa, which she could recite on demand.

Eventually she was obliged to take up residence in a private home. Everyone gathered there for her ninetieth birthday – Reeses, Owens, Carmarthenshire friends, old colleagues of Bert. On this occasion I was in a position to bring along her first great-grandchild. A new arrival in a family often presages a departure, but not on this occasion. Dorothy could not have been more thrilled to dandle one great-granddaughter, then another, on her knee. As they giggled and cooed at each other, as one baby girl after another made a grab for their great-grandmother's pebble-thick glasses, it was possible to catch a glimpse of the mother she must have been to her own small boys in the 1930s.

Eventually she entirely lost the use of her legs and stayed in bed where she started to talk of having lived a rich full life and wanting to go. When I visited her for the last time she barely spoke or even noticed our massed presence at the end of the bed.

Thirteen years after Bert made the same journey, they carried Dorothy's tiny coffin into St David's Church where she lay under the stained-glass depiction of Christ in Majesty which together they had endowed in 1962. His Grace the Archbishop of Wales did not attend on this occasion. The church was much emptier than it had been when she was the chief mourner: at ninety-six, she had lost all of her contemporaries. She was the last of the eighteen – the siblings of Meidrim and their spouses – to go. They started dying in 1958 and here she was forty years later, having survived them all. There was a hymn in Welsh at which I made a paltry stab. Then they took her to the crematorium and brought her ashes back to the churchyard and placed them in the ground next to Bert. For their two sons, doors would now swing open or click shut. My uncle began thinking about a permanent return to Wales while that afternoon my father left Carmarthen for the last time.

After my day on the Maes I head back along the Heads of the Valleys Road to the Rhondda Fach for a final choir practice. Tomorrow I am taking part in the most prestigious musical competition of the lot: the prize for the best male choir of over forty-five voices. Pendyrus have put themselves forward for their first National Eisteddfod since 1968 (when I was three). I have been yo-yoing along the M4, learning words and music for the very big day when one of the great choirs of Wales steps in front of the judges and the television cameras and takes on all-comers. It's the climactic moment of the Eisteddfod and brings the entire sequence of competitions to a close on Saturday afternoon.

It has been fiendish learning the music. Stewart Roberts has concocted a repertoire to fill a slot of fifteen minutes. One of the songs I already know: every choir has to perform the same test piece, which this year is 'Heriwn, Wynebwn y Wawr'. We are also having a stab at some operatic repertoire, a choral bauble plucked from Bellini's *I Puritani*. This being the National Eisteddfod, it's not in Italian. The Welsh words of 'Pan Seinio'r Utgorn Arian' ('When The Silver Trumpet Sounds') are, fortunately, repetitive in the bel canto style, although it does go on a bit and the words are ever so pernickety. Our third song is a lyrical ballad entitled 'Cenin Aur' ('Daffodils'), whose two verses are a heartbreaking lament inspired by the turn of the seasons and the impermanence of life. The problem here is that, to a perilous degree, the second tenor part clambers north into falsetto territory. In case there's time in the allotted space, Stewart has also lobbed in a traditional Welsh folk song called 'Hela'r Sgyfarnog' ('Hunting The Hare'). It's extremely fast for those of us not used to sight-reading in Welsh at seventy-eight revs per minute.

But I learn, I learn. The tried and tested methods work. For the two Welsh folk tunes, I simply recite them to buggery while in bed or the shower or on the M4. For this big practice the level of focus is intense. Stewart has brought in a distinguished Welsh conductor whose name escapes me to observe and comment. Our Welsh pronunciation is the perpetual bugbear: curl those *R*s. He has also plumped the choir with a variety of mop-haired and crew-cutted juniors, budding talents from the various schools where he teaches up and down Rhondda Cynon Taf. I stand next to one of them. He is even less word-confident than me, which is and isn't reassuring.

We are in full voice but, not wishing to put too much pressure on the more senior larynxes of Pendyrus, Stewart cuts the proceedings short. I could do with a couple more runs, to be frank, being still shaky on some of the less penetrable lyrics here and the odd notational chicane there. Stewart concludes with some heartfelt words of congratulation and encouragement – 'Gentlemen,' he says, 'I couldn't ask any more of you' – which we all lap up. It's followed by an injunction not to allow a drop of alcohol to pass our lips until after the performance.

Heading back to Mal's for the night, we speak Welsh. I worry that Mal has never heard me utter a single articulate thought. For a man who learned the language after he retired, when the brain ought by rights to be shutting down, his Welsh is remarkable. We watch the Eisteddfod highlights on S4C. Groups of poets are competing in teams, reciting short poems composed at speed. Judges loftily comment on their efforts, like schoolmasters marking an oral. The music of the poetry is manifest, but I can't say I understand much. Even Mal says he gets only about half.

The next morning two well-rested Pendyrus choristers prepare for the day ahead with a bacon sandwich, heavy on the butter and dripping with brown sauce. We are singing in the afternoon, but have a final practice somewhere on the Maes before lunch. There are shirts to be ironed, black leather shoes to be buffed. We pick up two more choristers, first tenor Gareth and his father Mel, an ex-miner whom Gareth encouraged to join. Having spent a life underground breathing in coal dust, Mel finds he's shorter of breath than the rest of us. We pooter down to Abercynon, the mouth of the valley, then head up past Merthyr towards the Heads of the Valleys Road where we park and catch the shuttle bus.

And so I enter the Maes in the jacket and tie of Pendyrus, the crest on my breast pocket. This feels validly Welsh. But there's more. Mal and I, Mel and Gareth and a few others are wandering along the tented street, the freshly dampened walkway glinting in the sun, when I hear a voice just off behind to the left.

'Pob lwc.' I don't initially twig that I'm being addressed, but turn and see a short barrel-chested man with a round face wearing a light-brown corduroy suit. 'Pob lwc,' he says again. Is he looking at me? He is, definitely. But why? I don't know him from … no, it can't be … it is! It's Dafydd Iwan, the president of Plaid Cymru and the musical conscience of Welsh Wales, who went to prison in defence of the language. And here on the Maes, as members of the Welsh-speaking public drift past and other choristers in their jackets wander about, he's wishing me good luck, of all people. I go over and shake his hand and ask him if he's coming along to hear Pendyrus compete. He's doubtless seen a thousand choirs sing, which explains the shoe-gazing evasion and muttered excuses. I don't mind in the slightest. The last time we spoke it was in English. This time, I am speaking Welsh to Dafydd Iwan on the Maes.

'Wyt ti'n adnabod pawb?' says Mal when I rejoin the group. Do I know everyone?

The day after competing in the National Eisteddfod I will have to go to New York. I'm determined to travel with a Welsh-language passport. Or a passport with lots of Welsh in it, such as I believe you can get if you apply in Welsh. I have taken the precaution of filling out my Welsh-language application form. I'm not quite sure if I can claim to have written it in actual Welsh, date of birth (*dyddiad geni*) and suchlike requiring answers in numerals. *Cyfenw*? At least my surname's Welsh, though one or two of its stablemates let the side down. Jasper Matthew Charles Bertram. When they ask my place of birth (*man geni*) I write 'Llundain'. There is no room to put Gower Street, the Welsh-sounding address of my birth.

The passport form is of course triply incomprehensible being (a) a passport form, (b) in official Welsh and (c) a daunting

combination of the above. Thank goodness for the English form
handed me by the post-office mistress in Machynlleth. That's only
singly incomprehensible.

For my passport photo I wear my Welsh rugby shirt. Next I book
an appointment at the passport office in Newport, handily arranged
as a stop-off on the way to choir practice. And this is where my plan
to enshrine my Welshness in an official document starts to go
wrong. I saunter over to the counter brimming with confident
goodwill. There's a pleasant-looking man uniformed as a representative of the United Kingdom Identity and Passport Service who
also wears an earring and a thin moustache.

'Hoffwn i gwneud cais am basport yn Gymraeg.' Note the soft
mutation of *p* to *b*, I think, as I look my man in the eye.

'Um, I don't actually speak Welsh, sir.'

'Oh.'

'No, I'm English. I just work here.'

'Oh.'

'Sorry about that, sir.'

'Is there someone I can speak Welsh to here?'

'Well, normally there is but they're on their break.'

'Oh.' I need to think on my feet. 'I want to apply for a Welsh
passport.' There's a pause.

'I'm … not quite sure what you mean.'

'A passport in Welsh. I've seen them.' In fact I've seen one. He's
looking a bit befuddled. 'I've filled out the form in Welsh.' I produce
the Welsh-language application form and brandish it, along with
my two passport photos featuring me in a Welsh rugby shirt.

'OK, let's have a look.' He takes the form and starts to check it.
'But I'm still a bit confused by this idea of a Welsh passport, sir. I
can't say I've ever seen one.'

'I could swear you can get one. With Welsh writing in it and things.' I may have been deceived. Or rather I may have deceived myself. I have tried to fantasise the Welsh-language passport into existence. But at least I can get a passport entirely made in Wales, even if it's in English.

'Could I see your old passport, please?'

Shit. I knew I'd forgotten something.

'Um, I left it in London.'

'I'm afraid I can't process your application without it.'

This is turning into a freshly baked catastrophe. I pull my Welsh-language passport application off the counter and head out of Newport. Human error is a terrible thing. The problem is that the clock is ticking. There's now not enough time left to guarantee having my passport issued in Newport. There's only one thing for it.

A week or so later I pedal in baking heat to the passport office in London and enter the teeming premises agleam with cycle sweat but tightly focused on the prize. The wait is much longer here, the system much better set up for inducing application-related neurosis. At least I've filled out the form in Welsh. That's something. They can't take that away from me. The electronic ticket numbers are read out by a computerised voice into which, unless I'm hearing things, they've programmed a clearly discernible tone of boredom and testiness. My number comes up. I head upstairs and come face to face with a uniformed representative of the United Kingdom Identity and Passport Service. He is large and hairy.

'I need to collect this later today,' I say, handing over the application and photos. Wearily he picks up the literature and starts to study it much as he has tens of thousands of applications before. Suddenly, his movements change in character as he flicks through the pages of the form, pupils darting up and down, across and back.

'What's this?' he says.

'It's my passport application form. It's in Welsh.'

'Blimey.' He gives it another once-over. 'We don't have any Welsh-language speakers.'

'But don't you know every word of the form anyway? It's exactly the same as the English one.' I wave my English-language form, which has come along for the ride. 'It's not as if my answers are in Welsh.' He can hear the distress in my voice.

'Look, given that you want the passport today, it would be a lot simpler if you quickly filled out that English form.' He's all emollience. 'It'll take just five minutes.' I sigh the atavistic sigh of the defeated Welshman and slap my English form on the counter. He even produces a pen and watches like a helpful parent as I fill in exactly the same answers as on my Welsh form. I conquer the temptation to put my city of birth as 'Llundain'.

'Have you got your photos?' At least I'm wearing my Welsh rugby shirt. They can't take that away from me. I cough up and stomp out of the building.

Four hours later I eagerly open my crisp new passport on the photograph page to find that they've somehow in the processing procedure contrived to bleed the colour out of my Welsh rugby shirt. It looks more Halloween orange than dragon red. Apparently I'm now Dutch. This really has been a demoralising exercise in step-by-step humiliation. My supposedly Welsh passport is about as Welsh as the Post Office Tower. I head back towards my locked bike, shoulders slumped, oppressed by the unfairness of it all. I'm about to pedal off when I think I might as well have a look at the inside front page, which says this:

EUROPEAN UNION
Yr Undeb Ewropeaidd

Then there's line of what I'm guessing is Scots Gaelic. Then:

UNITED KINGDOM OF GREAT BRITAIN AND
NORTHERN IRELAND
Teyrnas Gyfunol Prydain Fawr a Gogledd Iwerddon

In the final lines the order is inverted.

Pasport
PASSPORT

How typical that English needs to flaunt itself in self-important upper case. Must be an insecurity thing. I flick through to one of the back pages, where handy translations for various words are provided in the twenty-three official languages of the European Union. After English, and a long way before French and Spanish, German, Dutch and Portuguese, the other languages of empire and conquest, comes Welsh. Nationality/*Cenedligrwydd*. Sex/*Rhyw*. Date of expiry/*Dyddiad dod i ben*. Holder's signature/*Llofnod y deiliad*. This seems an appropriate moment for one's face to crack into a broad involuntary smile. Which mine now does, exultantly. It feels like I've finally and in the eyes of officialdom acquired Welsh nationality. I am Welsh. It doesn't quite say it in my *pasport*. But it might as well.

Maybe not everyone. But actually I do know people at the Eisteddfod aside from the members of Pendyrus. I poke my nose into the Learners' tent and spot a familiar face.

'Paned o de, os gwela di'n dda, James.' Cup of tea, please.

'O helo, Jasper. Ti'n iawn?' My Welsh tutor, who has volunteered to help wherever needed, really is the most unfazeable person. It's the first time we've met on Welsh soil, but in his tone of voice is an assumption that these casual meetings will happen on the Maes all the time. As I drink my tea I seize this opportunity to thank him for taking me on alongside his regular Welsh classes. His gaze wanders to his feet. I don't think he has any idea how much I mean it.

As it happens I also know someone else here. I bump into him outside a tented bookshop.

'Beth wyt ti'n gwneud yma?' What are you doing here? It's not a great joke, granted, but it's still a joke in Welsh.

'Sh'mae!' says the Archdruid of Wales expansively. Rather than his ceremonial garments, he's wearing a dapper light suit and tinted glasses. The face that lights up is somehow both round and sharp, receptive and assertive. He and Manon are all smiles, and so am I. However much he smiles, I'm rather nervous about mentioning my impending gift to the bardic tradition.

It's a bit intimidating speaking Welsh with an Archdruid. Jim grew up before and during the war and has lived his life entirely in Welsh. I have noted in his emails a tendency to deploy formal verb structures which Bishop William Morgan, the Elizabethan translator of the Bible, may recognise but which my L-plated brain finds challenging. Plus his front room is dominated by a tall carved wooden chair, the fruit of victory at the National Eisteddfod three years earlier. But I need to ask him about the rules of Welsh poetry, with a view to having a stab myself. So a couple of months before the Eisteddfod, I request a formal audience. The concepts under discussion being sufficiently complex, I additionally suggest that we proceed in English. He agrees, but with a rider.

'Please remember,' he says, 'that English is my second language.' Jim's accent is the closest that I've yet come across to one in which English words sound as if they could be Welsh. When he says 'brilliant', there's no flattening of the vowels. They come up as crisp and pure echoes of Welsh words like *gogoniant* (glory) or *diwylliant* (culture). He has led a rich full life in the heart of Welsh Wales. In the 1960s he was a Congregationalist minister in Carmarthen until his landmark translation of *Under Milk Wood* (1968) paved the way for a life in literature. As well as the Chair at the National Eisteddfod he has won the Crown twice. This is his first year as *Archdderwydd*. The job is at its busiest, he explains, in the Eisteddfod week itself, when he presides over various proclamations, as well as crownings, chairings and open-air ceremonies. For the rest of the year there are Gorsedd committees to run, honours to confer on new Gorsedd members, Celtic festivals to attend in the Isle of Man, Ireland, Brittany and Cornwall. Can he understand the languages of the latter, supposedly closest to Welsh? 'I can just about follow Cornish because it's very similar,' he says. 'Breton isn't at all.' During his term of office he also has to make it to one of the annual *eisteddfodau* held by the Welsh diaspora in Patagonia.

I decide to soften up the Archdruid with a question or two about Dafydd ap Gwilym, the great Welsh medieval bard with whom, in my quiet moments, I've been grappling.

'So, Jim,' I say, 'how good is he?'

'He is one of the foremost European poets. The difference from Chaucer, where we find it so difficult to understand, is that Dafydd ap Gwilym's Welsh is miraculously new. It's not that hard.'

'So why has no one ever heard of him outside Wales?'

'He's unsung,' explains the Archdruid, 'because he can't be translated. You lose so much once you start to translate *cynghanedd* into free verse. You've lost all the music.' *Cynghanedd*, which means 'harmony', is the word which encapsulates the bardic adherence to strict metre and internal consonance established in the Middle Ages.

'Unsung' is all too apt, therefore: in translation Welsh poetry speaks but it does not sing. But why do rules suit Welsh poetry? I wonder if there is a part of the Welsh mentality that thrives on conformity.

'I wouldn't argue with that,' says Jim. 'Because Welsh is a minority language and its existence has been questioned so many times, one draws strength from tradition. On the other hand it's the realisation that we have something unique. There is no similar scheme in any other language throughout the world. So why not use it? Why let it die?'

The basic unit of Welsh poetry, Jim explains, is the *englyn*, which in its most popular form has four lines. In the commonest type, the first line has ten syllables, the second six, while the third and fourth have seven each. So far so good.

'The first part is the ten-syllable line, which is broken up into seven/three, eight/two or very seldom nine/one,' he says. 'There is a connection. Let's call the split a dash. The three or two (or one) syllables have to harmonise with the beginning of the second line, with consonants or different rhymes. The second line itself ends with the main rhyme, non-accentuated. But halfway through that second line you have to have a consonantal echo. But then the stress is also important. The stress has to happen in the right place for it to harmonise.'

I listen. And listen. But the information struggles to settle. I sense it might all be easier with the help of a wall chart, a calculator and a brain transplant. The talk migrates away from poetry to other Welsh matters. We revert to Welsh. The Archdruid, who does most of the talking while I do most of the wondering what it all means, tells me a story about driving through the Brecon Beacons. He mentions a couple of place names – Aberhonddu (Brecon) and Mynydd Epynt – whereupon I hear the word 'Machlud'. I assume it's another place on the map of Wales.

'Lle yw Machlud?' I say to Jim. Where is Machlud?

'Ah brilliant!' he says. 'Lle yw machlud! I'll write a poem on that. Oh, you've given me a poem! Diolch yn fawr. Diolch yn fawr!' The Archdruid rubs his hands in glee. *Machlud*, he tells me, refers to the sunset. I've just asked where a sunset is.

I leave clutching a slim volume entitled *Singing in Chains*, vowing to compose a poem in Welsh if it is the last thing I do. The book is by his distinguished Gorsedd colleague Mererid Hopwood, tipped to be the first ever female Archdruid. The rules of *cynghanedd* are spelled out with admirable clarity. A child could understand what makes a Welsh poem so distinctly beautiful.

Try writing one yourself though. At least in part, *cynghanedd* boils down to elements one knows from English poetry: the play of rhyme, the bounce of rhythm and stress. But Welsh verse operates on an extra level. If you temporarily ignore the vowels in a Welsh poem, you can detect a pattern of consonants being repeated across the length of the line. Hopwood cites a verse by Dafydd ap Gwilym:

Yr wylan deg ar lanw, dioer
Unlliw ag eiry neu wenlloer;
Dilwch yw dy degwch di,
Darn fel haul, dyrnfol heli.

(Truly, fair seagull on the tide,
the colour of snow or the white moon,
your beauty is without blemish,
fragment like the sun, gauntlet of the salt.)

You don't need to understand Welsh to know that the original has a musical sensuality absent from the translation. Take the first line. In six apparently simple words the sounds *r*, *l*, *n* and *d* in the first half of the line are then repeated in the second half, in order. Then the third line breaks up into three sections: 'Dilwch/yw dy degwch/di.' The first two have an internal rhyme, while the first consonant in the second section is echoed in the third. 'And these,' says Mererid Hopwood, 'are two of the patterns that form the rules of *cynghanedd* as we still practise it today.'

I've got my eye on the basic *englyn* outlined by the Archdruid – four lines whose syllables are distributed thus: ten/six/seven/seven. Other rules to note: the second line has to finish on an unstressed syllable, while in the third and fourth lines, one must end with a stressed syllable and the other unstressed. And so I embark.

After a couple of hours' intense labour, including sundry false starts and fake trails, I hit a roadblock midway through the second line. There are a number of issues. I'm not entirely sure which of the four listed forms of *cynghanedd* I'm meant to be using. Also, the business of creating a sentence in which consonants echo along the line in strict order feels a bit like scouring a beach for identical pebbles. Finally, I have no clear idea of what I want to say. Some vague concepts about Welshness and my various Welsh tasks hover about in my head. I grow attached to a word I think I've coined – *tadiaith* (father tongue) – only for it to refuse to bed down into any meaningful sentence. Then I shuffle the signature verbs of my quest like a general moving battalions about on a scale map: *credu, canu, gweithio, siarad, chwarae, cystadlu, tyfu, eistedd*. But they are reluctant to configure themselves into a shape. And then a muta-tion gets triggered – gets *suffered* – and the daisy chain of conso-nants is thrown all out of whack.

I develop a headache, plus a feeling of desperation which locates itself in the urethra. I go back to the book and start looking for easier types of *englyn*. Words start to swim in front of my eyes. You can't write a poem without a thought in your brain. Then it strikes me. I practically slap my forehead. Of course! I've already written my first line. Unwittingly I blurted it out to the Archdruid. He thought he'd write a poem inspired by my accidental *cynghanedd*. 'Diolch yn fawr!' he said jubilantly.

And so I begin. The *englyn* I end up with after several more hours is free of sophistication. Its imagery is illogical, its sentiments cloying. It probably flouts a number of rules I don't know about. There's one word in the second line into which I have to crowbar the most tenuous meaning in order to make an internal rhyme. I can say without fear of contradiction that it is glib moronic tosh about the sun sinking bleakly in the east, if not for you then for me, and rising over Wales, which mutates my future from black darkness. As I say, melodramatic and nonsensical. I will make a point of never showing the Archdruid. Not ever. But it is my tosh. My Welsh tosh. And with it I am able to tack myself onto the end of the long and noble history of Welsh bards, the latest and the least.

Lle yw machlud llwm i chi?
Mae'r dwyrain yn fain i fi,
Codi'r haul yng Nghymru nawr
A threiglo fy wawr o ddu.

Familiar faces are mustering towards the north corner of the Maes. Graham, the choir secretary who invited me into the fold, has the commanding air of a brigadier before battle. The second tenors exude an air of readiness: Mal and Alan; Dai and Colin; the redoubtable Prof; Roy, who joined after me, waiting quietly. The top tenor French Horn is a-buzz. Barely out of their teens when Pendyrus last came to the National, they're now all over sixty. Jakey, hair as dark as it was then, was there in 1968.

Above us the pink pavilion shines obscenely whenever the light
stabs through gaps in the cloud. Through a door is a holding room,
filled with white-haired choristers in blazers of various hues: burgundy, black and, in Pendryus's case, navy blue. On a live video
feed piped in from the pavilion stage, one of our rival choirs is
bashing out its version of the test piece, 'Heriwn, Wynebwn y
Wawr'. As in Cardigan, we feel we can look everyone else in the eye.

I can't help noticing that the camera gets in good and tight on
choral faces. And it strikes me that, if you don't know the words,
you are going to look like a chump. Worse, you are going to look
unWelsh. Somewhere in my guts a butterfly clambers out of its
chrysalis and begins to flutter about in a businesslike fashion.
Another soon joins it. If a camera catches me Redwoodising in the
warp-tempo 'Hela'r Sgyfarnog' … it doesn't bear thinking about.
Trip over one syllable and you will never get the thread back. I have
the words in my pocket. I go into an emergency eleventh-hour
session.

'Wyt ti'n barod i ganu, bychan?' After a minute or so Mal
catches me at my revision. Am I ready to sing?

'Wrth gwrs!' Course! 'Dw i'n jus' siecio'r geiriau unwaith eto.'
Just checking the words one more time. Mal gives me a probing
look, smile half suppressed. We like having you in the second
tenors, it says, but don't you go letting anyone down now. Especially yourself. I suddenly need to rehydrate. By the water cooler a
choir in black tie is receiving a pep talk in Welsh. That'll be Côr
Meibion Taf, whom we thumped into third place in Cardigan.
They look suspiciously young. And very much swollen in numbers.
When we beat them there were barely thirty in the choir. They're
now double that. Hm. I get my water and retreat.

Clapping thunders through the loudspeakers. Another choir has
finished its fifteen minutes. Word spreads among Pendyrus that we

should now proceed to the next chamber to await our turn. All eighty of us form four long lines, each consisting of five second tenors, five tops, five baritones and five basses. The maths is relatively simple. Or it is until an instruction drifts back from somewhere even closer to the wings of the stage that choirs are actually standing in five rows, not four. Panic spreads like a bush fire. Choristers who have sung next to each other for a quarter of a century are not easily dislodged. Eventually, exasperated looks flung, flare-ups defused and deals struck, the four-row Pendyrus reconfigures itself into five rows for its most important musical moment in decades.

Throughout all this Stewart is standing quietly by a wall. The conductor is up for judgement as much as the choir, if not more. I go over to shake his hand. That winning grin of his is looking perhaps a little tight.

'Pob lwc, Stewart,' I say.

'I chi hefyd.' To you too. (Stewart prefers the formal mode of address.)

I resume my position at the far right of the back row. My flank's feeling a bit exposed. I put it to my neighbour – one of several schoolboys brought in by Stewart to fatten the sound – that maybe we should swap and he go on the end. He doesn't put up a fight. Now I'm in the winning position I occupied in Cardigan.

Pendyrus falls silent. One's breathing is becoming shallower, nails shorter. I do another word run-through of the two songs I know least. 'Awn ni hela'r ysgyfarnog' ('Let's go and hunt the hare'). 'Fe wylwn ni, o genin aur, o'ch mynd yn ebrwydd iawn ('We weep, o daffodil, that you leave so very soon'). All in working order. Any minute now I'm going to be on Welsh television, singing Welsh at the national festival of all things Welsh. If anyone had told me that two years ago ... or that the president of Plaid Cymru would

recognise me on the Maes … or that the Archdruid and his distinguished prose-writing wife would burst into the waiting area and
hurry over to find me and pump my hand and wish me luck …

Suddenly we're moving. An expert will be discussing our pros-
pects with a presenter on S4C. And now here's the green light.
Pendyrus's long-awaited return to the Eisteddfod will be their
subject. I feel like a sportsman emerging for combat as I follow the
long single line round the back of the stage, and am suddenly on
the national stage of Wales. The stage is aglow. Somewhere out
there beyond the lights an audience of several hundred can be
made out, including near the front – I've just spotted them – three
judges.

A hush descends. I am aware of cameras waiting to pounce on
telltale evidence of word-fail like a bird of prey scoping the floor for
the scuttle of rodents. As Stewart raises his baton I glue my eyes on
him and, I swear, don't remove them for the next fifteen minutes.

We embark with Bellini. I've often thought Welsh had an affin-
ity with Italian – the heavy commitment to the penultimate syllable, the many verbs ending in -io and -o, including seinio in the title
of 'Pan Seinio'r Utgorn Arian'. Pendyrus duly make the trumpets
sound with a bravura display of florid Latin melodrama. The song
reads like a public conversation, chatty and bustling, full of extrovert purpose. It goes on a bit, with lots of orchestral squiggles for
Gavin to impersonate on the piano. But the Italian flavours are rich
and colourful and, on a personal note, I am practically word perfect.
The all-seeing cameras won't have caught a sniff.

We glide into 'Cenin Aur', a ballad of haunting beauty into
which I could afford to put more facial expression but so tight is my
focus on Stewart's lyrical conducting that I may as well be Botoxed.
There is no piano accompaniment for this, so it's down to us to
conjure up an atmosphere. The bewitching harmonies spread a

lovely pall of Welsh melancholia across the floor of the pavilion as we sing of life's evanescence and man's empathy with the sad passing of the seasons. I'd be a pool of tears by the end of it if the dominant emotion weren't relief at mastering the second tenor's sinuous line, which slithers scarily high and topples towards the floor before curling up into the quietest, tenderest sigh of sorrow.

No sooner has the audience's appreciation melted away than we crash into the dissonant world of 'Heriwn, Wynebwn y Wawr'. The opening was delivered at full welly in Cardigan. This time, with amplification, we might as well blow a hole in the back wall of the pink pavilion. 'Miloedd ar filoedd sy'n amau bob dydd … !!' The lines feel like second nature to me now. Every word has made its way into my marrow, like songs sung in school and never yet forgotten. Every surge or drop in volume, each dynamic stress is like a feature in a much-loved landscape – a dramatic Welsh one, naturally. For some reason, familiarity does not allow me to relax and work on my facial performance. Later, when watching it back online, I see that this is the song in which a rogue camera chooses to seek me out and linger on my marble features. The level of concentration is chiselled on my face. I look like I'm successfully laying an egg of inconvenient diameter. My lips move to precisely the right specification. 'Mae'r dyfodol yn dechrau,' I sing. 'Mae'r dyfodol yn dechrau, yn dechrau, yn deeeechraaauuu.' The future is beginning. As Pendyrus sing the climactic words of this rugged paean to the power of song, here on the stage of the National Eisteddfod but also broadcast into homes across Wales, it's as if I can feel my own Welsh future joining hands with the Welsh past. How thrilled my grandparents would presumably be to know that a grandson of theirs, born in England and educated in Englishness, had somehow managed to paddle this far upstream towards the source of Wales and Welshness. 'Mae'r dyfodol yn dechrau … yn awrrrrrrrrrrrr.'

The future is beginning now! The *r* is rolled once more like an unfurling red carpet as Stewart turns to the audience and accepts forthright applause.

A single song to come, a brief merry afterthought to send us on our way. Let us go and hunt the hare, again without the piano, a harum-scarum chase across wide-open fields of song, words tumbling out at such speed that one or two go missing from the rear corner of second tenors. We're the only section with words, everyone else la-la-laing along, so the risk of exposure is considerable, but the long hours spent reciting pay off. With a final exclamation of national fervour – 'Cymru lân!' – all of a sudden the fifteen minutes' traffic of Pendyrus's time onstage is up.

Finally I can take my eyes off Stewart and look out past the lights towards an audience clapping hard and long. I note the judges writing. Pendyrus didn't put a foot wrong, surely. It was a Rolls-Royce performance, all effortless power and precision cornering. Welcome us back to competition with a gong, would you please?

Out in the open air, choristers are free to start unwinding. As the afternoon proceeds the sun stops vacillating and puts in a decent shift. The forecourt of the beer area is full of T-shirted wassailers while up on an outdoor stage Dafydd Iwan strums boisterously through the old favourites – 'Carlo', 'Yma O Hyd'.

After a contented hour or two in the sun we wander back for the adjudication. The tented stalls are closing for the last time, the streets of the Maes emptying. In the pavilion I sit in the wings on the right with Alan and Roy, my fellow second tenors. Just across the aisle the massed ranks of Côr Meibion Taf fill row upon raked row of seating. After a couple of minutes the judges make their way onto the stage. One of them approaches the microphone and starts talking in Welsh. I don't understand much amplified Welsh but there is no mistaking the moment when he announces, in reverse order, that of the seven competing choirs the one which has been adjudicated third best is Côr Meibion Pendyrus.

The heart sinks just a little. We haven't won. But we have been placed. The official line is that a placing will be deemed a success. Third is no disgrace. Until they announce the second-placed choir. Llanelli. Heads around me turn to one another in shock. Llanelli? Llanelli, it is widely agreed among my colleagues, are not in the same league as Pendyrus. What other enormities have the judges in store for us? Who can they possibly have picked for choir of the year? Instantly I can feel the result rise in my waters so am not at all thrown when Côr Meibion Taf, the black-jacketed mob across the aisle, leap to their feet like a football crowd and start hugging, yelling, fisting the air in triumph. As their exultant conductor emerges to collect the cup, Pendyrus choristers clap sportingly. But no sooner have we emerged into the open air and started following the human tide towards the exit than the mutterings begin.

Mutterings swell to splutterings in a pub in Tredegar, one of the smarter mining towns over in the next-door valley. A story fans around the floor that we have been the victims of a slippery inter-pretation of Eisteddfod rules. Côr Meibion Taf, whom we beat into third place in Cardigan when they could barely muster thirty chor-isters, were performing with an unfair advantage. So goes the rumour. Sure, our numbers were slightly plumped with the recruit-ment of half a dozen schoolboys. But theirs were mysteriously doubled – *doubled* – with the help of the chorus of the Welsh National Opera and the BBC National Chorus of Wales. There were up to ten from each, apparently. One of our number, who sings with the BBC Chorus, recognised a bunch of them. The talk is all of larceny, effrontery, skulduggery, conspiracy. And if it's one thing to lose to a choir packed with professional singers, what about Llanelli? Llanelli!

I'd be inclined to dismiss all of this but for the head-scratching of Stewart, who can't quite believe that we didn't at least finish second. Outside, shadows lengthen across the Valleys. Inside, the atmosphere fugs with grumbling about miscarriages of justice and brooding over murky politickings. I am in my Welsh rugby shirt by now, with Welsh rage boiling in my Welsh veins. I am as scandalised as the next Pendyrus chorister at the whims of judges and the tactics of rivals. I am appalled, truly. Something must be done, letters fired off, objections tabled. Cudgels taken up. But as the evening darkens, the beer swimming into our arteries mutates anger to sorrow and the old Welsh acceptance of fate's whims.

10

Cerdded = Walk

'I like wandering about these lonely, waste and ruined places.'

Revd Francis Kilvert (1871)

I AM BACK where I began. Across the broad waters of the Severn estuary the old bridge hangs suspended between two countries. As children, speeding to Carmarthen on the motorway, we used to look out for this staggering landmark for hours upon end. On a drizzly afternoon such as this we would never have found it until it was right on top of us. The magnificent struts are barely more than a rumour against a backcloth of grey August skies. That's England over there. Over here, under my feet, is the southernmost tip of what is known as the debatable land.

The dividing line between England and Wales has been nudged hither and thither like a boundary rope on a cricket ground. Along a turbulent corridor of terrain, tears and blood have been spilled, fists and swords swung. The current compromise is a botched job. There are some places with English names in Wales, others with Welsh names in England. And yet in the minds of both nations there is a border that everyone can sort of agree on. Over the centuries it has mutated from a fact into a symbol. And it starts here at Sedbury Cliff.

A notice on a big stone says as much: 'Llwybr Clawdd Offa'. *Llwybr* means 'path'. *Clawdd* means 'boundary' or 'fence'. Offa was the King of Mercia in the second half of the ninth century. More than a millennium ago, it was Offa who defined where Wales ends and England begins – or rather the bit of England that abuts Wales. The inhabitants of this island know little of figures in our collective history before the Norman landing in 1066. But this one name from the murky era of Anglo-Saxon primacy has imprinted itself on the very landscape in the form of a bank of earth, flanked by a ditch, which runs intermittently from the Severn estuary to the mouth of the Dee. And that's what I'm going to walk along, for 180 miles.

I say I. I mean we. For this bit of my quest, I am not alone. One hundred and eighty miles is a lot of yardage to cover on your tod. Coming in the opposite direction will be several solitary walkers, all of them men in their thirties or forties lugging rucksacks the size of coracles. I tend to agree with the Revd Richard Warner, who embarked on *A Walk Through Wales in August 1797* in the same week, 213 years earlier, in the company of someone he referred to as C—. 'Solitary pleasures are, at the best, but imperfect,' he explained in his opening dispatch; 'and with respect to travelling in particular, the gratification arising from it depends so much upon having a companion, with whom one can interchange sentiment, and communicate observation, as leads me entirely to coincide with Cicero in thinking that even a journey to the stars without society would be but a dull kind of expedition.'

This journey is to Prestatyn, at the other end of the Offa's Dyke Path, and I shall be walking there with E—. She and I have given ourselves eleven days to march up the eastern flank of Wales.

'Never heard of it,' people say when I tell them. 'What's that?' I need hardly add which side of the border these people live. But it's easy not to know about Offa's Dyke, even when it's right under your nose.

We turn our backs on England and set off downhill through a meadow. There's a slippery path cut into a conveniently raised rib of earth bisecting the field. This is to be the final test. I am going to measure out my Welshness in mileage and gradient, toil and sweat. It's only in the next field that I do a double take.

'Wasn't that it?' I say.

'Wasn't that what?'

'That raised bit of earth we just walked down. Wasn't that Offa's Dyke?' We look back up the hill. Give or take the odd hawthorn bush, it's quite distinct: a thick grassy spine interrupting the natural contour of the slope. So that's a good scholarly start then.

In mitigation, I'm not the only one who's missed it. A Mr Hutton, examining the remains of Offa's Dyke in 1803, reported that 'the traveller would pass it unheeded if not pointed out. All that remains is a small hollow which runs along the cultivated fields, perhaps not eighteen inches deep in the centre, nor of more than twenty yards width.' Whatever its physical size, its meaning cannot be mistaken. The Welsh have been known since time immemorial as the people who live on the other side of Offa's Dyke.

It's a bit of a bummer that we have to trudge through England for most of the first day. On the far bank of the Wye, whenever the path strays close enough, are tantalising glimpses of the land of my fathers. We are in that little tongue of Gloucestershire between the Severn and the Wye. Both sprout out of the earth hundreds of miles back on the bald flanks of Pumlumon in Mid Wales – I poetically recall that I've sipped the trickle that is the Wye's very source – and now the two rivers are surging towards reunion. I used to think the narrative of the two twisting rivers was a marvellous metaphor, but now that I'm wedged between them I can't quite work out what for.

The Archdruid should bash out an *englyn* on it, and all such mean-
ings would soon surface like a developing photograph.

Anyway, here we are in England. It's green and pleasant enough.
There are stubbly fields, a whole bunch of hedges. I have fed such
data into my calculations when pondering the key decision: which
way to walk – north to south, or south to north? I twist myself in
knots about this, much like the Wye writhing and swivelling down
there to the left. At first I judged it preferable to complete this
journey where it began, at the bridge. How very trim, I thought;
how jolly mathematical. But the more I looked at the map, the
more it seemed somehow regressive, like wishing for the womb. In
life we must stride away from what we know. Besides, the prospect
of fetching up in England at the end of eleven days and 177 miles
is indigestible. This whole venture is about walking towards Welshness. So south to north it is.

It's a scorcher as we leave Chepstow. The Revd Warner sounded
a jaded note as he trod the same road. The scenery, he scribbled,
'has already been described by tourists out of number, who have
been so particular in their details, as to leave nothing to be gleaned
by such birds of passage as C— and myself'. I must say I entertain
similar feelings as the path takes us into woodland where we start
to encounter day-trippers. They are shod in plimsolls, sandals, even
flip-flops as they walk the ancient border. Not a rucksack in sight.
'We are dykers,' I want to say after all of three miles. 'I'll thank you
please to step aside.'

But then the Wye took a grip on Warner's imagination as he and
C—clambered up an elevation and 'were suddenly astonished with
a scene grand and unbounded. Immediately under the cliff is seen
the Wye, following a course the most whimsical and sinuous that
can be conceived, and discharging its waters into the Severn.' We
stop and perch at Wintour's Leap, a similar spot slightly upriver.

It's so called because a royalist on horseback is said to have flown over the 200-foot limestone cliffs to escape chasing Roundheads. We look down at the loops of the muddy river. An apocryphal story, one suspects.

My backpack is insanely heavy. I've been told it becomes part of your anatomy after three days. Which means after fifty-two and a half miles, including today's frankly overambitious twenty-miler. It seems like a long process of acclimatisation. My fancy new breathable top – it would be beyond eccentric to do the dyke in my Welsh rugby shirt – clings damply to my spine. The rucksack, for the record, consists of 1 pr jeans, 1 shirt, 1 fleece, 1 pr shoes, 3 pr walking socks, 5 pr gentleman's briefs, 1 pr waterproof trousers, 1 anorak, 6 pckts crisps, 10 bars choc, 2 bottles water, 1 pr binocs, 1 copy *Kilvert's Diary*, 1 guidebook. It feels like 2 tons boulders. After half a morning on the dyke I know more or less how Aeneas felt as he carried his old man Anchises from the incinerated ruins of Troy. (The Welsh, lest we forget Gerald of Wales's theory, are ethnically Trojan.)

Once upon a time, of course, a change of clothes was a luxury for the gentlemen of leisure who went pedestrianising in Wales. George Borrow, setting out from Llangollen to traverse South Wales, packed into his small leather satchel a pair of worsted stockings, a razor, a white linen shirt and a prayer book. (The last two were reserved for Sundays.) He also had his boots resoled and his umbrella mended. In all weathers he must have looked a mess. On his summer outing from Llangollen to Anglesey he complains often of insupportable heat. But if the heavens opened he might find himself 'up to the knees in quags'. As for Warner and C—, having walked from Builth to Rhayader they entered the Angel Inn looking, he confesses, 'marvellously foul'. There was little for it but to pull on the same outer clothes the next morning. Warner packed 'a single change of

raiment, and some other little articles for the comfort of the person'
into a specially customised pocket of his coat 'that sweeps from one
side to the other, and allows room sufficient for all the articles necessary to be carried'. C— had extra-large pockets sewn in each side
of his. They regretted their choice when, passing three gentlemen
in Cardiganshire, they noted that each 'carried a handsome leath-
ern bag, covered with neat net-work, which, being suspended from
the right shoulder by a strap, hung under the left arm, in the
manner of a shooting-bag'. To Warner and C— the arrangement
looked not only ergonomic and comfortable, it also 'gave the wearer
much less the appearance of a pedlar than attached to us'.

After a few sweaty miles walking along a high escarpment
through old forests we come to a glade where, beyond a clearing
between trees, there is a lovely distant prospect of Tintern Abbey.
Wordsworth returned to this bend in the river when still a young
man in 1798. Meditating on the sublimity of the place, he found
memories of its many 'forms of beauty' still miraculously clustered.
' … oft, in lonely rooms,' he quivered,

> … and 'mid the din
> Of towns and cities, I have owed to them
> In hours of weariness, sensations sweet,
> Felt in the blood, and felt along the heart;
> And passing even into my purer mind,
> With tranquil restoration.

Whenever marooned too long at the wrong end of the M4, that's
sort of how I feel about Welsh landscapes all the time now. We get
the poem up on my phone and read quite a lot of it out loud.
Neither of us has ever been to the mother abbey of the Cistercians
in Wales. How it beckons seductively in the flat bright light. I think

of my uncle Teilo, in the last monastery still extant in Wales where brothers work and worship in the old Cistercian way of which Gerald so approved. We are all for deviating into Wales to pay our respects. It's only a mile out of our way in total. But at the signpost to Tintern and without a second thought we drop the idea like a stone. An extra mile? We've still got fourteen to go.

Onwards, alongwards, down to the Wye where we lunch on its bank, the peace and solitude broken only as intermittent cars yammer by along the A466. A swan floats regally past, parked on driftwood. The way to travel.

'That's Wales across the river,' I say, just so we're both in the loop.

And that's where it stays for much of the first day. Technically we're in what Offa deemed to be Wales, but one can't entirely ignore the reality that England snatched it all back again. Not that there's much sign of the dyke round here. The views of various valleys are of course marvellous; one's spirits soar at all the right sights. But as the afternoon lengthens I'm inclined to think mostly of suffering feet and groaning limbs. The advice from all and sundry was to train hard for this multi-marathon, but the memory of being smashed to smithereens in rugby has cast a long shadow.

The good news is that we've crossed the border. 'Croeso i Gymru'. I feel perky as anything as we tear up the Kymin – two miles swallowed up in a trice – and find ourselves gazing out at most of Monmouthshire. I have borrowed binoculars for just such an occasion. Mountains recede as far as the eye can see. I try to work out which one's which. The ones clustering around Abergavenny are easy: Sugar Loaf, Blorenge, Skirrid. Some people refer to these and other Welsh peaks as hills, but they really must keep their English traps shut. Henry James, who persisted in thinking he was in England, describes how he and a companion 'scrambled up the little Skirrid'. However, from his description of it – 'the aspect of a magnified extinguisher … the grassy cone … as smooth-faced as a garden mound' – it is clear he'd confused it with the Sugar Loaf. We sit in silence and watch the west. This is why we came.

The less said about day two the better. It's a mere twelve miles, ten fewer than yesterday factoring in a missed signpost in a darkening forest. But that's much more than enough. One's body has largely shut down. Legs cooperate only under the direst duress. The Offa's Dyke signposts send us across soft arable undulations, but I am old and weary. And tetchy. I've gone right off the Sugar Loaf, which like an attention-seeking tot plays a tiresome game of peek-a-boo behind a fringe of hills. As for the Skirrid …

'I'm thinking of compiling a list of Welsh mountains there's no point in climbing.' This over lunch at the top of a meadow from where we can look at a cinemascopic array of peaks. My walking companion looks at me quizzically.

'Starting with the Skirrid. It's meant to have a famous notch in it. The summit was split in two on the day of the Crucifixion. I've never seen the notch once. So you can put that on the list. An entirely pointless mountain.'

'What else is on the list?' E— chooses to humour me.

'I'll get back to you on that.'

The afternoon unfolds at snail's pace. A mile is an infinitely flexible concept. We are down to fewer than two of them an hour despite easy terrain. Crusty little churches in Llanfihangel Ystum Llewern and Llantilio Crossenny are not enough to keep spirits from wilting. On the map, Llangattock Lingoed seems somehow to be getting further away.

'Preseli,' I say. 'No need to climb that.' Preseli is the mountain in Pembrokeshire that loomed over my grandfather's childhood. Silence. Maybe I should just compile the list in my head.

'The Black Mountain.' Now I'm being provocative. E— has a soft spot for the Black Mountain, though she's not been up it. (No point.)

'Aren't we doing that tomorrow?'

'That's the Black Mountains. Plural. Totally separate.'

We keep going. Fields come and go, and kissing gates and ODP signposts. We refuel on *bara brith* at the moated White Castle, scene of dire conflict once, now stormed by tots unstrapped from car seats. Will this afternoon ever end? A squad of shiny horseflies have mistaken my sweaty head for dung. The mind grows heretical.

'Snowdon.'

'What?'

'You heard me.'

'Why Snowdon?'

'Too big.' My mood is marvellously foul. 'And crowded.'

That's one thing I will say for day two. We meet barely a soul. This corner of Wales is ours, all ours.

We roll in at six o'clock, lower limbs as flexible as marble. The list of what's still to come is suddenly daunting, starting with day three: Llangattock Lingoed to Hay-on-Wye: 19.5 miles. Then Hay-on-Wye to Kington: 14.5. Kington to Knighton: 13.5. Knighton to Churchtown: 12 (strenuous hills!). Churchtown to Buttington Bridge: 16.5. Buttington Bridge to Trefonen: 16.3. Trefonen to Llangollen: 13. Llangollen to Bwlch Penbarras: 18.6. Bwlch Penbarras to Prestatyn: 20.7. Apparently the path crosses the border nine times.

The distances look increasingly monstrous but compared to others who have trekked across Wales they are nothing. 'A walk of six and thirty miles from Caerwent to Usk,' noted Warner breezily. On another day: 'We set off for Rhaiddar-Gowy, a town at the distance of thirty-two miles.' One morning they did eleven miles before breakfasting in Abergavenny. Borrow perambulated no less stridently. 'Having now walked twenty miles in a broiling day I thought it high time to take some refreshment.' One day he left for Holyhead, 'seventeen miles distant', at four in the afternoon. He walked the fourteen miles from Llangollen to Ruthin and then back again. 'I always walk in Wales,' he advised an Italian staying in the same hotel in Snowdonia. 'Then you will have a rather long walk, signore; for Bangor is thirty-four miles from here.' He boasted that he could cover four and a half miles an hour.

And then there is Kilvert. Saturday, 26 February 1870: 'A lovely morning so I set off to walk over the hills to Colva, taking my luncheon in my pocket, half a dozen biscuits, two apples and a small flask of wine. Took also a pocket book and opera glasses … Very hot walking.' After a twenty-mile round trip, he was back in time to dress for dinner.

Francis Kilvert served as curate in Clyro in Radnorshire for seven years from 1865. The diary he kept of his daily rounds, much of which was destroyed – it's presumed by his widow – was exhumed and published in the 1930s. It is a priceless record of country life in Victorian Wales. Kilvert had a huge relish for oral history gleaned from elderly parishioners, the more sensational in flavour the better. But long swathes might have been written in any century. The local characters who live and breathe in his pages – wizened peasants, mannered gentry and voluptuous farm girls, wassailers and drovers fighting outside the Sun Inn in Clyro – are somehow timeless archetypes. He also had an extraordinary eye for the rural rota, for nature's intoxicating variegations, the turn of the seasons from crushing heat to withering cold. As he walked tirelessly about the Wye Valley, his response to the world around him gilded his prose with lush Wordsworthian tints.

Of the parish's scenes of solitude he wrote, 'There dwells among them a spirit of quiet and gentle melancholy more congenial and akin to my own spirit than full life and gaiety and noise.' Kilvert developed such a profound attachment to the Black Mountains and the hills around Hay and Clyro that, although he was no Welshman, they have since become known as Kilvert Country.

We approach Kilvert Country at the southern foot of the Black Mountains. The route to Hay-on-Wye is long and high. And rain is confidently predicted. We start early. At eight in the morning after a mile or so I am pleased to report that I look over my left shoulder and can see the indisputable notch in the summit of the Skirrid. They call it Holy Mountain though its forked profile looks much more like the wrathful work of the devil. We cross the road and the railway that lead into England and head sharply upwards. As we gain height, clouds close in, rain spits, sheep scatter. Heather smothers the tops and the mountain falls away on both sides. Nowhere can there be a clearer sense of walking along a frontier than on the Hatterall Ridge. Hang-gliders or suicides have a clear choice up here: to hurl themselves into England or into Wales. National temperament seems written into the landscape. To the right, England exudes a rolling, self-satisfied contentment while Wales retreats towards the horizon in a series of wild convulsions.

Through binoculars I look out obsessively for Waun Fach, the summit of the range whose pimply peak nature in its wisdom has made visible only if you're this high up. Thanks to the weather it's all change. Cumulus crashes against the eastern wall of the ridge like a gigantic wave. Gusts of wind push clouds across the protean mountainscape as if drawing curtains back and forth in front of a stage set. One minute you see nothing, the next the Vale of Ewyas is laid at your feet. Llanthony Priory materialises at the floor of the valley, another Cistercian relic open to the skies. 'On our left we passed the noble monastery of Llanthony in its great circle of mountains,' recorded Gerald of Wales coming down the valley from the other end as part of the Archbishop of Canterbury's great caravan of proselytisers eight centuries earlier. It's less a circle, in fact, than a long narrow canyon 'no more than three arrow-shots in width'. Gerald noted approvingly that the abbey was 'roofed in with sheets of lead'. Thanks to the Reformation, you now have to imagine the roof.

There's something perfect about Llanthony. It's rumoured that St David lived there as a hermit, which was enough to persuade one and then another hermit to follow suit until an Augustinian monastery was endowed, then a priory built. One night in 1327 it housed the dethroned Edward II, shortly to be murdered. The young Turner captured Llanthony's lonely ravishing essence, then Walter Savage Landor bought the estate in 1807, fired by dreams of picturesque rural seclusion. But his stay was short-lived. When he vanished irascibly abroad, he left his creditors and Mother Nature to continue the process of dilapidation.

In the spring of 1870 Kilvert made a memorable pilgrimage over the Gospel Pass from the north. The day trip brought out his hot-tempered side. 'What was our horror,' he exclaimed, 'on entering the enclosure to see two tourists … postured among the ruins in an attitude of admiration.' One of them was pointing out features of interest among the remains. 'If there is one thing more hateful than another it is being told what to admire and having objects pointed out to one with a stick. Of all noxious animals too the most noxious is a tourist. And of all tourists the most vulgar, illbred, offensive and loathsome is the British tourist.' He and his companion had the long walk home to Clyro to calm their nerves. 'We were rather tired with our 25 miles' walk, but not extraordinarily so.'

The Offa's Dyke Path continues for mile upon mile along the

ridge, past Lord Hereford's Knob to the rounded summit of Hay Bluff from where the spectacular work of the Wye, the valley carved by its passage as it wanders carelessly off into England, now becomes apparent. We can see most of Radnorshire. Somewhere down there, buttressed on the other side by yet more hills, are Kilvert's haunts, Hay-on-Wye and Clyro. Off to the left is the northern flank of the Black Mountains, lined up like ships' prows as if forever jostling for position. The only way from here is down, four sapping miles across long sloping moorland.

Hay is asleep in August after the second-hand bookshops have closed. Those who have walked over the ridge are soon asleep too. Three days and fifty-three miles are up. We are officially acclimatised, as is clear from the furious pace set the next morning as we cross the glistening Wye and head into the hills above Clyro. I hope Kilvert would approve of our failure to visit his church and point sticks at his memory. Instead, we pass along his wooded paths. 'The beauty of the view was indescribable,' he said of the valley. Behind, the Black Mountains stand sentry on the horizon. After a few steep miles we reach the village of Newchurch, where Kilvert one May morning was slightly disgusted to find the clergyman's young daughters busy castrating lambs. 'But I made allowance for them and considered in how rough a way the poor children have been brought up, so that they thought no harm of it, and I forgave them.' Kilvert had a soft spot for young girls. To one of them in the Newchurch school he offered a kiss for every correct sum. He doesn't specify her age, but it's clear she flirted with him outrageously. 'Shall I confess that I travelled ten miles today over the hills for a kiss, to kiss that child's sweet face? Ten miles for a kiss.'

The diaries of his that survive are a catalogue of pining for unobtainable females, some too grand, others too young. When he returned to England in 1872, he and the entire neighbourhood with him seem to have gone into mourning ('These people will break my heart with their affectionate lamentations'). Among the parting gifts he took away with him was *Wordsworth's Complete Works*. In 1877 he returned to the Wye as vicar in Bredwardine, just over the border. In his fortieth year, his search for a mate came to an end when finally he married. Within months he had died of peritonitis.

The path leaves Kilvert Country and rises onto Hergest Ridge, halfway along which we walk into England. I haven't made a note of how many counties you can see from the top but it's presumably several. I produce my opera glasses, as Kilvert would have called them, and survey the lumps and miscellaneous humps of the West Country: the Cotswolds, the Malverns, a couple of odd-looking paps somewhere off in Herefordshire. To the west, of course, the drama is altogether more operatic. A bunch of Brecon Beacons, the Black Mountains, possibly Pumlumon looking like a ne'er-do-well scruff in the back row. Somewhere to the north, faint shadows suggest themselves. The magnificence stills the tongue and swells the heart. And look, nudging out from round the side of the Black Mountains, now decidedly to the south, is the good old Skirrid – hurrah! – to which my feelings are now entirely charitable as it raises its two fingers out to piddling English peaks.

Sixty-six miles down.

The next morning the wind is raising its fists, and the skies have a thuggish edge. At the top of a blustery hill we keep our long-awaited appointment with Offa's Dyke, which has come along from England. It carves a field in twain, running in from the east. We reach it, take a left and follow it. And follow it. For miles and miles, for days and days. It's not much to look at, you think as you look at it. It's a mound of earth. It would hardly hold back a Welsh marauder. The dyke's footling size provokes comparable sniggers to those unleashed at the knee-high Hadrian's Wall.

In places the boundary is indeed unassuming. But 1,200 years on, at other points it is still very remarkable. Offa's engineers took care to heap the earth up from the Welsh side, so at its highest points a Mercian on the dyke would have towered ten feet over a Welshman in the neighbouring ditch. There are points over the next few days when I stand on the Welsh side and – imaginarily stripping away the foliage, the trees and bushes, the breaches in its flanks made by badgers and rabbits, the cows and sheep peacefully grazing on its grassy crest – I am looking at a Saxon prototype of the Iron Curtain.

There seems little doubt that where all it needed to be was a boundary line, that's what it was. Where it needed to be a fortification, it swelled to altogether more threatening dimensions. It did the trick, not just in the reign of Offa but for centuries afterwards. 'There was a time,' Borrow's guide in Llangollen tells him, 'when it was customary for the English to cut off the ears of every Welshman who was found to the east of the dyke, and for the Welsh to hang every Englishman whom they found to the west of it. Let us be thankful that we are now more humane to each other.'

The dyke puts me a pickle. No aspiring Welshman should grow too fond of any symbol of English oppression. But the Welsh have long since adopted as their own the Norman castles erected to suppress them. Offa's Dyke, being predominantly in Wales, has also been subsumed into the heritage. Besides, nowadays you have a different physical relationship with it. In the old days Welshmen will have come at it perpendicularly. No one will have walked the length of it. So the scale of the achievement is really only clear to modern hikers.

The sheer obsessive relentlessness of it takes the breath away. The shape it cuts across the rolling landscape, admitting no impediment as it scales the likes of Herrock, Llanfair, Selattyn hills and plunges down the other side, resembles the twisting track of a sub-terranean serpent. And everywhere it passes, the view to the west is unimpeded. If you were standing on the dyke, you would have seen the Welsh coming.

It was built, it is thought, in the final dozen years of Offa's thirty-nine-year reign, once Welsh resistance to Mercian suprem-acy in the borderlands had been quashed. The closest contempo-rary account is from the Welsh-born Bishop Asser's *Life of King Alfred*, written perhaps a century later. He refers to 'rex nomine Offa qui vallum magnum inter Britannium atque Merciam de mari usque ad mare fieri imperavit' – a king named Offa who ordered a great wall to be between Britain and Mercia from sea to sea. Offa was evidently as ruthless as any of Wales's other conquerors. William of Malmesbury, the Anglo-Norman historian, noted after another century had elapsed that 'in the same character, vices were so palliated by virtues, and at another virtues came in such quick succession upon vices, that it is difficult to determine how to char-acterise the changing Proteus'. In *Beowulf*, the great Anglo-Saxon epic, there is an encomium to another older Offa, a king who through military might had successfully fixed a border with a neighbouring enemy. One scholar suggests the lines are 'hard to account for unless it was a compliment to his great Mercian name-sake'. A thirteenth-century deed refers to 'Offediche' in Shropshire.

According to Speed's Chronicle, the dyke's construction was not without incident. Marmodius, the defeated King of Wales, arranged with other enemies of Offa to 'brake down the banke of this forti-fication, filling up again great part of the ditch' and then attack Offa's court. The guerrilla campaign was soon snuffed out, Mar-modius conquered and his vassals taken hostage. And work on the dyke resumed.

The scale of the achievement was not fully acknowledged by academe until 1955 when Oxford University Press published *Offa's Dyke: A Field Survey of the Western Frontier-Works of Mercia in the Seventh and Eighth Centuries AD*. That publication date is deceptive. Sir Cyril Fox, the study's author, first accepted the commission from the National Museum of Wales and the Board of Celtic Studies of the University of Wales as a young man thirty years earlier. He spent eight summers poring over the dyke and its off-shoots, from 1925 to 1932. 'It provided the finest possible introduction to Wales and the Welsh,' he wrote, 'and largely accounts for the affection I have for both.' Like Warner he took a companion, a Mr Dudley W. Phillips who brought his fiddle and a chatty disposition, along with a willingness to be a human yardstick in photographs of the dyke. 'The survey of Offa's Dyke was certainly a laborious undertaking,' Fox wrote, 'both in field and study, and is perhaps tedious to read. But I venture to think that it was worth doing.'

Fox devoted those summers to measurement, assessment, cataloguing. Of constructed earthwork he measured 81 miles, spread over a distance of 149 miles. Taking soundings at forty different points, he calculated the bank's average height to be over six feet, and its breadth nearly sixty feet. His conclusion was that the earthwork was begun in the middle nearest to the heart of Mercia, continued to the north, while the southern sections where the border was less contended were the last to be built. It was constructed, he thought, by experienced engineers working to the plans of one controlling designer, but that responsibility for building it was possibly taken on by landowners across whose territory the dyke passed. Hence some of its sudden changes of direction. Discrepancies in size and profile between sections, in misalignments and overlaps suggested to him that such works were completed by different gangs.

He feels certain that Offa spread the cost. 'I doubt whether the King who built the Dyke expended a single penny on labourers,' writes Fox. It must have involved many hundreds using basic tools and working in all weathers. Not for Offa's men with picks and shovels the pleasure of digging and heaping huge mounds of earth in the summer months. If the dyke took only eleven years to finish, including many sections which would have been much higher than they are today, no wonder Fox concluded his somewhat dusty academic appraisal with an exclamation: 'What an astonishing effort for a small state of farmers and peasants this eighty miles of earthen wall and excavated ditch represented!'

The hiker cannot avoid the same conclusion. Even when it's raining old women and sticks. Halfway through day five the heavens open between the easily confused Kington and Knighton. They finally close again at the end of day nine, at Buttington Bridge, sixty-five miles later. The rain is never quite of the torrential variety which dissuaded even Borrow from venturing out. But intermittently it persists. I note that things are going to take a turn for the worse while munching on a sandwich on a hill looking south to the distant Black Mountains along an avenue flanked by Hergest Ridge and Radnor Forest. Beyond, jutting proudly to attention in my opera glasses, are the twin turrets of the Brecon Beacons: Pen-y-Fan and Corn Du. From thirty-five miles off they are no more than tiny hints on the horizon. I can't take my eyes off them. Then a dark cloud swoops across and they are no more. In a trice, Radnorshire has disappeared altogether. We are alone with the slithering dyke.

In due course it becomes apparent that my Gore-Tex boots, recently purchased and guaranteed to keep the water out, are fundamentally permeable. We trudge over green damp hills, searching for consolation. A laminated notice strapped to a gate across a bridge soon promises it. 'Use the facilities behind the chapel in Dolley Green.' How friendly. Trust the Welsh to offer a welcome (we have crossed back into Powys). We traverse a valley floor and come upon a quiet cluster of houses. There's a sign to a loo at the back of a sturdy red-brick Baptist chapel. I loiter. A man outside a house greets me in a thick accent from one of the southern states of America: Georgia, it turns out; the Baptist minister, I presume. He and his family, he explains, are off back home after six years. 'It's been a good ministry,' he's saying. 'We've converted six people, including our sons.' Excluding the sons, youngish boys with mullet haircuts whom they have home-educated, that's a strike rate of one conversion every eighteen months. 'You believers?' he says. I now realise why the loo is advertised to hikers for miles along the ODP: it's a honeytrap. 'Er, not as such,' I say. My efforts to believe in any of the Welsh ways, from Cistercian to Congregationalist, have already proved abortive. 'Save thee,' he says. I thank him. He adds, 'Some people don't like it when I say that.'

As we move on, E— confirms that the loos are covered floor to ceiling with billboards, stickers, posters, pamphlets, leaflets, all designed to lure the abluting hiker to the path of righteousness. We have our own path to follow, plus our own brand of baptism, as we clamber over exposed hills. Even a herd of cows we pass is shelter-ing under conifers so you can see only their legs. We descend into Knighton, the traditional mid-point of the ODP, wishing the world were a warmer. drier place.

Day six brings no relief. Only twelve miles. Most of them verti-cal. Up. Down. Up and down. A bit of along. Up and up. Down and down. Wales can't claim responsibility for this purgatory sup-plied by Shropshire. The dyke hares over them unimpeded. At points we are reduced to climbing for ten paces, then resting, eleven then resting, twelve then resting and so on. One would be grateful for rope ladders and the odd zipwire. At one point we lose our way and are ensnared in a head-high bracken forest sprouting from steep slippery mud. One's thick socks, dried out on radiators overnight, are now wringing again. No sooner do you conquer a hill than it's required that you plummet all the way down to cross yet another footling rivulet in the valley floor. On the plus side, one can feel one's gluteal mass solidifying into granite. There are occasional treats. A long path over one hill is lined on both sides with wild raspberry bushes which, without a care for other dykers, we strip like locusts. It makes a change from the hundreds and thousands of plump blackberries lining the ODP in August.

We bump into a flock of sheep being removed from one field and on to another. The farmers are sensibly shod in knee-high rubber. I think I may be developing trench foot. Crossing an old drovers' route the dyke grows to impressive proportions. Below us we can see most of Montgomeryshire. The dyke plunges downwards and we with it until it is slinking along the backs of gardens. It was the occupants of one such property that Fox asked in 1928 if the locals knew what Offa's Dyke actually was. 'His reply though indirect was not ambiguous. "You put your head inside the back-door of Bob Jones's cottage there; tell him he was born the wrong side of Offa's Dyke, and see what happens."'

It is becoming apparent that each day on the dyke is like a journey from innocence to experience, hope to despair, and maybe even from youth to death. You start out each morning as springy as a freshly born lamb. Yes, it helps if the sun blesses you with its bounty, and if the fields are as flat as Holland, both of which suddenly happen on day seven. But neither is obligatory. The first two or three miles are painless like childhood (especially if you have popped a precautionary painkiller). By elevenses, you're refuelling your way into your teens. When you sit down to lunch you have pushed hard through your twenties and feel the need to settle, in this case to sandwiches, crisps, chocolate, an apple. Suddenly everything becomes hard work. You are now in the breeding years of your mid thirties and bewilderingly exhausted, but the hard yards must be traversed until middle age gradually restores your mojo and for a brief deceptive phase you are a contender again. Then the reality of exhaustion kicks in. For the final few miles you plummet headlong towards geriatric enfeeblement, prey to twinges and aches, malfunction and dolour. Eventually you can go not a step further. The mind is technically willing, but the body has been pushed too far. You lie down and close your eyes and wait for oblivion.

This happens to us eleven days in a row.

We are now passing one hundred miles. I look at a map and cannot quite believe how far up towards North Wales we've traipsed. The dyke races along the current border for a mile or two. Frustratingly, the path keeps to the English side of the line. Wales is precisely four yards away. I itch to trespass into the land of my fathers. I am desperate to be in Wales. At a certain point I can stand it no further: at a gateway I plant my feet on Welsh soil, stop and aim a satisfying arc of piss into England. In such visceral ways does one demonstrate one's *Cymreictod*. Across a watery valley Powis Castle is a dull orange smudge.

On day eight the dyke forges forward along the horizontal with a masculine sense of purpose while to its right the sashaying Severn flashes its flirty curves like a street-walker. We tot up twelve miles before lunch – a record – and reach our digs so precipitately that we decide to carry on for two miles into tomorrow's schedule. This is what it feels like to be fit. The day ends at Carreg-y-big where the unimpeded hilltop view as the sun slants across Mid Wales yields a brilliant display of mountainous activity. Pumlumon is clearly

parked on the horizon. I'm pretty sure those are the Arans, impor-
tant-looking hulks just a mile or two as the crow flies from Hedd
Pugh's farm in Cwm Cywarch. And far off in the distance is the
unmistakable silhouette of Cadair Idris.

Day nine brings faint annoyance at the Boundary Commission
and its arbitrary choices. We pass English villages called Nantmawr,
Tyn-y-Coed, Trefonen, Craignant, Bronygarth. Clearly they've
been stolen by England. My huff lightens as we cross the Afon
Ceiriog and re-enter Wales. A red plaque on the bridge notes that
it was near here in the Berwyn Mountains that the Battle of Crogen
took place in August 1165 between the army of Owain Gwynedd
and Henry II of England 'as Wales fought for its freedom from
English domination'. The plaque is too polite to mention who won.
(The Welsh did.)

And now a sad moment looms. We are parting company with
the dyke. It swerves off to the east to follow a course into the outskirts of Wrexham. Those who designed the ODP chose to take it
through more pleasing pastures, such as Chirk Castle now materialising not far to our right. 'A noble edifice it looked,' said Borrow,
who walked here with his wife, stepdaughter and a guide, 'and to
my eye bore no slight resemblance to Windsor Castle.' The Borrow
party crossed the fields, rang on a bell and were shown round the
ancestral home of the royalist Middletons. 'We had never seen in
our lives anything more princely and delightful than the interior.'
For us a rule established at Tintern applies: no tourism if it's a yard
off the path.

Before the morning is out the path has crossed an even more
spectacular landmark. We walk along the flank of a canal full of
idling longboats piloted by, for the most part, gentlemen with a
wheel in one hand and a preprandial glass of red in the other. The
canal veers round to the right and by some miracle throws itself for

300 metres across a wide chasm cut by the River Dee, which roars distantly underneath us. Pontcysyllte – which sounds thoroughly romantic in Welsh but merely means 'connecting bridge' – was completed in 1805. Its architect Thomas Telford would later create the suspension bridge over the Menai Strait at whose construction Wordsworth marvelled. But this levitating waterway, which ferried slate down from the quarries of the Eglwyseg Mountains, seems somehow the more astonishing. 'Ancient Rome was celebrated among nations for her bridges and aqueducts,' enthused the *Cambrian Quarterly Magazine* in 1831, 'but modern Wales surpasses her.' Never mind that the actual experience of walking across it induces weak knees and queasiness. Borrow's guide advised him that this was 'the finest bridge in the world', adding that it made him feel sick. 'I too felt somewhat dizzy,' conceded Borrow, 'as I looked over the parapet into the glen.' It is indeed nerve-racking that there is nothing between the canal and the drop. One too many glasses of red and a longboatman could easily topple the forty metres to certain death. We pass over the other side with relief.

After a few miles along the canal path in the shadow of the bristling Trevor Rocks, we stumble into Llangollen, walk through the town and up the hill to a large black-and-white cottage on the edge of a cascading stream. It's not on the ODP, but rules are there to be broken. More than anywhere in eighteenth-century Wales, it was Llangollen which fed fashionable notions of the romantic and the sublime. Thomas Pennant, the great Welsh travel writer of the era, declared that there was no other place 'where the refined love of picturesque scenes, the sentimental or the romantic could give further indulgence to his inclinations'. Bizarrely, these fantasies of an alpine wilderness on the doorstep of England were channelled through a pair of spinsters who settled in this very property in 1780. Lady Eleanor Butler and her younger companion the Hon.

Sarah Ponsonby both hailed from noble Anglo-Irish families and flouted the marital plans hatched for them to elope and spend a blissful half-century luxuriating in each other's company in the house they grandly renamed Plas Newydd – New Hall. They were retiring but certainly not shy. Polite Georgian society knew of their case and collectively accepted them. Visitors flocked across the border to pay their respects – mostly a long procession of the titled, and even royalty. No doubt their celebrity derived partly from their aristocratic roots, which the ladies were themselves careful to insist upon. Would we have heard of the Ladies of Llangollen who dressed like men had they been commoners? As it was, they became part of the tour of North Wales, as much as the nearby Cistercian ruins at Valle Crucis and the castle at Dinas Brân glowering down at the town from its crest across the Dee. Among their visitors was Arthur Wellesley, later to become the Duke of Wellington, who within a year would sail for Spain to engage in war in the Peninsula. Walter Scott, whose novels they devoured, visited them when Lady Eleanor was ailing. Wordsworth on hearing of Lady Eleanor's ill health in 1824 sent a slightly palsied sonnet from Ruthin which alluded to 'Sisters in love, a love allowed to climb / Ev'n on this earth above the reach of time'.

Precisely what the love consisted of has never been conclusively established. 'Nobody knowss if they were lessbianss,' says the audio guide at Plas Newydd in a soft, sibilant North Walian accent. Byron, writing when a student at Cambridge in 1807 of his romantic fondness for a fellow undergraduate, knew all about the rumours: 'We shall put Lady E. Butler and Miss Ponsonby to the blush,' he boasted. Seven years later, presumably in acknowledgement of their status as romantic pioneers, he sent the ladies a copy of *The Corsair*.

The ladies first passed through Llangollen in 1778 after crossing from Waterford. They had a prodigious day of tourism, having no idea yet that they would have another half a century to take in the sights. They walked to 'an Abbey called Valede Crucis' then made their way to Chirk Castle. But first they clambered up to Dinas Brân and the overhanging crags of the Trevor Rocks to look upon 'an extensive Prospect … of the Beautifullest Country in the World'. They will have ached the next day.

We are certainly in North Wales now. My blistered heels tell me as much, as does the Scouse catarrh tingeing the Llangollen accent. Clambering up towards the crenellated silhouette of Dinas Brân on day ten I feel a stab of longing. It's certainly not a longing for England, but it is for not walking, which England represents. Two days and thirty-eight miles to go.

The sun is fierce, the wind sharp at the top. Borrow climbed up to these charismatic ruins more than once, and on each occasion experienced mild irritation. 'I do not think I saw the Wyddfa then from the top of Dinas Brân. It is true I might see it without knowing it, being utterly unacquainted with it, except by name.' He was right. Snowdon (Yr Wyddfa) is not visible. Not yet. We head north under the grim Eglwysegs. Scenes such as these routinely coaxed the same sort of adjectives out of Georgian visitors. Where they said 'awful' we say 'awesome'. Even the sternest English naysayer would concede that these are mountains, not hills.

In due course rock gives way to moor, and as rain revisits we wander out across bare, cold, bleak heather into forest where red toadstools and fat heavy ceps line the path at the edge of the woodland. Mile upon mile. Step upon step. Eventually we rise onto a headland from which, not long after lunch, there is a miraculous sight. I whip out the opera glasses.

'Look!'

'What?' E— is not sure what she's meant to be looking at.

'At that. Over there.' There is longish pause.

'I can't see anything.'

'That's the point.'

Twenty-five miles to the north, a misty tabula rasa fills the horizon. Journey's end is visible. The faint outline of turbines embedded in the Irish Sea twizzles in the wind. And in the fore-ground, fanning out along the corridor of the Vale of Clwyd, we can see most of Denbighshire. Awesome.

'We came into a most pleasant, fruitful, populous, and delicious vale,' said Defoe when he reached this point in his tour, 'full of vil-lages and towns, the fields shining with corn, just ready for the reapers, and the meadows green and flowery, and a fine river, with a mild and gentle stream running thro' it.' He fell with relief on the Arcadian valley, so trimly organised and sprouting with well-kept crops, after his exhausting journey across the wilds of North Wales. Had he wandered up onto the top of the range he'd have seen his enemies patrolling there on the western horizon, the razor-sharp peaks of Snowdonia glowering not thirty miles away, and even further off to the south, the mountain he called 'Kader-Idricks'. And if he'd cared to look to the east, he'd have seen the Dee, an angry torrent back in Llangollen, now wide and becalmed as it con-venes with the sea this side of the Wirral and Liverpool. But Defoe sensibly kept to the valley floor. 'We had a prospect of the country open before us, for above 20 miles in length, and from 5 to 7 miles in breadth, all smiling with the same kind of complexion; which made us think ourselves in England again, all on a sudden.'

We keep to the heights, blanketed in downy purple heather. Green paths loop over tall bosomy hills of the Clwydian Range as the tenth day makes way for the eleventh and last. By the final morning there are twenty-one miles to go till we meet the sea in Prestatyn. We walk hard and fast. At the end of one long hard pull uphill I am no more out of breath than as if swanning along a city pavement. We swoop northwards. As the hours pass, the market towns of Ruthin and then Denbigh down in the valley gradually recede on our left flank. I have a new awareness: so this is how it feels to be intensely fit and alive, to have a body in which you can entirely trust. The last lunch after many miles is taken on the top of a rounded hill, looking to the west where those crags in Snowdonia – the Glyders, the Carneddau, Tryfan, Yr Wyddfa – serrate the horizon. A cloud clings to the famous peak, the highest place in Britain this side of the Highlands. I could watch this spectacle for ever.

We rise to our feet and carry on, as one must. And instantly spot a problem. Hips, shoulders, thighs, joints, backs choose this particular moment to jostle for attention. E—'s knees moan the loudest. Downhill paths turn instantly infernal. Bit by bit the contents of her rucksack make their way across into mine. The signposts pointing the way are remorseless. Chocolate offers no consolation, nor energy bars nor even tea taken after crossing the A5 via a footbridge.

How shocking to see cars scarring the ineffable peace of Wales, which we have traversed without once meeting a dual carriageway. The end must therefore be nigh, if only Prestatyn did not also seem to be retreating somehow. I miss a turning and off we wander from the ODP. An extra half-mile in such circs – a quarter there and a quarter back – is not easily swept under the carpet. Two fuses shorten. There are seven miles to go. Seven miles! If you told your teenagers you were about to lead them on a seven-mile walk they'd laugh at you and carry on channel-hopping. And we've done two seven-mile walks already today.

Ever so slowly, Wales disappears under our feet. There are no more sheep. We stumble through cow pasture and wheat field until down to our left the path draws back the curtain on trim suburban outskirts. The pastoral Vale of Clwyd has come to this. In terms of visual stimulants, the journey is as good as done. The sun is weakening now as the path rises onto a ridge before plummeting sharply into Prestatyn proper. The descent is agony. My feet are – no exaggeration (or not much) – killing me. The first commercial building we spot in town is a funeral director's. My boots all but walk me in. We pass down the high street, incongruous in shorts and thick socks. A pub looms on the left. Offa's Tavern. There can be no more suitable place to end this glorious trek up the rib of earth planted in the landscape of our imagination. We push through the door thirsting for liquid relief, to be met by a stale stench of weak lager and tinny speakers pulsing. A dozen drinkers variously prop up the bar, play slot machines and poke one another in the chest. The room simmers with negative energy. One man leans in and asks if we've just walked the Offa's Dyke Path. His eyelids are heavy with drink; beery fumes fog the air between us. I've never felt the need to get out of anywhere faster. We must reach the sea. Prestatyn, someone kindly tells us, is bisected by the railway, so we should take the overpass and keep walking north.

These are the hardest yards: half a mile to the sea along wide roads. Starkness on the edge of town. We are hobbling to the end of Wales. Tomorrow's paralysis has already come. My feet burn with each step. I have wandered the length and breadth and depth of Wales. Now Wales is running out. So this is what it feels like to grow old and suffer betrayal by one's own body. Once upon a time my father crossed Offa's Dyke. Now I have crossed the other way. Kiss me quick, sing shops hawking beach tat. A brute leisure complex protects the shore, as factual as a Norman castle. Somewhere beyond a wall, sea and beach and sky vanish into one another. We halt at the end of Wales.

11

Parhau = Endure

'This perhaps is what is meant by *hiraeth*: a lifelong yearning for
what is gone and out of reach.'

Alice Thomas Ellis, *A Welsh Childhood* (1990)

WHERE DO I DRAW THE LINE? I set out to turn myself into a
Welshman and am curious to know when such a mission can be
described as accomplished. I've paddled, worshipped, worked,
sung, spoken, played, competed, farmed, composed and walked
my way towards Welshness. With more success in some cases than
in others. I've got Welsh in my passport. I've described myself as
Welsh in the 2011 census. What's left?

I know I am reaching full immersion when I have my first dream
in Welsh. Like all good dreams it addresses a deep-rooted anxiety,
in this instance about losing my mind. I can no longer think of the
words for things. I visit an old people's home to see if I can get
myself tested. At the reception desk they are not remotely interested in my condition. After all I'm only forty-six. I get up and
make to leave. I'm just walking out of the plushly carpeted sitting
room when I notice a male figure sitting in a high-backed armchair
to the right of the door. He is wearing a beautifully cut green tweed
three-piece suit. I instinctively know that this is my grandfather.

When I sit by the armchair to talk to him Bert addresses me in colloquial Welsh which I understand and answer. The conversation is
far more intimate than any exchange we have ever had. Our heads
lean in so that they almost touch. A beautiful warm smile plays on
his face; his blue eyes glisten. He is even chuckling.

I wake up, not in the middle of the dream, as you usually do, but
at the end.

Twenty-five years after my grandfather died, I stand in the rain
where the cattle grid once guarded the entrance to Mount Hill. A
man happens to be outside the door to which a postman once bore
a letter addressed 'Bertram, Carmarthen'.

'Can I help you there?' There's an undertone to the voice: a
Welshman's home is his castle. For all he knows I might be plan-
ning a break-in.

'My grandparents bought this house in 1936,' I say. 'My father
and uncle grew up here.'

'Mr Rees?' he says more warmly. 'Would you like to come in and
look around?' The owner introduces himself as Monty Griffiths.
Monty of Mount Hill.

'When I bought the house off Mrs Rees,' he tells me, 'I said to
her, I said, "Mr Rees was a butcher now, wasn't he?" "No," she said,
"my husband was a dentist!" "That's what I meant," I said. "A
butcher."' Monty mimes my grandmother tutting. 'He was missing
two fingers, wasn't he? I was terrified of him as a boy, I was.'

We walk along the corridor into the house, past the old drawing
room where Dorothy's portrait of her mother Nain sitting primly in
an armchair used to hang. It's now in my attic. Standing in the hall,
which is of course smaller than I remember, I see that the kitchen
where my grandmother conjured up those Christmas lunches and
trolleyed them into the dining room for Bert to carve is now a
bedroom again. Mrs Griffiths has a taste for highly floral linen. The

dark old snooker room where as teenagers we spent our entire time, sunk down the little run of stairs, is the kitchen once more, now glinting with mod cons. Some of the old atmosphere still clings to the sitting room where my grandfather would smoke his pipe in the corner by the fireplace. The surfaces are still laden in the Welsh way with an absolute riot of brass and china knick-knacks. And yet the house sounds different. The hall no longer clinks and tinkles the way it does in my memory. Soon after moving in, Monty tells me, he put his foot through a floorboard in the hall, established that the whole house was riddled with rot and had it gutted.

I ask if I can go upstairs to the old attic bedroom. At the top of the short winding staircase Monty holds open the door. The ceilings slope in as much as ever but the three beds in a row have gone, and so too the poltergeist in the dark alcove which used to haunt us after lights out. Instead, in a house where classical music-making once took place, the middle of the room is occupied by a large shiny drum kit. It is and isn't a change. Forty years after we'd wake up at six on Christmas morning and set off a furious racket, the new owner is still putting our bedroom to traditional use.

I am a Welsh teacher now. The new academic year is beginning, there is a fresh intake of Welsh-language beginners, and James has put out an email to several Welsh speakers. He needs classroom assistants. One Thursday evening at the London Welsh Centre I walk into a large basement room which teems with perhaps thirty-five people who have volunteered to learn the language. It is a sight to lift the heart. I park myself at a table with six new learners as James begins the business of introducing the Welsh alphabet with its rogue extra letters – *ll* and *dd*, *ch*, *ff* and *rh*. Faces are pulled as the class grapples with the new consonants. Puzzled looks sprout at the news of odd Welsh vowel sounds. Soon we are learning to introduce ourselves.

'Belinda dw i. Matthew dw i. Julia dw i. Alison dw i. Rhys dw i. Pascale dw i,' they say.

'Jasper dw i.'

They have brought along the usual array of incentives for wanting to try Welsh. They are married to/about to marry Welshmen/Welshwomen. They grew up in Wales and want to communicate with a Welsh-speaking parent. One wants to improve on her forgotten GCSE Welsh to land a job back in Caerphilly.

At the end of the first lesson James teaches them some basic phrases of greeting and farewell. One of them is *tan y tro nesaf* (till next time). After our ninety minutes are up each Thursday evening, I repeat the phrase like a supplication, hoping that uttering the words will make them come true, that everyone I say it to will indeed come back next week. But Welsh as usual sets a cat among the pigeons and there is the expected attrition across the term. Languages are not for everyone, especially not in adulthood, especially not this language with its inimical grammar and tongue-twisting sounds. The first mention of mutations (*Croeso i Gymru*) pastes dread and confusion on several faces, and sends the odd initiate running for the hills. One academic has funding to do a paper relating to Welsh, but after week two we don't see her for dust. I never quite establish exactly why a nervous middle-aged Sri Lankan wants to learn; by week three he doesn't, and is gone. The woman with GCSE Welsh moves back to Caerphilly. But the majority refuse to let Welsh defeat them. One man scratches his head at the speech exercises set by James and long after half-term still appears to have learned absolutely nothing. But he keeps coming back, as bold in the face of the odds as a cockroach in a nuclear holocaust.

Along with one or two other volunteers, I patrol the tables, listening and advising, testing and correcting. They look at me as if

I'm a guru whose Welsh wisdom runs to unfathomable depths. Now and then I have to put them right on that, mostly when some bog-standard lacuna in my knowledge base is exposed. For this reason I entirely avoid the table furthest from the front where James has exiled all the Gogs, the ones who want to learn Welsh as spoken in the north. As for everyone else, when they ask I answer as best I can. And I slip them extra bits of contraband vocab, insist they write it down, and suggest that they make sure to learn it before next Thursday. Steady tapping breaks the stone, I tell them. Towards the end of the term I sense that my adopted table starts to dread my approach. They have me down as a hard taskmaster. The problem is that I care. My enthusiasm can barely be contained. We have a language to save. This, I realise, is how evangelists must feel all the time. I am here to spread the word. The words.

The task in hand is summed up in a single, beautiful double meaning. *Ysgol* is the Welsh for 'school', but also for 'ladder'. I have a vision of all Welsh speakers, from the Archdruid up on the very highest rung all the way down to the beginners clambering onto the lowest. We are every one of us on the same ladder, each climbing in the same direction. It is the responsibility of those higher up the ladder to extend a hand downwards and help pull up the ones on the rungs below. Thus was I hauled towards competence by James, an adult learner, and now I in turn am reaching out to those below.

I am more determined than ever that, before my journey is completed, my girls will come to Wales and experience some of its wonders just once before they take their own paths into adulthood. I'd rather not witness their quarter Welshness entirely wither as it has with other descendants of Meidrim. Not on my watch. A carefully prepared cocktail of begging and emotional blackmail wears down their defences until eventually one gives in and the other domino soon topples. E—, a convert to Welsh walking, is coming too.

We drive through the dark until in wisps of fog the road heaves up into the heart of the mountains and over the Llanberis Pass and down to a cottage at the foot of Crib Goch. We have a two-day window. On one of them – we're not sure which – we are going to the very top of the land of their fathers.

Yes, to complete Project Wales I am striking Snowdon off my list of Welsh mountains there's no point in climbing. Next morning rain spatters the window. *Mae hi'n bwrw glaw*, as they say; lit. 'it's striking rain'. The forecast for tomorrow is no better. Today therefore is the day to make a dash for it.

It's flattish walking up to the first of the lakes, then an easy climb towards Llyn Llydaw, which, more than a mile in length, stretches away towards the forbidding wall of Y Lliwedd, rising into invisibility. We bisect the lake, then skirt its northern bank. It is no mystery that Arthur's legend hangs about this place like a persistent mist. The still surface of the water, its bottom strewn with boulders, could easily be pierced any minute by a thin female arm bearing a silver sword. Behind us an epic landscape falling away across the valley is a muted rumour in dull midwinter daylight. The silence would be all-engulfing were the flanks of the mountains not alive with a hundred plump streams bustling down from the clouds as if bringing urgent news from on high.

Many millions have walked here before, hundreds of thousands of them each year. William Wordsworth stayed overnight to watch the sun rise over Wales. George Borrow marched his daughter up and walked all the way back down to Bangor. H. V. Morton took the train to the top with miserable tourists who hated the wind. Among your predecessors, I tell the girls, is your grandfather, who came up here in 1938, a five-year-old crying all the way to the top.

On this day we are more or less alone. Cold and damp have evacuated the mountain. A seagull, which has drifted inland in search of lunch, patrols overhead. The path works a way upwards alongside a foam-white cascade, which crescendos over an approaching edge. Glaslyn materialises, a more intimate, secret lake hemmed hard into the side of the face. (*Glas*, curiously, means both 'blue' and 'green'.) The only way now is semi-vertical, and treacherous with departing snows. As we gain altitude the views grow murkier until Glaslyn sinks below the cloud line while we rise into nothingness. Silence descends. There are no streams up here and the mists muffle noise so that voices sound soft and immediate. We could be indoors were it not for the cold, the intermittent rain and the gradient.

When the change comes it is instant. The path zigzags its way up onto a ridge. A pugnacious wind greets us, fresh from Greenland. The shelter offered by the mountain has gone and walking grows unpleasant. We take a left and follow the path through thicker snow, without a clear sense of how near the summit is – it's far too blowy for map-reading – but dimly aware that this mountain can't go on rising for ever. The telltale track of the railway joins from the right. The train, it goes without saying, is not running today. Soon we make out the faint silhouette of a nearby building. It must be the summit cafe, shut and abandoned. The summit is upon us. My daughters are ahead now and racing towards the man-made cairn that rises as if on a Wagnerian stage set, E— not far behind them. They are already at the top in triumph as I, bringing up the rear, trudge up the steps. Part of me wants the climb to end, another part to go slow and stretch a moment that will not come again.

'You're at the top of Wales, girls,' I say, for want of anything more oratorical. Millions have stood on this point. On a boiling day the first great Welsh travel writer Thomas Pennant, who came half the way by horse, claimed he could see Yorkshire, Scotland, Ireland and the Isle of Man from here. We can't see a thing. But you can at least sense how the Welsh word for Snowdonia – Eryri – tacked across into English. This is the original eyrie, haunt of eagles. I coach them to say Eryri. A reservoir of Welsh information is dammed up inside me. I want to direct their attention to the various Welsh peaks I've been up, always to find Snowdon staring across at me: Cadair Idris, Yr Eifl, the Clwydian range, Arenig Fawr, Aran Fawddwy. But today we are unable to stare back. Down there, I want to say, is Porthmadog, where your great-grandmother Dorothy grew up, and Dolgellau, where she went to school. A bit of you is bred of this heaven.

I want to share all this in these freezing celestial mists. But not much gets said at 1,085 metres in early January with an ambient temperature dragged down by 80 mph winds. Instead I thank them all for coming up here to be alone with me at the very pinnacle of Wales. They smile, cheeks pink and eyes alive, and ask if we can go back down now.

(The next day it absolutely pisses down.)

From the emptiest place in Wales to the fullest. Wales are at home. And so am I. I hear the familiar chords cue up the famous tune for the umpteenth time, played as ever by the brass band in regimental red. I've been this way before – the Welsh crowds rising to the rafters, the words of the anthem poised on tens of thousands of lips, the team braced to sing.

I've been this way, but never quite so far. With half an hour to go to kick-off, I am back in the jacket of Pendyrus and walking up through the corner tunnel out onto the pitch of the Millennium Stadium, marching along the edge of the sacred turf to the far side where seats are slowly filling to sing 'Calon Lân'. I have learned the words to this and other hymns and arias. In all my feverish imaginings I never dared build this particular Welsh castle in the sky.

'Calon lân yn llawn daioni …' we sing, the melody levitating into the floodlit night. A pure heart full of joy. In front of me my fellow second tenors Mal and Alan, Colin and the Prof. Stewart, relieved of conducting duties this evening, has chosen to join us. Sadly our number has been depleted. Roy, the quiet, wiry widower who joined the choir after me, has died within the past month and been sung to his rest by members of Pendyrus.

'Bread of heaven, bread of heaven,' we sing. 'Feed me till I want no more, want no more …' And the thousands join us. Haydn James, whom I first saw as a tiny dot from high up in the back row of the stadium, is now my conductor. We sing Max Boyce's 'Hymns and Arias', the sound one part Caruso to two parts gelignite, then 'Sosban Fach'. The red seats of the Millennium are filling. Behind us the visiting squad is grunting and thudding through warm-ups. I turn to watch bones shake and oval balls spin through the air under the tall H-shaped posts.

As the teams jog back inside, we march round to our final position near the players' tunnel. In front of me three tiers crammed with Welshmen and Welshwomen rise towards the roof, thousands and thousands of them looking down at Pendyrus out on the grass of the greatest rugby stadium on the planet. I cannot go any further into the heart of Wales, I tell myself. 'Heey Juude …' (Not everything about the song sheet is indigenous.) Once again my eyeballs gently toast as fire jets spit from pitch-side barrels with growing urgency. The tunnel starts belching pink smoke, the Tannoy whips the gathered multitudes into a frenzy and the visitors, then, to a climactic detonation of din, the hosts, sprint out to join us.

'WALES! WALES! WALES! WALES!'

In front of us they go through the business of lining up, shoulder to outsize shoulder. They have never seemed nearer, never seemed more colossal. The crowd now stands to the visitors' rumpty-tumpty anthem, which we alone in the stadium know how to sing. Silence descends in the great secular cathedral of Wales. The air is pregnant with the approaching noise. High in the gods I had to stand mutely during the national anthem the first time I came to the Millennium. Latterly I've been Redwoodising. I have never sung the anthem all the way through by heart, and yet it has not been necessary to learn the words. They have somehow flowed into my bloodstream. Now I'm down on the pitch. Over this last threshold is the end of my quest. I open my mouth. Breathe. And with my compatriots, sing.

Mae hen wlad fy nhadau yn annwyl i mi.

In front of me the wall of Welsh voices heaves into musical life. The old land of my fathers is dear to me, we sing. This is how giants must sound as they wake from their slumber in Eryri.

Gwlad beirdd a chantorion, enwogion o fri.

We invoke celebrated bards and singers, such as those who have consented to guide me in the ways of Welshness. To whom I am eternally in debt.

Ei gwrol ryfelwyr, gwladgarwyr tra mâd
Tros ryddid gollasant eu gwaed.

In unison a whole stadium recalls the spirit of Welsh warriors who once spilled blood for national freedom.

Gwlaaad (= country)!

This one resonant syllable comes up six times in seven lines.

Gwlaaaaad!

I don't think I have ever sung a single word with more heart (= *calon*).

… pleidiol wyf i'm gwlad.

I am indeed partial to my country. The anthem is going far too quickly. If I could choose a Welsh moment of mine to last more or less for ever it would be this. The final couplet approaches, the great imprecation. As long as the sea walls protect this pure beloved domain …

Tra môr yn fur i'r bur hoff bau,
O bydded i'r hen iaith barhau.

… O let the old language endure! I sing these words – written in Pontypridd in 1856 as the Victorian Age plotted to legislate Welsh into extinction – with quite extraordinary force. Holding the highest note on *iaith* (= language), I am simply shouting in tune, though drowned of course by the thousands of voices rising into the night. O let the old language endure. *Parhau* = endure, continue. The stadium vibrates with approval and fervour. Our anthem has worked its spell yet again as few anthems can.

Choristers of Pendyrus have no time to turn to one another and smile. The teams are already shaking hands and we must make a rapid exit towards the corner tunnel. Yes, I think as I start walking rapidly, I *am* welcome to Wales. The players are making for their separate ends of the pitch. But I am listening hard to the Tannoy.

I've requested a small favour of Rhys the Voice, my contact with the microphone. The Welsh Rugby Union will frown – they've banned this sort of thing – but I've asked if I can speak to Wales through him. A hush descends as the fifteen Welsh heroes assume battle positions. The whistle will sound the second we have stepped off the grass. Listen now, as I leave the pitch, listen. Suddenly, the amplified words of Rees the Voice reverberate around the entire Millennium Stadium.

'YMLAEN, CYMRU! COME ON, WALES!'

Acknowledgements

My instinct is to give thanks to the whole of Wales, but that might be overdoing it. But I would like to acknowledge the many descendants of Corn Gafr who have been helpful in a variety of ways. My father Simon Rees and my uncle Brother Teilo Rees have allowed their memories to be tapped again and again. Thanks also to my mother Jacquy Rees, my brothers Rupert Rees and Ted Rees and my daughters Pascale Rees and Florence Rees. Cousins who have also kindly shared their knowledge are Hugh Rees, Andy Rees, Claire Rees, Philip Rees, Alys Russell, Steve Phillips, Elizabeth Moody, Catherine Moody and Elizabeth May Rees.

I would also like to express my thanks to the many Welsh people who have been generous with their time and knowledge. Chief among these is James Dodd, who helped me learn to speak a great and noble language. Any deficiencies in these pages and elsewhere are entirely mine.

I am also indebted to Leighton and Rhian Jones, not only for their considerable hospitality in Cardiff, but also for introducing me to the Archdruid Jim Parc Nest, also known as Jim Jones, and Manon Rhys; to Rhys Jones, also known as Rhys ap William and Rhys the Voice, who introduced me to Brian Lewis of Unity Mines and Haydn James of the Welsh Rugby Union. To all of them the words barely cover it, but thank you very much indeed/*diolch yn fawr iawn*.

I can never adequately express my gratitude to Pendyrus Male Choir for keeping a welcome in the Rhondda Fach. My particular thanks go to conductor Stewart Roberts, chairman Creighton Lewis, joint secretaries Graham Clarke and John Lewis and the committee, as well as the second tenor section, who were wonderfully tolerant of my incursions. Most of all I would like to thank Malcolm Long for his unfailing hospitality on my many visits to Penrhiwceibr.

The Pugh family of Blaencywarch were extraordinarily kind and patient as I learned the rudiments of sheep farming: to Hedd and his wife Sian and their sons Dewi, Owain and Carwyn, and to Hedd's mother Margaret, I am deeply indebted. My thanks also to Helen Davies of the National Sheep Assocation, Wales Region.

Early on in my week at the National Language School in Nant Gwrtheyrn it became clear to my fellow students in *Cwrs Uwch* that they may well find themselves wandering into these pages. I would like to express my thanks to Roisin Willmott, Helen Davies, Richard Fairhead, David Smith and John Richards for their tolerance and understanding but most of all for their conversation. I would also like to thank our teachers Pegi Talfryn and Eleri Llewelyn Morris.

Various Welsh luminaries allowed themselves to be grilled by me. My particular thanks go to Bernard Thomas, Bryn Terfel, Dafydd Iwan, Alun Ffred Jones, my rugby uncle Elgan Rees and the minister Towyn Jones of Capel Yr Annibynwyr in Lammas Street.

Thanks also are due to Gareth John, press officer at the Welsh Assembly Government, Ceri Jones and Beverley Jenkins of Visit Wales for helping with accommodation on the Offa's Dyke Path, as well as former ODP Officer Jim Saunders for his indispensable advice.

I would also like to thank the following: Gareth Rees (probably no relation), Catrin Griffiths, Monty Griffiths, Giles Smith, Hattie Longfield, Ian Warrell of the Tate and Martin Fowler of the Coracle Museum.

James Gill of United Agents took a diligent interest in Welsh matters, despite playing for another Celtic team. I am grateful to him and to Andrew Franklin of Profile Books. It has been a pleasure to work with my editor Lisa Owens, with whose wisdom (try as I might) I have found it impossible to disagree. And I am going to thank my father a second time for scoping the manuscript for errors of fact and – *rhaid cyfadde* (= it must be admitted) – judgement.

Finally, my lasting thanks to *fy nghariad* Emily (née Thomas) for travelling with me into Wales, towards Welshness.

Bibliography

Barker, Juliet, *Wordsworth: A Life* (Viking, 2000)

Borrow, George, *Wild Wales* (Fontana, 1977)

Bradley, A. G., *In the March and Borderland of Wales* (Houghton, Mifflin and Co, 1905)

Brake, Julie and Jones, Christine, *Teach Yourself Welsh*, 2nd edition (Hodder Education, 2003)

Clowes, Dr Carl, *Nant Gwrtheyrn: Rebirth of the Lost Village* (Ymddiriolaeth Nant Gwrtheyrn, 2008)

Dafydd ap Gwilym, *A Selection of Poems*, ed. Rachel Bromwich (Gomer, 1982)

Davies, John, *A History of Wales*, revised edition (Penguin, 2007)

Defoe, Daniel, *A Tour Through the Whole Island of Great Britain* (Penguin, 1971)

Fox, Sir Cyril, *Offa's Dyke: A Field Survey of the Western Frontier-Works of Mercia in the Seventh and Eighth Centuries AD* (OUP, 1955)

Gerald of Wales, *The Journey Through Wales* and *The Description of Wales*, tr. Lewis Thorpe (Penguin, 1978)

Holmes, Richard, *Shelley: The Pursuit* (Penguin, 1987)

Hopwood, Mererid, *Singing in Chains: Listening to Welsh Verse* (Gomer, 2004)

Hunter, David, *The Offa's Dyke Path*, 2nd edition (Cicerone, 2008)

Johnson, Samuel, *The Letters of Samuel Johnson*, ed. Bruce Redford (Clarendon Press, 1992)

Jones, Christine, *Teach Yourself Welsh Grammar* (Hodder Education, 2007)

Jones, Francis, *Historic Carmarthenshire Homes and Their Families* (Brawdy Books, 1987)

Kilvert, Revd Francis, *Kilvert's Diary 1870–1879*, ed. William Plomer (Penguin, 1977)

King, Gareth, *Modern Welsh: A Comprehensive Grammar*, 2nd edition (Routledge, 2003)

—— (ed.), *Modern Welsh Dictionary* (Routledge, 2007)

Little Book of Meat Facts: Compendium of Welsh Meat and Livestock Industry Statistics 2010 (Hybu Cig Cymru)

Mackenzie, Revd Henry, *Essay on the Life and Institutions of Offa, King of Mercia* (Hamilton, Adams and Co, 1840)

Mavor, Elizabeth, *The Ladies of Llangollen* (Penguin, 1973)

Morton, H. V., *In Search of Wales* (Methuen, 1932)

Parker, Mike and Whitfield, Paul, *Wales: The Rough Guide*, 2nd edition (Rough Guides, 1997)

Potter, Beatrix, *Hanes Pwtan y Gwningen* (Frederick Warne, 1979)

Rees, Elizabeth, *Celtic Saints, Passionate Wanderers* (Thames and Hudson, 2000)

Rowling, J. K., *Harri Potter a Maen yr Athronydd*, tr. Emily Huws (Bloomsbury, 2003)

Thomas Ellis, Alice, *A Welsh Childhood* (Michael Joseph, 1990)

Vaughan-Thomas, Wynford and Llewellyn, Alun, *The Shell Guide to Wales* (Michael Joseph, 1969)

Warner, Revd Richard, *A Walk Through Wales in August 1797* (Bath, 1798)

Williams, Gareth, *Valleys of Song: Music and Society in Wales 1840–1914* (University of Wales Press, 1998)